Lou

Lou

FIFTY YEARS OF
KICKING DIRT,
PLAYING HARD,
AND WINNING BIG
IN THE
SWEET SPOT OF
BASEBALL

LOU PINIELLA

WITH BILL MADDEN

HARPER

NEW YORK · LONDON · TORONTO · SYDNEY

HARPER

FIRST HARPER PAPERBACK EDITION PUBLISHED 2018.

Designed by Bonni Leon-Berman

Library of Congress Cataloging-in-Publication Data has been applied for.

ISBN 978-0-06-266080-0 (pbk.)

18 19 20 21 22   LSC   10 9 8 7 6 5 4 3 2 1

This book is dedicated to my wonderful wife, Anita. For the past fifty years, she has been my rock, my loving companion, and the mother of our three amazing children, Lou Jr., Kristi, and Derek.

I also want to thank my parents, Margaret and Louis, for the love and encouragement they gave me all their lives.

CONTENTS

CHAPTER 1

Glory in the Sun

The sun was just beginning its slow rise above the Fenway Park grandstand behind home plate, and you could already feel the tension in the air as we climbed off the team bus and began making our way to the visiting clubhouse for what would be the biggest and most fun baseball game of my life. What an absolutely glorious October day for a sudden-death Yankees–Red Sox baseball game that was to decide the 1978 American League East title, with brilliant sunshine and temperatures in the low seventies that couldn't be more perfect for everyone, fans and players alike—with the lone exception being the unfortunate guy called on to play right field.

Which, in the Yankees' case, was going to be *me*.

I didn't know this until I got to the clubhouse and saw the lineup posted that had me hitting third in right field and Reggie Jackson batting cleanup as the designated hitter. For the most part, Bob Lemon, who'd taken over as the Yankees' manager from Billy Martin in late July, had been switching Reggie and me back and forth from right field to DH. Reggie had played right the previous two games at Yankee Stadium, but he'd had his problems in right in Fenway through the years, and while Lem never said anything to me, I just figured he wanted Reggie fully in his comfort zone and his mind on hitting.

Right field at Fenway Park is trickier than most parks—if you ask me, it's the toughest right field in the American League because of the contour of the wall that wraps around from the "Pesky Pole," at 302 feet in the right field corner, to as deep as 380 feet in the right-center bullpen area, all of it only about five feet high, which means the fans are right on top of you. And on cloudless, sunny days, as Monday, October 2, 1978, was shaping up to be, right field at Fenway can be downright treacherous on fly balls, especially line drives, once the sun makes its rise above that grandstand.

The air in the clubhouse was businesslike as we dressed for this final battle with our archrivals, absent the customary in-house verbal hijinks that during the season provided both tension-reducing levity for us and entertainment for the writers. We'd been through so much to get to this point, overcome so much adversity, that now it was time for fulfillment. We didn't look at it as "do or die." We looked at it as "do." We just didn't know how it would be done. No one could have ever foreseen it getting done with Bucky Dent's bat and my glove.

The only world championship ring I wear is from 1977, but that's because it was the first one for me. Without a doubt, however, the most fun season of my life was 1978. We had perhaps the most balanced lineup of professional hitters in baseball, perfectly suited for Yankee Stadium—lefty power in Reggie; Graig Nettles and Chris Chambliss for that short right field fence; and high-average right-handed gap hitters in Thurman Munson, Willie Randolph, and myself, who each took advantage of the stadium's vast left-center field. Roy White, a versatile switch hitter, could hit second, sixth, or seventh, and at the top of the lineup we had the speed of Mickey Rivers. And starting out in '78, we had a rotation of Catfish Hunter, a future Hall of Famer; Don Gullett, my roommate, who'd been the ace of the 1976 "Big Red

Machine" Cincinnati Reds; Ed Figueroa, who'd won fifty-one games over the previous three seasons and would go on to win twenty in '78; and Ron Guidry, who, in 1978, had one of the greatest seasons of any pitcher in history—leading the majors with a 25–3 record and 1.74 ERA. Over the winter, George Steinbrenner, taking a page from Noah about having two of everything, signed Goose Gossage, one of the premier closers in the National League, to team up with our own Sparky Lyle, who'd only been the American League Cy Young Award winner in '77. So this was a well-constructed, championship-caliber baseball team, with few weaknesses, a team of pressure-tested players who knew how to win.

It's understandable, though, if Yankees fans weren't so sure of that during the first half of '78, and began harboring serious doubts about the team's ability to repeat as world champions. We started off losing four of our first five games, and Goose especially had a rough period of adjustment, coming in as he did as the designated "co-closer" with Sparky, who was one of the most popular players on the team. (It didn't help either that Goose and Billy got off on the wrong foot in spring training when Goose refused Billy's order to throw deliberately at the Texas Rangers' Billy Sample, and the two never mended fences.)

In his first game as a Yankee, Goose came up the loser on Opening Day in Texas when he gave up a ninth-inning homer to Richie Zisk. He blew the save and gave up three more runs in three innings against the Brewers in his next game, five days later. Then, a week after that he was completely demoralized when he threw away a sacrifice bunt by the Blue Jays' Dave McKay to let in the winning run in the ninth inning in Toronto. After that game, we watched in silence as poor Goose sat at his locker crying.

Years later, we were having a couple of beers after an Old-Timers'

Day game at Yankee Stadium, and Goose, seemingly still hurting, could not forget how absolutely devastating those first couple of weeks had been for him.

"They gave me Sparky's job on a silver platter and what do I do but start off with the worst stretch of my entire career," he said. "They always talk about the '78 Yankees and the great comeback. Well, it wouldn't have been a great comeback if it hadn't been for me! But the beauty of that team was that, in the face of disaster, they'd be laughing like kids on a Little League field. After that awful game in Toronto in which I threw that damn bunt twenty feet into the stands or wherever, I'm collapsed in my locker, my head buried in my uniform top, and I look up and who's standing in front of me but Catfish, who said, 'Hurry up and get dressed now. We're taking you out to dinner.' From that point on, I realized what a special group you guys were. They knew how to cut the tension. Whenever I'd come into a game after that, Thurman would come out to the mound and say, 'Okay, Goose. How do you plan to screw this one up?'"

Cut the tension we did. After that rocky first week, we started getting our footing, and through the first two months we were hanging right there with Don Zimmer's Red Sox, a couple of games out of first place. But then the injuries began to set in. It started with Catfish, finally experiencing the toll of pitching *626 innings*—you read that right!—his first two seasons with us ('75–'76), going down with a rotator cuff issue with his shoulder on May 9. We didn't get him back until mid-July, by which time we were trailing the Red Sox by double digits. Actually the *way* we got Catfish back was a kind of a miracle in itself. His shoulder had been hurting since midseason '76, and it was assumed he was probably going to have to get cut on. But while he was in the hospital having his arm examined in late June, one of our team doctors, Maurice Cowen, tried a unique procedure on him in which, after putting him under an anesthetic, he began stretching and manipulating Catfish's shoulder. It was something Cowen had tried earlier on Gullett with some success. When Catfish came out of the anesthetic, he found he could once again cock his arm and throw with no pain. This continued for the rest of the season. On days he was pitching, we'd be sitting in the clubhouse and you could hear the popping in Catfish's shoulder from the trainer's room where Cowen was doing his manipulation thing.

There was also a period in late June/early July when we were without both Randolph and Dent, our second base–shortstop combo. And while he didn't miss many games, Thurman was banged up with assorted injuries the first four months, specifically his knee and his shoulder—at least that's what we surmised, because Thurman would never tell anyone where he was hurting or if he even *was* hurting. I only know it affected both his throwing and his power. Through the first 81 games in '77, he was hitting .315 with 11 homers. At the same juncture in '78, he was batting .288 with just 4 homers. He was also having increasing problems with his throwing, to the point where, right after the All-Star Break, Steinbrenner suggested to Billy that he move him to right field for a while to give his arm some extra rest. He didn't go back to catching regularly until August 3.

Meanwhile, with Zimmer managing with the pedal to the metal, the Red Sox kept winning and winning into July, gradually pulling away. By July 5, our deficit had reached ten games, and then we went into the throes of seven losses in eight games. The most crushing loss during that stretch was the Sunday getaway game in Milwaukee right before the All-Star Break, in which the Brewers—with Mr. Steinbrenner looking on from the private box of the Brewers' owner, Bud Selig—completed the series sweep, 8–4, and Gullett left the game in the first inning clutching his shoulder. Donnie had experienced periodic shoulder soreness for a couple of years, and for a while Dr. Cowen's manipulations had kept him going, but as

I watched him from right field, slowly trudging to the dugout after retiring only two batters, an uneasy feeling came over me that this time it was real bad. I was right. His rotator cuff was completely torn. Just like that his career was over.

After the game, Mr. Steinbrenner was frantic. We were playing lousy, we'd just gotten Catfish back only now to lose Gullett, and the pressure of a season slipping away was building all around us. I really think at that point Mr. Steinbrenner had given up on the season, and if he were alive today he'd admit that. Over the break, he announced a series of changes he wanted to implement. In addition to the Thurman move to right field, it was determined that Mike Heath would be doing the bulk of the catching and that Gary Thomasson, our fourth outfielder, was going to start playing center, leading to media speculation that Mr. Steinbrenner was getting ready to break up the team and trade almost anyone, starting with Rivers.

Things would only get worse before they got better, as our tough streak culminated in an infamous blowup on July 15 between Reggie and Billy that resulted in Billy's resigning as manager in Kansas City. We'd opened the second half by splitting two games with the White Sox at the stadium, then, with Rivers restored to center field, had lost three more in a row to the Royals. It was in the tenth inning of the final game of the Royals series, July 17, with no outs and Thurman on first, that Reggie incurred Billy's wrath by twice attempting to sacrifice—after Billy had wiped off his initial bunt sign—and wound up popping out. Billy and Reggie had been at odds all season, mostly over Billy's stubborn refusal to hit Reggie in the cleanup spot. After the game, which the Royals won, 9–7, Billy was in a fury in his office. It was later reported in the papers that a clock radio was in pieces on the floor and Billy, after blowing off the writers, was on the phone with George and his team president, Al Rosen, demanding that Reggie be suspended for insubordination.

Mr. Steinbrenner really had no choice. What Reggie had done was inexcusable, and so they docked him five days (four games) and about $9,000. Believe it or not, the players were mostly oblivious to all this commotion going on in Billy's office—by this time we'd become almost immune to the continual Billy-Reggie histrionics, and it was probably just coincidental that we went on the road to Minnesota and Chicago and proceeded to win five in a row without Reggie.

But if Billy won a victory there over Reggie, it turned out to be a Pyrrhic one. As soon as Reggie returned to the team that last game in Chicago and addressed all the writers, saying that he didn't think what he had done was an act of defiance and adding that Martin hadn't spoken to him since spring training, another fuse was lit. When one of the writers showed Billy those quotes he erupted all over again, and later after a few drinks at O'Hare Airport, where we were waiting for our plane, he made the fatal remark to Murray Chass of the *New York Times* about Reggie being a "born liar" and George "a convicted one," in reference to Mr. Steinbrenner's conviction for making illegal campaign donations to President Nixon in the Watergate scandal.

The next thing we knew, when we got to the ballpark in Kansas City the following afternoon, Billy had resigned and Lemon was coming in as our new manager. Goose, you have to understand, hated Billy, but he nevertheless kind of summed up the mood of the team at that point when he said there was very little reaction among the players. "If anything," he said, "there was a sense of relief. We were all sick and tired of all the Billy-Reggie bullshit. I'm probably the wrong guy to be saying this but if you ask me I don't think we would've won in '78 if Billy had stayed as manager."

Billy could be difficult for a lot of players. But between the lines, in the dugout, he was a great manager in my opinion. I learned more from him than any other manager I played for. His problem was he wanted to be the headliner. He liked teams he could manage, teams that played fundamentally sound baseball with not a lot of egos, which we were. Unfortunately, Reggie *had* to be the headliner. They were two volatile personalities who didn't like each other. Mr. Steinbrenner always maintained that in New York you *do* need stars, and I agree with that. In Reggie he got the biggest star in the game when he signed him as a free agent after the 1976 season, and Reggie helped us, no question. His heroics in the 1977 World Series stand for themselves. But the constant clashes with Billy made it hard on all of us. The manager has to get along with his star players—I made a point of that when I was managing. But Billy didn't care, and that was why he kept getting fired.

The other thing was this constant friction between Billy and Al Rosen, the president and general manager of the Yankees in 1978, which went back to when they were bitter rivals as players in the 1950s, Billy with the Yankees and Rosen with the Indians. Billy looked at Rosen as an outsider and didn't like taking orders from him, and he complained about not being consulted on player moves. And as Rosen himself says, "I couldn't warm up to Billy Martin if I was embalmed with him."

So when Billy self-destructed at the airport in Chicago, this was Rosen's opportunity to bring in his own man and old Cleveland teammate Lemon, and it proved to be just what everyone needed at that time. Lem was immediately a calming influence. His first-day clubhouse address to us was brief and simple: "You guys are defending world champions, so just go out and play like you did last year. I'm just gonna put what I feel is the best lineup for that day on the field, try to make the right pitching changes, and stay out of your way as best as I can."

Lem could not have been more correct. As Reggie himself would later say, "Bob Lemon was exactly what we needed after Billy. A tough old guy with an even disposition."

Around the same time Lem took over, the Red Sox finally started to slump—they went 13–15 in July—and we began slowly rebounding from our lowest ebb of fourteen games back in fourth place, on July 19. A week later, we'd gotten it down to eight, and I remember a bunch of us sitting around the clubhouse having a few beers after a game and agreeing we could still win this thing. All we needed was to keep playing the way we were capable of and whittling it down with an eye on that four-game series in Boston in September. There was also one other factor that, in retrospect, Lem especially credited for calming things down and keeping us in a "taking care of business" mode: on August 10, all the New York newspapers went on strike, and they didn't come back until November 15. The daily "Bronx Zoo" Yankees soap opera was officially shut down.

Still, our deficit was at six and a half games when we got to September, but that was when the Red Sox, whose veteran players Carlton Fisk, Rick Burleson, Carl Yastrzemski, George Scott, Fred Lynn, and Jerry Remy had all been battling assorted injuries of their own, started to wear down and hit the skids. From August 25 to September 6, we went 12–2 at the same time the Red Sox went 8–5, and as we rolled into Boston for that four-game September series, which we'd had our eye on since July, we were only four games back, with a chance to leave town in first place.

It was right around this time we were all feeling pretty good about the way the season had turned around, and I was kidding around with Catfish that I was thinking about getting an Afro—just like Oscar Gamble, our happy-go-lucky "free spirit" outfielder in '76 whom we'd traded to the White Sox the following April in the deal for Bucky. Oscar had the supreme Afro, so much so that Topps had made a special baseball card of him.

"You do that," Catfish said, "and I'll pay for it. I wanna *see* this!"

So our confidence level had never been higher, and I'm sure the Red Sox could feel it. For the next four days, Fenway Park must have felt like the Alamo for the Red Sox and their fans. We won the first two games 15–3 and 13–2, and then Guidry pitched a two-hit, 7–0 shutout in the third game. One of the things I always admired about Zimmer was the "riverboat gambler" mentality he had as a manager. He knew his x's and o's but wasn't afraid to manage against 'em at times. I think, in that respect, he made Joe Torre a better manager with the Yankees. Joe was basically a conservative by-the-book manager, but when he hired Zim as his bench coach, all of a sudden the Yankees were doing a lot of different things, more squeezing, stealing, and hit-and-running.

But in the fourth game of this series, Zim made the gamble of his life, which still has Red Sox fans scratching their heads: instead of pitching his ace, Luis Tiant, on three days' rest, or Bill Lee, his veteran lefty (whom he admittedly had no use for), he chose a soft-throwing rookie left-hander, Bobby Sprowl—who had started only one other game in the big leagues—to stem the Yankees' tide. We thought it was a decoy, that if Sprowl got in trouble early he'd have Tiant or Lee warming up in the bullpen.

But that was not the case. Sprowl was understandably nervous and couldn't even get through the first inning, walking four batters. We scored three runs in the first, two more in the second, and pounded out another 18 hits in completing what came to be called the "Boston Massacre." We left Boston tied for first place, and, as promised to Catfish, I went to a hair salon and got my hair rolled up in curlers with this greasy stuff all over my head. When it was done, I had a frizzy hairstyle, this magnificent Afro perm, for the first time in my life, and, true to his word, Catfish paid for it. I really liked it, too, but more important, so did my wife!

Zimmer later defended the Sprowl decision, maintaining that his pitching coach, Johnny Podres, had insisted the kid had major-league stuff and was confident he could give them at least five or six innings. As for Lee, who had long been Zimmer's nemesis, openly feuding with him and calling him names, Zim pointed out that after getting off to a 10–3 start, Lee had lost his next seven decisions and had to be pulled from the rotation. I could understand Zim's lack of confidence in Lee, but in a game as big as that one, with your lead down to one and first place on the line, don't you at least have to bring back your ace?

After the series, Zimmer got a lot of criticism in the Boston papers for not resting his veterans enough in the first half of the season. But while that may have looked valid for a time in early September, it is a tribute to both Zimmer and the makeup of that Red Sox team that, instead of completely collapsing after we caught and moved past them into first place, they won 12 of their last 14 games, including eight in a row at the end, to force the one-game playoff.

We finished the season almost as hot, winning six in a row to maintain a one-game lead right up to the final day, when, against the Indians at Yankee Stadium, we had a rejuvenated Catfish (who'd won nine of ten decisions in August and September) ready to close it out for us. But after giving up only four runs in his previous three starts, Catfish simply didn't have it. The Indians knocked him out in the second inning, touching him up for five runs, including a couple of homers. On the other hand, Rick Waits, an unsung lefty, pitched one of the best games of his career for the Indians, a five-hitter, and we were flattened, 9–2. We later learned that after Tiant pitched a 5–0 shutout over Toronto in the season finale, the Red Sox rubbed it in by posting "Thank you, Rick Waits" on their center field scoreboard.

If this hadn't been as consequential a game as it was, I might have taken the occasion to start needling Catfish on the bus to the airport.

We were famous for that. I loved getting on Catfish for giving up homers—he gave up 374 of them in his career but, remarkably, 250 of them were solo shots. That was his style. He challenged hitters— "Here it is, hit it"—but if he gave up a home run it was seldom preceded by him walking anyone. Whenever we'd come in to Kansas City, Catfish would start up, eager to remind the whole bus that the Royals had traded me after the 1973 season and replaced me in the outfield with Jim Wohlford, a .260 singles hitter who had only 21 homers in fifteen years in the majors (mostly as a part-timer).

"Here we are. Here's the town where Lou got beaten out of a job by Jim WOAH-ford. Jim F-ing WOAH-ford. They got rid of Lou here to make room for Jim F-ing WOAH-ford! That's what they thought of Lou here!"

I had to listen to this shit every damn time we came in to Kansas City.

Well, I had to defend myself, and Catfish's penchant for giving up homers gave me the perfect fodder.

"All I know, Catfish, is you've given up so many damn homers at Yankee Stadium I've gotten to know everyone in the front row of the bleachers on a first-name basis! They've declared the right field bleachers at Yankee Stadium a hard hat zone! When you're pitching, I'm no longer bringing my glove to the outfield. I'm bringing a jai alai cesta!"

Oh, we had fun. But whenever I had a bad game, I tried to make sure not to be on that first bus back to the hotel. I'd linger in the clubhouse and take the second bus, which was usually mostly the writers, broadcasters, and support people. Because it didn't matter who you were. If you struck out a couple of times, made a couple of errors, stranded a bunch of guys in scoring position, gave up a couple of homers, you could expect an unmerciful verbal beating from Catfish, Sparky, Munson, Nettles, Rivers, and Co. You had to be able to take it.

On our way to LaGuardia for the short flight to Boston after that last game, however, there had been no such verbal sparring. For one thing, Mr. Steinbrenner was on the bus, and he was steaming. Losing the last game was bad enough, but earlier in the month, with the Red Sox and us running neck and neck, American League's president, Lee MacPhail, had held a coin flip in his office on Park Avenue to determine home field advantage in the event we ended up tied. George had been in Tampa, so he'd sent Rosen over to MacPhail's office to do the flip. As Rosen later told it, he called heads and the coin came up tails, but when he got back to the stadium and called Mr. Steinbrenner to deliver the bad news, the Boss went ballistic on him, screaming, "Ahhhh, I've got the dumbest people in baseball working for me! How in the hell could you be so stupid to call heads when everybody knows tails comes up seventy-five percent of the time?"

That Steinbrenner! Sometimes he could be so irrational, you were just astounded.

Once on the plane, Mr. Steinbrenner was sitting up front with Rosen, and I could see he was very quiet, making everyone extremely uncomfortable around him, so I decided to take it upon myself to try and loosen him up a little. As soon as we were airborne, I walked up the aisle and stood next to him.

"What do you want?" he grumped.

"I just wanted to tell you, Boss, that even though you guys didn't do your job getting us home field advantage, we're gonna do ours tomorrow and you're gonna get an extra gate out of it as well."

He looked at me as if I were crazy and shouted, "Get out of here, Piniella!"

Nevertheless, I'm sure Mr. Steinbrenner was fully aware that we'd taken the liberty of packing for Kansas City and the American League Championship Series, beginning on Tuesday.

When we got to the hotel, I decided to go to bed early, but as I lay there my mind was spinning and I couldn't get to sleep. Finally, after tossing and turning for about an hour, I got up, got dressed, and went around the corner to Daisy Buchanan's, one of Boston's most popular watering holes, to have myself a Jack Daniels. I walked in, looked around, and, lo and behold, a whole bunch of my teammates were in there, drinking and laughing and having a great time. Right there and then I knew we were gonna win the next day.

Of course, it didn't hurt my confidence knowing we also had the best pitcher in baseball, Guidry, going for us, albeit on short (three days') rest. In his previous two starts, both complete games, Gator had given up only one run, to bring his record to 24–3 with a 1.72 ERA. Having used his best, Tiant, to get the last-game win, Zimmer countered with Mike Torrez, the big, strapping right-hander, also pitching on three days' rest. Mike had been with us the year before and had won two World Series games against the Dodgers, so we knew him well. He was a workhorse—250 innings for the Red Sox in '78—and a great competitor.

From the start, I could see Gator wasn't quite as sharp as he'd been his previous two outings. In the second, Yastrzemski got him for a leadoff homer that got the Fenway Park crowd worked up and on their feet, and the Red Sox nearly broke through for another run the next inning when George Scott led off with a double and was sacrificed to third, only to be left stranded when Guidry retired the next two batters.

In the sixth, I could see Gator was starting to lose a little off his fastball. Rick Burleson led off with a double to left and was singled home by Jim Rice for a 2–0 Boston lead. Right after the Rice single, with the Red Sox's left-handed power hitters, Yastrzemski and later Fred Lynn, coming up, I moved about four to five feet closer to the right field line to guard against them pulling Guidry. Yaz grounded out, but after we issued an intentional walk to Carlton Fisk, Lynn hit a long drive toward the right field corner that I was able to run down.

In his 2001 autobiography, Zim recalled his reaction to the play from his vantage point in the Red Sox dugout: "When Lynn hit the ball, I said to myself, 'That's extra bases for sure and two more runs for us.' But as I jumped to the top step of the dugout and craned my head to see where the ball was going to land, I was dumbfounded to see Piniella right there to catch it. I later asked him: 'Why in the hell were you playing so close to the line?' That's why Piniella was a great manager. Ordinarily, a hard thrower like Guidry, you don't ever figure anyone is gonna pull the ball off him. But Piniella was smart enough to see he'd gotten tired. He used his ingenuity and that catch as much as anything was what won that playoff game."

But Guidry later said he wasn't at all surprised I was in position to make the catch. Remember, this was a very close-knit team and we knew each other well, knew each other's instincts. "Lou was not the fastest outfielder or the flashiest and probably wouldn't have wanted to be out there if it was his choice," Guidry said. "But he knew batters and understood pitchers and always put himself in the best possible position to make a catch. When Lynn's ball went up, I thought right away, *He'll catch it*. I hadn't even looked to see where he was playing. It was like that with all of our outfielders. I never had to position them. They knew how to play the hitters, and if the ball hit their glove, they caught it. All of 'em, that is, except Reggie!"

All day long the fans in right field, especially this one guy, had been heckling me. After I made the catch, which put me face-to-face with them right against the right field wall, I momentarily considered handing the ball to the guy as a souvenir. I quickly thought better of it, however, and instead I just yelled at him, "Take that, you asshole!"

Even though the Red Sox still had a 2–0 lead and Torrez looked strong, I just had a feeling the third time around the lineup we were going to start making some noise of our own to counter the Fenway crowd. And then it started. After Nettles flied out to start the seventh, Chambliss and White both singled. Next, Lem sent up Jim Spencer to pinch-hit for Brian Doyle, who'd been a backup infielder for much of the season and had been called back up from the minors in late September to take over at second base when Randolph went down with a hamstring injury. Spencer was our number one left-handed bat off the bench, but Torrez was able to retire him on a fly to left, bringing up Bucky, our number nine hitter, who was hitting .243 with 4 homers for the season.

Ordinarily, Lem probably would have also pinch-hit for Bucky in that situation, but with Doyle now out of the game, he had no more infielders. After taking the first pitch for a ball, Bucky fouled the next one off his left ankle and began hobbling around, writhing in pain. This went on for a couple of minutes, and we wondered if Bucky was going to be able to stay in the game. While he was hobbling all around, Rivers, who was in the on-deck circle, yelled at him that his bat was chipped and handed him another one, which the bat boy borrowed from Roy White.

I remember watching all this from the dugout and expressing my surprise at Torrez, who was just standing there on the mound and not taking any warm-up pitches. As he even admitted to me years later, it was a fatal mistake. Once Bucky finally got back in the batter's box, Torrez threw him a fastball, belt high and inside, that got just a little too much of the plate, and Bucky drove it high in the air to left. We all leaped to the top of the dugout to see the flight of the ball, and for a moment it looked like Yastrzemski was going to be able to either catch it, or get a carom off the Green Monster. But then I saw him dropping his head, and it was like a pin had pierced a balloon and Fenway Park went eerily silent as Bucky toured the bases for one of the most improbable big-game three-run homers in history. As Bucky is fond of telling people: "Whenever people would come up to me and ask me how many home runs I hit in my career, I used to joke, 'Only one, but it was a big one.'"

After the homer, Rivers walked and Thurman doubled him home to make it 4–2. What I've always found so ironic is that Bucky's homer completely overshadowed the tack-on homer Reggie hit leading off the eighth, which actually proved to be the winning run, Reggie once again being "Mr. October"—only nobody remembers it.

In the bottom of the eighth, with Gossage now pitching for us, the Red Sox closed to within 5–4 on RBI singles by Yastrzemski and Lynn, and just like that, it was a nail-biter again. The first two Red Sox batters in that inning hit balls to me in right, one by Jerry Remy that went for a double and the other by Jim Rice that I was able to catch. But as I came back to the dugout after the inning, I told Lemon that, with the sun now high over the grandstand roof, I just couldn't see balls hit to right on a line drive trajectory. My private hope was I wouldn't have to deal with that in the ninth.

But with one out, and Burleson on first via a walk from Goose, my worst fears were realized when Remy hit a soft liner over the infield right at me—and right in the sun. I saw the ball when it left Remy's bat, then lost it as it was going over the infield. But I didn't panic and didn't let Burleson know I'd lost it. I took a couple of steps backward to give myself a little more time to recover when the ball came out of that sun, and hopefully to keep it from getting past me. As it was, it dropped a few feet to my left. I lunged to cut it off and was able to pick it up on one hop and fire a throw over to Nettles at third. Again, the key was not to show panic, and because he wasn't sure whether I was going to catch the ball, Burleson hesitated and stopped at second. I'll say this, my throw to Nettles was one of the best throws of my career.

The play, of course, loomed ever larger when Rice, up next, flied out to me in right center—this time the ball was in the air and not blocked by the sun—for what would've been a game-tying sac fly had Burleson advanced to third. Now it came down to one final moment of intense drama—Goose, tiring himself after facing thirteen batters in relief, versus Yaz, the Red Sox icon who'd been the hero and the American League MVP in the Sox's 1967 "Impossible Dream" pennant season. It was only fitting, and I can only imagine how absolutely shocked—and immediately deflated—the Fenway fans were when Yaz, who'd already knocked in two of the Red Sox's runs with his homer in the second and an RBI single off Goose the inning before, hit this sky-high pop-up to third. Watching from right field, I felt as if time stood still, waiting indefinitely for the ball to come down into Nettles's glove.

Looking back, I find it amazing to see how fragile that win was, and my play ended up counting for a lot more than I realized at the time. As Goose later recalled, "Our entire season was decided on that one play Lou made on Remy. It's as simple as that."

There's nothing more fun than playing in a game like that, in which you can cut the tension with a butter knife. That's how you're supposed to respond. Don't let the situation overwhelm you. When it was over, we knew we had just beaten the second-best team in baseball. No challenge would be greater than this one.

CHAPTER 2

The Tampa Red-Ass

You've heard the phrase "came from humble beginnings"—well, that was me, although I never realized it or felt it at the time.

I was born August 28, 1943, in Centro Español Hospital on Bayshore Boulevard in Tampa, Florida, one of four hospitals in Tampa that practiced socialized medicine, and for my first seven years I lived with my parents, Margaret and Louis, both Spanish immigrants, along with Mom's parents, her two brothers, Mac and Joe Magadan, and Mac's wife, in a three-bedroom house, with an outhouse in the back, on Conrad Street, just off North Howard Avenue in Tampa. Both my uncles, Joe and Mac, had a huge influence on my baseball career, taking me out to play and teaching me the game in my formative years, and after I turned pro they would use their summer vacations to go see me in whatever cities I was playing in.

In poker or anywhere else, where we lived was what you would call a "full house." A few years later, when my brother Joe was born, we finally had to move to a bigger house in West Tampa Heights. Joe was a good athlete, too, but he was afflicted with polio as a young man. He's always been an inspiration to me.

At dinner my parents and my uncles would sit around the table and talk baseball, and the conversations regularly would become quite loud and heated. They all had strong opinions, and it's fair to say there were many arguments in our household over the game of baseball. Always, though, there was a sense of family. We didn't have a lot of money, but we were rich in everything else that really mattered.

In those days, West Tampa, along with Ybor City, was the center of the cigar industry, with at least fifty cigar factories within a five-mile radius, and most of the people working in them were immigrants from Cuba and the northern part of Spain. The factories are almost all gone now, victims of the slow but sure demise of the Tampa cigar industry, which began in 1959 when Fidel Castro took over in Cuba and cut off the supply of Cuban tobacco to the United States.

My whole world back then existed in a seven-block area of North Howard, and my mom would not allow me to stray from there. Only after I became a teenager would I ride my bike over to the causeway that connects Tampa and Clearwater and go crabbing. I'd bring a big sack with me and walk along the grass flats, catching blue shell crabs, bringing back three dozen or more to the neighborhood. I'd keep a dozen or so for us, which my mom would cook up in a big pot with hot sauce and put over spaghetti, and then sell the rest.

Along that North Howard strip, which is mostly boarded up and abandoned today, was the West Tampa Bank, a clothing store, a library, a coffee shop, a linoleum tile store, a movie house, a hardware store, a barber shop, a meat and poultry store, and a social club—which was really a kind of smoke-filled gambling hall where the men of the neighborhood would play cards and dominos for money. Around the corner was the local fish market, owned by Sam Castellano, one of our American Legion baseball coaches. This was a very strange fish market. It would open at nine o'clock every morning but by nine fifteen Sam would say he was out of fish! We always found that rather curious, but whenever we'd ask our parents why Sam always ran out of fish so quickly, they'd just smile and shrug.

In the middle of the neighborhood was Rey Park, where we spent our days playing on the swings and playing basketball. The park was too small for baseball, so we invented our own "minibaseball" game: cork ball, in which we'd wrap up a cork with tape and use a broomstick for a bat. On weekends there'd be cockfights in West Tampa, and all the old men with their Panama hats and cigars would be waving fistfuls of dollars, betting on the little gamecock roosters in their fight for survival. And on more than one occasion I remember sitting in the barber chair only to have the barber interrupted from cutting my hair by the butcher next door running into the shop chasing a chicken with a cleaver.

We spoke only Spanish at home, and it wasn't until I started at Saint Joseph's Catholic grade school that the Salesian sisters taught me English. Saint Joseph's was a dilapidated old wooden building—so dilapidated there were places you could stick your foot right through the floor. When I was in the fifth grade, Saint Joseph's moved to a new building a mile away, but that didn't make the Salesian sisters any less easy when it came to discipline. I felt the wrath of their rulers on my knuckles many times, all the way up to eighth grade, when I graduated and went on to Jesuit, the all-boys Catholic high school about a mile north of Saint Joseph's and a block away from where the Tampa Bay Bucs stadium is now. My mom insisted that I go to Catholic school because that's where she'd gone and she liked both the education and the discipline. Me? I missed not having girls in my class.

Jesuit was about the toughest academic school in Tampa. My freshman year, they gave you an exam to determine what "college prep" group you'd be in. I wound up in the "B" group, but two of my closest boyhood friends, the Iavarone twins, Malio and Carmine, didn't do so well on the entrance exams and bolted to the public Memorial Junior High (and later Hillsborough High in Seminole Heights) after just one week! Not that it hurt either one. Their father had a pizza restaurant on Buffalo Avenue, and after graduating from Hillsborough, they, along with their brother Gene, went into the restaurant business, operating three of the most popular and successful eateries in all of Tampa. It was while he was working for the Tampa recreation department one summer that Malio met Mike Ilitch, a student at the University of Tampa who was the recreation supervisor, and took him to his father's restaurant one night. After the meal, Ilitch marveled to Malio: "Your future is in pizza!" He meant it too. Malio listened, and his steak house on Dale Mabry Boulevard, with its legendary pizza, was the "in" meeting place of Tampa for over thirty years, where the Tampa cognoscenti from all walks of life, sports figures like George Steinbrenner and John McKay, generals from MacDill Air Force Base, politicians, and even gangsters held court regularly. As for Ilitch? He did even better with pizza, founding the Little Caesars franchise and becoming the billionaire owner of the Detroit Tigers and the NHL Detroit Red Wings.

Jesuit was about a half mile away from Al Lopez Field (named for the Tampa legend and baseball Hall of Famer who managed the 1954 Cleveland Indians and the 1959 Chicago White Sox to the World Series), where the Cincinnati Reds played their spring training games, so when spring rolled around I was one young man whose fancy turned to baseball. My buddies and I made a habit of skipping school, alternating writing "sick notes" to our teachers, and standing behind the left field fence at Al Lopez Field during batting practice, running down baseballs, which we would then sell for twenty-five cents until we had enough money to buy a ticket. This was where I got to see so many of the heroes of my youth—Ted Williams, Stan Musial, Mickey Mantle—close up when they'd come to Tampa to play the Reds. Unfortunately, my truancy capers came to an abrupt and embarrassing end one day when I was sitting in the stands and was confronted by Father Lashley, the prefect of discipline at Jesuit, who happened to be taking in the game himself.

"You're sick, huh?" he said.

"Uh, well," I stammered.

"Come see me in my office first thing tomorrow morning."

The next day I reported to Father Lashley's office and he presented me with a pile of about fifty to sixty sheets of paper and instructed me to draw donkeys on each sheet, cut them out, and write "I am a jackass" on them. Looking back now, for a Catholic school that was always conducting fundraisers, Jesuit sure didn't seem to care about the price of paper.

My mom worked in the Morgan Cigar Co. as an assistant comptroller. My father worked for the Curtiss Candy Co. as a regional sales supervisor—his territory was from Clearwater across the bay from Tampa all the way out to Orlando in the middle of the state. Both of my parents were athletes—my dad was a pitcher in the Tampa semi-pro Intersocial League on Sundays, and my mom, who was 5'9", had been an all-state center on her high school basketball team, Our Lady of Perpetual Help in Ybor City, in the 1930s and also hit cleanup and played first base on the boys' softball team. This may come as a bit of a surprise, but both of them also had tempers. I would go every Sunday to watch my father's games at Cuscaden Park in Ybor City, just east of West Tampa, and serve as the bat boy—these were big social events, with the park regularly packed with 1,000 to 1,200 people, although later when my Jesuit high school team played our archrival, Jefferson, there, the crowds were even larger. Quite a few times, however, I'd watch my father get kicked out of games for arguing calls with the home plate umpire. I guess that was where I first learned the magic words with the umpires that could guarantee you an ejection.

With my father traveling so much during the week, it was up to my mom to really raise me, and she was my coach, my mentor, and my protector, who both encouraged and disciplined me. At my basketball games in the winter and my baseball games in the summer, she was my most vocal fan—sometimes too vocal for the referees and umpires. There's a story—which I swear I never saw and has never been documented—about my mom hitting a basketball referee over the head with an umbrella. But because she gained such notoriety with high school refs and umpires, the tale endured and became part of West Tampa lore. My mom was very opinionated and she knew the game, and years later, when I was managing, she wouldn't hesitate to call me up and question some of the moves I made in games.

So I guess you could say I am a product of my environment.

When I was six and my younger brother, Joe, was born, my mom quit the cigar company and went to work for my father. But we needed to get our own house. So in 1953 we moved to West Tampa Heights—which was considered to be "upscale" compared with West Tampa—to a larger three-bedroom house on Cordelia Street, and I remember in 1954 we also got our first TV set, an old DuMont with the rabbit ear antennae, just in time for the World Series between Al Lopez's Indians and the New York Giants. Our new house was right across the street from a playground called Capaz Park, where my mother was later the director and which now has been rechristened as the Lou Piniella softball field.

When I reached my teens I gravitated to Macfarlane Park, less than a half mile away, where everyone would spend most every day in the summers playing pickup baseball games from eight o'clock in the morning till ten at night, when the park closed. That's the way it was in Tampa—we went from the playground leagues, to the Pony League and American Legion ball, playing nonstop baseball. It's why Tampa was, and still is, a baseball hotbed, as evidenced by so many players—myself, Tony La Russa, and Ken Suarez in the '60s, and later Fred McGriff, Luis Gonzalez, Wade Boggs, Dwight Gooden, Lance McCullers, Tino Martinez, Gary Sheffield, Rich Monteleone, and my cousin, Dave Magadan—all making it from the Tampa sandlots to the big leagues.

Macfarlane was a huge swath of land that stretched across a few acres and had a golf course running through it. La Russa grew up in a house right across the street from Macfarlane Park, and on a few occasions when I'd be playing golf there, I hit some balls into Tony's backyard.

We played most of our high school and American Legion games in Macfarlane, which had no fences, and when I went to the University of Tampa we held our workouts there. But on Tuesday and Thursday nights and for the doubleheaders on weekends, the games were played in Cuscaden Park in Ybor City, which had lights, a large grandstand that could seat well over one thousand fans, and a short left field fence—kind of like Fenway Park—with no fence in either center or right. It also had, adjacent to it, the best swimming pool in the city, and after our games I particularly enjoyed cooling off at the pool and checking out all the girls from the public schools.

La Russa and I were high school rivals (he went to Jefferson) but in the summer we were teammates—he played shortstop, I pitched and played left field—on the same Post 248 American Legion team and the West Tampa Pony League team. Tony just *looked* like a major-league player. His uniform was always perfectly creased and bloused and fit him to a T; he was always the captain of the infield, directing cutoffs and throws to the right base, and he could do everything with the bat. I still remember, a couple of years later in June 1962, when the Kansas City A's owner, Charlie Finley, came to town and signed Tony for $100,000, a brand-new Pontiac, and money for college. It was the first big bonus anyone from Tampa ever got. I said to myself, "Damn! I'm a better player than he is. What am I gonna get?"

For his part, La Russa apparently agreed with me. As he told me years later, "There was never any doubt in my mind that you were our best player. I was just a little more composed."

Our Post 248 American Legion team, which had a third future major leaguer in our catcher, Ken Suarez, went all the way to the state finals in 1960 before losing to Miami. I've tried to forget the crushing way we lost. With two outs in the ninth inning, we were winning by a run and Miami had a couple of runners on base when the batter hit a fly to left center that should have ended the game. Both myself and our center fielder, Paul Aldridge, called for the ball but then held up at the last second as it dropped between us and both runners scored.

Years later, this play still stings—not just me, but my teammate Tony La Russa as well, who saw it this way: "I remember watching from shortstop and saying to myself, 'That's it, Paul's got it.' But Lou was 'the guy' on our team and he wanted to catch the last out. We were shattered. We'd all had the same dream. I remember back at the hotel after the game, Lou barricaded himself in his room. He was so devastated."

About the only consolation we had was when we got home to Tampa, we found out our West Tampa Pony League All-Star team, which had lost its first game in the double elimination tournament, had gone 4–0 in our absence, and could go to the finals in California if we could win a doubleheader against two other teams that had only one loss. And that's what we did. Two days later, we were on a plane to Ontario, California, for the Pony League World Series.

It was the first plane trip for any of us, and we were all really pumped. But on one of the off-days before the first game, our coaches arranged to take us on a hiking trip to nearby Mount Baldy. I remember not being particularly too enthused about the trip and staying back when all the other kids began walking down this hill to a waterfall. When I finally decided to join them, I was running really hard to catch up and tripped on some rocks and began tumbling down the hill toward a cliff that had a hundred-foot drop. If it hadn't been for a giant boulder, which stopped my momentum, I would probably have been killed. As it was, I was hurt really badly, my left ankle chipped, with a mild concussion and cuts and bruises all over. The doctors in the hospital did a good job of patching me up, enough so that I could play in the game the next day. But my ankle was really messed up—I could hardly put any weight on it—and I had to play left field instead of pitch, which La Russa and I agreed was probably the difference in the game since I was the best pitcher on the team. It was also the last time we would all play together.

The ankle bothered me the rest of the time I was at Jesuit, although I actually had a better senior season—statisticswise—in basketball than the year before, when I set a single-game scoring record with 57 points against Brandon High School. I had a really good jump shot and averaged about 32 points per game my senior year and was named to the Catholic school all-American team. I might have liked to have played football as well in high school—I had a good arm and the coaches said I could've been a good quarterback—except my mom prohibited me on account that her brother, Joe, had gotten seriously hurt in college, nearly losing a kidney, playing football for Loyola of New Orleans.

While I ultimately made my mark in baseball, the most influential person in my young life was my basketball coach at Jesuit, Paul Straub. What a wonderful man was Coach Straub. He'd lost both his legs and had a permanently disabled right hand from injuries he suffered at Guadalcanal in World War II, but you'd have never known it. Despite having two wooden prosthetic limbs from the knees down, he could travel the court almost as fast as we could. Years before at the University of Tampa, the football coach there, "Chelo" Huerta, teamed up with Coach Straub on a trick in front of the freshman recruits to demonstrate how tough they were going to have to be to play football at Tampa. As Huerta launched into his "toughness" dissertation, Coach Straub sat on a bench nearby in long pants and a T-shirt, reading a magazine, when this other guy, who was playing darts, suddenly wheeled around and fired a dart into Coach Straub's leg. The looks of terror on the faces of the recruits satisfied Huerta that he'd made his point.

From Coach Straub I learned values, the will to compete, and, most important, teamwork. He was extremely patient with me with my temper—I was constantly being fouled—impressing on me that, for the good of the team, I had to restrain myself and not get a technical. It wasn't easy. One particular game against our archrival, Jefferson, there was nothing Coach Straub could do when, on a fast break, I went up for a layup and was flagrantly fouled by, of all people, Victor Noriega, the cousin of my future wife, Anita. I immediately came up off the floor throwing punches, and in a matter of seconds the stands emptied onto the court and a full-fledged riot broke out. My mother was right in the middle of it, and maybe that's where the umbrella story got started. When I retired from playing with the Yankees in 1984, Coach Straub was one of the people, along with my family, who I brought to New York for the day the organization had in my honor. He was that important to me.

At the same time, the baseball coach at Jesuit, Jack O'Connell, and I did not get along, so much so it cost me my senior year in the spring of 1961. I joined the baseball team late that spring, right before the first game, because the basketball season had extended all the way to the regional finals. Nevertheless, O'Connell told me he wanted me to start that first game. My arm wasn't nearly in shape and my mom told me not to risk an injury that could possibly derail my baseball career. The fact was, the year before, O'Connell would start me in one game, then bring me right back in relief the next game, and my mom thought he was abusing my arm. "If you ruin your arm, what are you gonna do?" she asked.

So I told O'Connell I wasn't going to be able to pitch that first game and he said, "If you don't want to pitch, then just quit"—which is what I did. One of the biggest regrets of my life is missing my high school senior year of baseball. It killed me sitting in the stands and watching my teammates that whole spring and not being a part of it because of my own stubborn pride. Who knows what kind of bonus money I might have been offered? As it was, my parents wanted me to go to college anyway, and I wound up going to the University of Tampa—which in those days consisted of only one building—on a kind of dual scholarship for baseball and basketball, but because I was living at home, I got to keep the extra money for room and board. It wasn't $100,000 and a new car, but I was, in effect, getting paid to play baseball after high school.

The baseball coach at Tampa, Sam Bailey, was quite a character. He'd gather us around before practice and scream, "None of you guys here is worth a damn! The only reason you win is because of good coaching!" Then he'd blow his whistle and order us to start running around Macfarlane Park, shouting, "I want to see nothing but asses and elbows!" One time, when a few of our players complained to him about having trouble with their footing because of all these sand spurs on the ground, ol' Sam screamed, "Sand spurs! Sand spurs! I'll show you sand spurs!" and then picked up a handful of them and stuffed them in his mouth! In a few seconds, he was bleeding all over his mouth as we just stood there dumbfounded. From that day on, we called him "Sand Spur Sam."

Sam was really a football coach who assisted Huerta in the fall and coached the baseball team on the side. He didn't know a whole lot about baseball, but I liked him and enjoyed playing for him that one year. We did, however, have one altercation. My grandfather came to most of my games and liked to park his car behind the left field fence so he could talk to me between innings. He also would bring me one of those big Cuban sandwiches to eat before the games. But this one day he was late and didn't get to slip the sandwich through the fence to me until the start of the second inning. With no time to eat it, I stuck the sandwich in my glove and hoped no one would hit any balls to me. But as fate would have it, the first ball hit in the inning was a fly to left, and as I raced over to make the catch, the sandwich exploded in my glove, lettuce, cheese, pickles, tomatoes, and salami flying all over the place. Everybody was looking at me, laughing uproariously at my buffoonery, and Sam came running out of the dugout screaming, "What the hell is going on out there?" He promptly took me out of the game, and the next day I had to run a few extra laps around Macfarlane Field.

Midway through my freshman year at the U. of Tampa I made the decision to quit school and pursue my baseball career. My ankle had really bothered me all through the basketball season and I could see I needed to concentrate on one sport. The only problem was going to be the scouts' ability to convince my mother that I had major-league promise and needed to turn pro now, not in three years. What it took was a provision in the contract I signed with the Cleveland Indians in which $7,500 was held back to pay for the rest of my college. And I did try to complete my degree after turning pro, taking night courses at the U. of Tampa in the off-season while working in the National Shirt Shop during the day. I did this for four years until something else far more meaningful for my life than a college degree happened: I met and married Anita Garcia.

I didn't know Anita when I was in high school or when I was first taking classes in college. I only knew of her. In her freshman year of high school she and my friend Malio Iavarone were elected home-coming king and queen of their class. Later on, after she graduated from Hillsborough High School, she was elected Miss Tampa and went on to compete in the Miss Florida pageant. I actually didn't meet her until a few years later, after I'd started playing pro ball—the first time at Ponce De Leon Park in Ybor City, where she was the park director, and later at a semipro football game in Tampa in which one of my former baseball teammates at the U. of Tampa, Ronnie Perez, was playing. At the time, Anita was dating Ronnie, and I sat in the stands with her and Ronnie's parents. After the game, Anita and Ronnie went on a date and I came home with Ronnie's family.

But then a few months later, she and Ronnie quit dating, and I asked him if it was all right with him if I called her. He gave me his blessing and I gave her a call, only to be told by her that she was busy. The same thing happened when I gave her a second call. I was basically shy and after two turndowns, I was getting very discouraged. Nevertheless, I decided to give it one more try, only this time I prefaced my question by saying, "I'm gonna make this very simple. I'm a baseball player and in baseball it's three strikes and you're out and you already have two."

She would later say that the problem with the first two times I called her was that it was last minute. But when I laid it on the line, she knew the pressure was on her. As she later told me, "If I turned you down one more time, that would have been it. You wouldn't ever call again." And she would have been right.

I was a Latin kid from Tampa and I always had wanted to marry a Latin girl from Tampa. I knew almost from the very beginning Anita was the one. For that first date I know I must have made quite an impression on her when I took her to a Pizza Hut.

"Here he was, telling me how he was this professional baseball player, but instead of taking me to Bern's Steak House, he takes me to

Pizza Hut," said Anita. "He then explained that if I stuck with him, we'd be regularly dining on steaks. The fact was, I was making more money as a schoolteacher than he was."

Afterward, we went to a little club for drinks and dancing. This was November 1966 and we dated steadily all that winter and got engaged. The following April, I flew home from the Indians' spring training camp in Tucson to get married at the Temple Terrace Country Club. Because my grandmother had just died, my mother didn't want any music at the wedding—which I know didn't go over too well with Anita's family. They were a large Italian-Spanish family who loved dancing but were also very strict with their three daughters. But if that wasn't disconcerting enough for her, our honeymoon was spent not in Bermuda, the Bahamas, Aruba, or Hawaii but in Portland, Oregon, the home of my new team, the Indians' Triple-A affiliate in the Pacific Coast League.

I know those first couple of years being married to a minor-league ballplayer couldn't have been easy for her. She had hardly ever been out of Tampa, and now here she was, on the other side of the continent, alone with no friends while I was on these long Pacific Coast League road trips. But we both grew to really like Portland and, in retrospect, the Pacific Northwest became a very big part of our lives.

In the winters, Anita, who majored in art and education at the University of Florida and South Florida, taught first grade at Broward Elementary while I was selling clothes and continuing to take classes at U. of Tampa. She had forty-five students but always said that I was her forty-sixth after putting up with me that whole first summer in Portland. The fact is, I was never much of a student and gradually became less and less interested in getting my degree. In the winter of 1968 I had two courses, zoology and square dancing, the latter being one of those gimme courses that everybody took just to be assured of getting an A or a B. But while zoology was just a matter of studying, square dancing was a much bigger challenge for me because I had two left feet. Leading up to the final exam, Anita helped me practice every night. But after cramming all night for the zoology exam, I was just too tired to do any square dancing so I blew off the final exam. Nevertheless, I was surprised a few days later when they posted an F for the course next to my name. It turned out, after I inquired (too late), that the final exam had been a *written* exam! All I had to do, they told me, was to basically just show up. That was it for me! And the record will forever show the final course I took in college was square dancing—which I managed to fail.

It was all right, though. I had already met and married the girl of my dreams. Now it was time to fulfill my baseball dream.

CHAPTER 3

Have Bat, Will Travel

Anybody who ever cared to check out the long, nomadic road I took through the minor leagues before eventually reaching the majors after seven years and four different organizations could only come to one conclusion: there must have been issues with this guy—and they would be right.

There were plenty of them, starting out with temperament and moving on to stubbornness, lack of discipline, and the inability to hit the breaking ball. As good an athlete as I had been in high school, I'm sure the baseball scouting reports on me were not particularly overwhelming. I didn't have great speed. I didn't possess raw power, and I didn't have any certain position, other than somewhere in the outfield. What I did have was basic baseball instincts and intellect, which don't usually show up in the scouting reports.

Even though I missed playing baseball my senior year, scouts told me they'd seen enough bat potential in my sophomore and junior seasons to warrant a bonus of around $50,000. Instead, because my parents wanted me to go to college, I wound up agreeing to sign for half that with the Cleveland Indians after taking my final exams of my freshman year at the University of Tampa. By going to Tampa, it kept me in front of a lot of the same scouts who'd seen me in high school and on the sandlots. But the Indians' scout, Spud Chandler, who won an American League Most Valuable Player award as a pitcher for the Yankees in 1943, was the most persistent. The day after the baseball season ended, he was sitting in front of my parents' house with a contract for $25,000 and instructions to report to the Selma (Alabama) Cloverleafs, the Indians' farm team in the lowest-rung Class D Alabama-Florida League.

My uncle Mac drove me from Tampa to Selma and my introduction to the last segregated league in professional baseball. My manager at Selma, Pinky May, had been managing in the Cleveland system since 1952 after a brief five-year major-league career as a third baseman with the Phillies during the war years. He was a really good guy who lived in Saint Petersburg, just like Chandler, and made me feel at home, even if the environment in the Deep South was a bit unsettling. Selma had only three traffic lights in its downtown—that was it. At night, the boll weevils would invade the ballpark in droves from the river that ran alongside it, and they often stopped the games. On the way home from night games, we'd get so hot we used to pick up a couple of watermelons, spike 'em with vodka, and sneak into the town swimming pool with some of the southern belles.

The ballparks in the Alabama-Florida League were all tiny, most of them kind of run down, and one of them, in Andalusia, had no fences! It was there where, in one game, I hit an inside-the-park home run—a line drive to left center that got between the outfielders and just kept rolling. I hit only one other inside-the-park homer in my career—against the Yankees, no less—a drive into the monuments in left center of the old Yankee Stadium off Fritz Peterson. The ball went over the head of my later great friend Bobby Murcer, who, un-characteristically, didn't get a good jump on the ball. Years later, every time I brought that up to Bobby, chiding him for having so little respect for me as a hitter, he swore he didn't remember it.

As I said, there were other elements of my Selma experience that were a little unsettling for a kid who grew up in Tampa, which was kind of a melting pot of whites, Hispanic immigrants, Cubans, and blacks. We all played together in the high schools and sandlots and didn't really know from race. So I wasn't used to seeing "whites only" drinking fountains and public restrooms, and it didn't really dawn on me until we were about a month into the season that the league was all white. It turned out that 1962 was the final season of the Alabama-Florida League. When the national association of minor leagues decreed it would have to integrate for 1963, Alabama governor George Wallace refused, and the league was disbanded.

One of the first things Pinky May did for me when I reported to Selma was give me a new pair of baseball spikes. The ones I had, he said, were too big, and he handed me a pair of Wilson kangaroo spikes. They were too tight when I first put them on, but then Pinky put them in a shoe stretcher and for the first time in my baseball career I had a comfortable shoe. Pinky did find out quickly I was a red-ass, but somehow he tolerated me. There was no running water in the dugout and instead they had a big rain bucket filled with ice water. But on too many occasions, I got pissed off after making an out and kicked it over—which didn't endear me to my teammates—and was probably why they got immense amusement the time I flung the ladle in disgust into the bucket after striking out and then fell headfirst into the bucket trying to fish it out.

When I turned pro, I was strictly a pull hitter, and I was able to get away with that in Class D ball and all the way up to high A ball the following season, when I hit .310 with 16 homers and 77 RBI at Peninsula in the Carolina League. But after hitting a decent .270 with 44 RBI in 70 games in my first season as a pro, I was a little surprised when, that winter, the Indians left me unprotected in the minor-league draft and I was the first player selected by the Washington

Senators. I was home in Tampa when I got a call from the Senators'
general manager, George Selkirk—another former Yankee who held
the distinction of having replaced Babe Ruth in right field (inher-
iting his number 3 uniform as well) for them in 1935. Growing up
in Tampa I hated the Yankees—I rooted for the Indians and the Red
Sox—and yet all of a sudden early in my career I was getting inter-
twined with them. At Selma I'd been making $650 a month, but be-
ing as I was selected in the draft for the Senators' forty-man roster,
I expected major-league money. I didn't know they could pay you
less than that, and much to my dismay Selkirk sent me a contract for
the same $650 a month. I wrote a letter back to him expressing my
dissatisfaction and he sent me a letter back saying the Indians had
been very generous to me. So much for that negotiation.

I reported to the Senators' spring training camp in Pompano Beach
in '63, and it was there where I got a real indoctrination to the finer
points of the game from two of their veteran players, Don Zimmer
and Jimmy Piersall. Piersall, who had been a Gold Glove, All-Star
outfielder with the Red Sox and Indians, was especially helpful to
me with my outfield play, showing me how to go back on balls and
to throw to the right base. The Senators sent me to Peninsula, which
as I said was a few notches higher in the minor leagues, but as far as
race conditions were concerned, the Carolina League was not that
much different from Selma in the Deep South. I didn't like that when
we stopped for gas and food on road trips, the black players had to
stay on the bus and wait for us to bring food back to them, and in
most towns they had to stay in separate black hotels. It was a terrible
situation that we had no control over.

Still, in spite of the cultural challenges, I was very satisfied with
my season at Peninsula, hitting .300 and all, and in my mind, I was
ready to show what I could do against Triple-A pitching or better.
I bought a '57 Chevy that summer and during the day I'd go to the

tobacco auctions in North Carolina, which were a reminder of my childhood when both my parents worked in the Tampa cigar companies. But then, in the last week of the season, I had a party at my house in Newport News and somehow (my mind remains hazy to this day about this) I ran my left arm through a glass door—a gruesome cut that required about twenty-five stitches. Right before that, my manager, Archie Wilson, told me there was a possibility I might be called up to the big leagues. (Dare I mention that, in a very brief major-league career, Archie Wilson played seven games for the Yankees in 1951 and '52?) Instead, I went home to Tampa and then was assigned by the Senators to a winter ball team they had there, presumably to make sure I had fully recovered—and not torn any tendons—from my party accident. It was bad enough I hadn't regained any strength in my arm, but on top of that, against much more experienced pitchers in the winter league, the Senators found out I couldn't hit the slider. As a result, I really struggled and really got the red-ass, crushing more watercoolers and bat racks than baseballs.

Then, just before I was supposed to report to spring training the following February, I got a notice that I was about to be drafted into the army. When I called Selkirk to inform him, he was furious.

"Why didn't you tell us about your draft status sooner?" he bellowed. "We could have gotten you into the reserves."

Fortunately, the Senators were able to get me into a National Guard outfit in Washington, but while I was away in basic training, they also got rid of me. On August 4, 1964, I became the "player to be named later" in a trade the Senators had made the previous March with the Baltimore Orioles for a major-league pitcher, Buster Narum.

As soon as I got out of the service, I got a call from the Orioles' general manager, Lee MacPhail, welcoming me to the club and asking me to report to its Class C Aberdeen, North Dakota, team in the Northern League.

"Even though it's a lower-class ball," MacPhail said, "because you're doing this for us, if you do well there we'll call you up to the big club in September."

I hit .270 with 12 RBI in Aberdeen's last 20 games and, as promised, the Orioles called me to the big leagues. My manager at Aberdeen was Cal Ripken Sr., and Cal Jr. was the bat boy. Besides Cal Jr. there was another future Hall of Famer on that team: Jim Palmer, who jumped right to the majors in 1965. Unlike me, Palmer was in the majors to stay. My calling lasted just those last couple of weeks of the '64 season, most of which were spent as a spectator on the bench. Hank Bauer—yet another former Yankee—was the Orioles' manager, and it was very clear to me he had little time for an inexperienced kid called up from A ball.

On September 4, I got my one and only major-league at-bat when Bauer summoned me to pinch-hit for Robin Roberts against the Angels at the Coliseum in Los Angeles. I ran the count to 3-2 on Fred Newman, a right-hander, before grounding out to short. When I got back to the dugout, Roberts came up to me and said, "Hell, I could do that!" Years later, Roberts would live in Temple Terrace, Florida, where I lived, and every time I ran into him I never let him forget how he left me feeling thoroughly intimidated after my first major-league at-bat.

The following spring, I reported to the Orioles' major-league camp in Miami, where Bauer and I became much more acquainted— although from my standpoint, not for the better. We were staying in the McAllister Hotel in downtown Miami, not far from the hot spots on Biscayne Boulevard. One night, my roommate, a pitcher named Steve Cosgrove, and I were in one of them throwing back a few Jack Daniels well past curfew when a little bit before two, the bartender came over and poured us a couple more shots.

"These are from a gentleman across the bar," he said. We couldn't make out who he was pointing to so we just waved "thanks," finished our drinks, and went back to the hotel. The next morning at the ballpark, Bauer called us over before the workout.

"Where were you last night?" he demanded.

"Oh, we went to bed early," we replied.

"Early my ass!" Bauer said. "That guy who bought you the drinks last night was *me*! I hope you enjoyed 'em because today you're gonna pay for them."

With that, he ordered us to start taking laps in the outfield, back and forth, starting on the warning track, from right field to left field, all while the game was going on and he could watch us from the dugout. Thank god he called off the dogs in the fourth inning. A couple of days later, the Orioles had a game in Tampa against the Cincinnati Reds and I was part of the traveling squad—presumably, I thought, because it was my hometown and I'd be getting a chance to play before my family and friends. But for nine long innings, Bauer let me sit on the bench, and I never got into the game. It was something I never forgot—to the point where when I became a manager in the big leagues, whenever we had a road game in spring training, I checked with all my players to see if anyone had family or girlfriends in those towns, and I always made sure to get them into the games.

Not long after, Bauer sent me to the Triple-A camp in Daytona Beach, and from there I was sent to Bainbridge, Georgia, where the Orioles' Double-A Eastern League Elmira team—which I'd been assigned to—was training. I had a couple of days to report and I used all of it, pulling into Bainbridge around 2:00 a.m. The team was lodged in an old army barracks, and after picking up my blanket, sheets, and pillow, I got into my cot and began to quickly doze off. Suddenly, a few minutes later there was this light in my face, being held by a little guy with a crew cut, screaming at me, "Who the hell do you think you are?"

This was my introduction to Earl Weaver.

I'm groggily rubbing my eyes, trying to see, and Weaver is scream-ing, waking up everyone in the barracks.

"You can thank this guy here for waking you all up," he yelled. "This is what happens when you get here late!"

That whole year at Elmira I felt Weaver's wrath. He was tough. He was profane, and he was relentless when it came to adhering to his rules, instructions, and his way of doing things. But he was also all about winning, and in retrospect, much as I hated him, playing for him that season was probably the best thing that could have hap-pened to me because he taught me the importance of discipline and team rules. I can also understand why he maybe didn't think much of me as a player. It was cold, damp, and dreary those first couple of months in Elmira—I had never played in cold weather before—and I really struggled with it. But what I especially struggled with was the slider—I just couldn't pick up the spin on it—and so I had the worst season of my career, hitting .249 with 11 homers and 64 RBI in 126 games.

Temper, of course, was also a problem. We were playing a game in Reading, Pennsylvania, and with two outs in the top of the ninth inning, down by a run and runners on first and second, I had a 3-0 count and hit a triple. As I'm standing on third base, feeling quite proud of myself for knocking in the tying and go-ahead runs, Weaver, in the third base coaching box, says to me, "That's gonna cost you fifty bucks."

"What the hell?" I said.

"I had you taking 3-0," he said.

The next day, he confronted me in the clubhouse and demanded his fifty dollars. When I told him I didn't have it, he started to grab for my wallet.

"Don't touch my damn wallet," I shouted at him, and from there it escalated into a big argument.

"You're never gonna play in the big leagues," Weaver said.

"Why?" I said.

"Because you're too big of a red-ass!"

"You're a helluva example," I countered, and with that Weaver suspended me for three games.

Two days after he suspended me, I was sleeping at home and I heard this knock on the door. One of my roommates, Mark Belanger, opened the door, and I heard this clomping up the stairs. It was Weaver.

"One of my outfielders got hurt last night and you're in the lineup today so get your ass out of bed!"

From that day on, Weaver and I actually got along the rest of the season.

When I failed to make the adjustment to the slider that whole season at Elmira, the Orioles took me off their major-league roster. It was very deflating. I had gotten used to going to the major-league camp in spring training, and despite my struggles with the bat, Weaver had told me that he was going to take me with him to Triple-A Rochester the next year. Instead, over the winter the Orioles traded me back to the Indians, once again for a player to be named later. I flew out to Arizona to the Indians' camp in Tucson and was greeted by their manager, Birdie Tebbetts, who immediately caught me by surprise by telling me they wanted to make me a catcher. Tebbetts was a former catcher himself, so maybe that's what gave him this idea, but I never knew why and thankfully the experiment didn't last too long. The first pitcher I caught was "Sudden Sam" McDowell, the Indians' flame-throwing ace who threw a 100 m.p.h. fastball and a curveball that broke just as hard. I especially couldn't handle his curveball, and his fastball practically knocked the glove off my hand.

After about three weeks of this I went into Tebbetts's office and told him I'd had enough. He had this knowing grin on his face and

I was thankful my catching days were over. One of my everlasting fond memories of that camp was meeting—and being befriended by— Rocky Colavito, the great Indians slugger who had led the American League in RBI the year before and went on to hit 374 homers in the big leagues. The first night, Rocky took me out to dinner and made me feel at home, made me feel like I was a big leaguer, even though I wasn't, and that was a thrill.

I was actually in one of the first rounds of cuts and sent to the Indians' Triple-A team in Portland, Oregon, where the manager there, Johnny Lipon, was about to have a profound influence on my career. At Triple-A, the pitchers were more experienced, and as such, I was seeing more and more breaking balls and having the same lack of success with them as I had in Elmira. Finally, one day Lipon called me into his office for a talk.

"Do you want to stay here or go back to Double-A?" he asked.

"I want to stay here, of course," I said.

"Well then," Lipon said, "we've got to fix your batting mechanics. You're not going to be able to stay here if you keep on pulling everything. Tomorrow we're gonna start changing you. I'm gonna teach you how to hit the ball to the opposite field."

With that, he handed me an old Nellie Fox bat with the thick "milk bottle" handle, which he'd taped up so I had to choke up on it. The next day, with Lipon throwing to me, I had to hit four out of five pitches to the opposite field. We did that in practice and then he ordered me to do the same thing in the games. I was allowed to pull the ball only one time in each game; the other three to four at-bats I had to go to the opposite field and up the middle. Lipon also instructed me to stay inside the ball more and wait on the ball in order to get a better look so I wasn't swinging at so many bad pitches. He didn't want me trying to hit home runs, but rather concentrating on hitting the ball to right field and right center. I had been used to standing almost right on home plate, but Lipon got me off the plate and helped me stride more toward the pitcher than to shortstop, while staying closed longer so I had more time to see the pitches. The purpose of choking up was to guard against getting jammed with the ball. Every day he'd have me come out early and make the effort, and soon I started to feel really good knowing the curve was coming, and I could hit the ball up the middle.

Lipon was a great mentor but besides working with me on my hitting, he, like all my other managers, had to frequently talk to me about my temper. "You've got to control yourself or else one day you're gonna really hurt yourself." He was so concerned about me—and a couple other red-asses on our team—that he went so far as to install a punching bag in our dugout for us to take out our frustrations on. I came close to proving him right in 1967 when, after grounding into an inning-ending double play, I took my frustrations out on the right field wall, throwing my glove at it and kicking it furiously. I'd forgotten it was a portable wall, and after about my third kick, it fell on top of me. It took the whole bullpen crew to extricate me. Lipon didn't even bother to run out there, and when I got back to the dugout he thankfully didn't say anything. I was embarrassed enough.

I was hitting about .150 when Lipon first called me in, but by the end of the '66 season, I was at .289. Still, one year at Portland hitting .289 with not a lot of power wasn't going to get me to the big leagues. My second year at Portland I hit .308 with 8 homers and 56 RBI in 113 games, but in the scouts' and the organization's eyes I was still a guy who didn't have great foot speed, and was an average outfielder with not a lot of power. I know Alvin Dark, the Indians' manager, must have felt that way because I was about the only prospect on that Portland club who didn't get called up to the majors at some point that season.

The next year at Portland everything started to come (except the speed). I was hitting .317 with 13 homers and 62 RBI—hitting the ball to all fields—when I ran into an outfield wall hard and suffered a separated shoulder. I could barely pick up my arm. Just when I thought I was finally ready for the big leagues, another setback. The Indians did call me up at the end of the year but I was still hurting and got into just six games without a hit.

As the season came to an end, I began to assess my career such as it was. I'd been bouncing around the minors for seven seasons, and the realization began to stare me in the face that maybe I wasn't going to make it in this game. I went home to Tampa after the season, knowing that in November there was going to be a draft for the two new American League expansion teams in Seattle and Kansas City, and I'm thinking to myself if I don't get picked in the expansion draft, if I don't make it to the big leagues, I'm gonna hang it up. I wasn't making any money playing baseball—the most I'd made was $1,200 a month in Triple-A—and I'd gotten married to Anita in 1967. She was still making more money than me, teaching first grade in the Tampa school system. You can't support a family on $6,000 a year, and during the winter, while I was going to school at night to try and get my degree, I got a second job selling clothes in Tampa.

The day of the draft I was calling the local newspaper, the *Tampa Tribune*, all morning to find out if anyone had taken me. Finally, on the third round, I got a call from Marvin Milkes, the general manager of the new Seattle Pilots, welcoming me to his team. It was a brand-new team, one with low expectations, but I was elated. I'd seen a lot of Seattle playing in the Pacific Coast League for three seasons, and I really liked the city. But when I got to the spring training camp in Tempe, Arizona, I was a little surprised to see most of the hitters the team had drafted were right-handed—Tommy Davis, Tommy Harper, Rich Rollins, Wayne Comer—and I wondered privately how this was going to work out. The Pilots' manager was Joe Schultz, a paunchy, grizzled old baseball lifer who you knew had not been hired for the long term but rather just to shepherd the team through its first season. Schultz had been around in baseball since the early '30s and had managed in the minors since 1950. He was not what you'd call a taskmaster, and this being a veteran team, he didn't have a lot of rules either. Every day we'd come to the park and his message was the same: "Pound some mud and drink some Bud!"

I liked Schultz and got along with him fine, but as the spring went on I wasn't getting a whole lot of playing time and I began to worry whether I would make the team. After being taken in the third round of the expansion draft, I figured I was gonna get a good look in spring training, but that wasn't the case. I remember one time Schultz came up to me in the clubhouse and asked me, "Where you playing tomorrow?" When I told him I didn't know, he snapped, "Goddammit, Piniella, you're supposed to know where we're playing."

"It's not where you're playing," I countered, "it's *how* you're playing!"

He didn't like that answer, and I remember saying to myself I should've kept my mouth shut because here we were coming to the end of camp and I was just waiting for that call to the office—the call I'd gotten so many times before—where the manager tells me I'm going back to the minors. Sure enough, on the next-to-last day of camp, Schultz called me into his office, where Milkes and the team traveling secretary were also.

"Good luck," Schultz said.

"Good luck?" I said.

"We just traded you to Kansas City, the other expansion team," Milkes said.

In return the Pilots got Steve Whitaker, a left-handed-hitting outfielder who had previously been a top prospect in the Yankees' system, and a right-handed pitcher, John Gelnar. That now made three times I had been traded before ever making the majors to stay, with the new Kansas City Royals now being my fifth different organization. I was an official baseball vagabond.

I left Schultz's office and went back to my apartment to pack my bags for the flight home to Florida. The Royals trained in Fort Myers, but the next day they were playing the Phillies in Clearwater, just a few miles from Tampa, and I was looking forward to making my Royals debut in front of my family and friends. Before I left, I got a call from Cedric Tallis, the Royals' GM, who I have to say was one of the strangest people I ever knew in baseball. Cedric called to welcome me to the Royals and to assure me I was going to be part of the big-league team. He also gave me a raise from $10,000 to $12,500. I felt like a rich man. All the while, however, he was talking in an *English accent*! Through the years I got to know Cedric pretty well, as the GM in Kansas City and later when he came over to the Yankees as the assistant GM for them. (I actually had a bit of a hand in that after he was forced out as Royals GM in 1974. He had traded me over to the Yankees the year before, and when Gabe Paul, the Yankees' GM, was looking for an assistant, I told Mr. Steinbrenner they couldn't find a better baseball man than Cedric and urged him to hire him.)

That Royals team that won four AL West division titles from 1976 to 1980 was almost entirely put together by Cedric, who made tremendous one-sided trades for Amos Otis, John Mayberry, Hal McRae, and Larry Gura, and drafted or signed George Brett, Freddie Patek, Dennis Leonard, Paul Splittorff, Willie Wilson, Frank White, U. L. Washington, John Wathan, and Dan Quisenberry for the organization. Cedric never got his due credit for all of that. He was a great baseball executive and judge of talent. At the same time, though, he had the persona of Peter Falk's Columbo, the seemingly absentminded TV detective, and oftentimes it was hard to tell just where he was coming from. In my second contract negotiation with him, in 1970, we were talking numbers in his Municipal Stadium office when, all of a sudden, Cedric reached under his desk, pulled out a putter, and started putting golf balls.

Another of his eccentricities was when he'd be engaging in conversation about baseball and all of a sudden burst into a dialogue re-creating his battlefield experiences in World War II. When he was with the Yankees, he delighted in flummoxing the New York writers by interrupting an interview and saying cryptically: "We have to worry about the Indians." No one ever knew if he was referring to the Cleveland Indians (doubtful, since they were always at the bottom of the division) or real Indians. Cedric would never say, but he took great fun in periodically greeting the writers by raising his palm and saying "How!"

By this time, I probably should not have been at all surprised when I showed up at Jack Russell Stadium in Clearwater for my first game with the Royals to find that their manager, Joe Gordon, was yet another ex-Yankee. This was getting almost eerie—the scout who signed me, two of my first general managers, and now three of my first six managers, all ex-Yankees. I was somewhat taken aback when I saw the lineup card, in which he had me leading off and playing center field. It was Johnny Lipon at Portland who had moved me from center field to what I presumed would be a semipermanent corner outfielder in 1966, and I had never led off a game in my life.

But on the second pitch of the game, I hit a home run over the right-center-field wall. The wind was blowing out that day, but I got three hits and made an immediate impression on Gordon. After breaking camp, we played a pair of exhibition games against the Cardinals in Kansas City and filled old Municipal Stadium to capacity. In the first game, I tried to further impress Gordon by running over the Cardinals' catcher Tim McCarver at the plate—much like Pete Rose's jarring bowl-over of Ray Fosse in the 1970 All-Star Game. The

KC fans loved it but McCarver was enraged and came up screaming, "What are you, *crazy*? This is *spring training*, man!" Fact was, Mc-Carver was a bona fide major leaguer and I was just a wannabe major leaguer.

I was still leading off and in center field on Opening Day against Tom Hall, a lefty with the Twins whom I had faced in the Pacific Coast League, so I knew him a little. In my first at-bat I hit a double to left field. You never forget your first major-league hit, and this first game as a Royal I got three more, including a game-tying RBI single in the sixth, and we won, 4–3, in twelve innings. After eight nomadic years of struggle, work, and doubt, I had finally arrived.

Now all I had to do was prove I should stay there, and thankfully that's just what I did. After three games, Gordon moved me from center field to left and down in the lineup, initially to fifth, then to third, and I went on to have a really nice first season in the big leagues, .282, 11 HR, and 68 RBI. Nice enough to be named, at twenty-six, the oldest Rookie of the Year in history. It was a proud moment for me—and especially for my wife, Anita.

All through my development years in the minor leagues, Tom McEwen, the local sports columnist for the *Tampa Tribune*, seemed almost too eager to chronicle my struggles and temper tantrums in his Sunday column, which always began: "Over breakfast of corn flakes, scrambled eggs, sausage, hashed browns, rye toast and cof-fee . . ." and then he'd go on to say why "Lou will never make it to the big leagues." So the day after I won the Rookie of the Year, Anita got herself a paper plate and stapled a piece of lettuce and some bacon to it and put it in a box along with the newspaper article of my winning the Rookie of the Year, sprinkled some corn flakes over it, and added a note saying, "All those things you wrote about my husband never making the majors, try this with your breakfast!"—and mailed it to McEwen.

Of course, my rookie season was also not without incident. In mid-July, we flew into Chicago from Anaheim and had an off-day before a three-game series with the White Sox. My roommate, the pitcher Wally Bunker, and I decided to take advantage of the day off to hit some of the nightspots on Rush Street. I don't remember too much of that evening, only that when we got back to the Executive House, where the team was staying, I was soaking wet. It must have rained. Anyway, I went to sleep only to be woken up by a phone call early in the morning. It was Cedric Tallis calling from Kansas City.

"You're in a lot of trouble," he said. "What the hell did you do last night?"

"I don't know what you're talking about, Cedric," I said. "I only know I went out for a couple of drinks with Bunker and came in wet."

"Well, you better get up," Cedric said, "because Joe Gordon is coming up to your room and you're gonna have to tell him what happened."

I had no idea what was going on. A few minutes later, Gordon was knocking at my door and as I let him in the room I could see he was very distressed—enough so that when he saw the minibar he helped himself to a glass of gin. It turned out Bunker had apparently gone sleepwalking and wandered down to the lobby in his underwear. He had forgotten what room he was in and went around pounding on every door, shouting "Piniella! Piniella! Let me in!" The guests at the hotel had complained that there was this man running around the hallways in his underwear, and they had used the name "Piniella" to describe him. The hotel manager was in a panic and called the Royals, threatening to report this disturbance to the police and have me arrested. Somehow it got resolved without anyone's being arrested, and Bunker got off with just a fine from the Royals.

That first year for the Royals we won 69 games and finished in fourth place in the American League West, far exceeding most everyone's expectations for a start-up franchise. For that reason, we were all a little shocked when, five days after the season, Gordon announced he was quitting as manager. In his press conference, Gordon cited the fact that it had been eight years between managing jobs when he signed on with the Royals, and a lot of changes in the game had happened in the interim. For me, 1969 was an especially great year: I'd finally made it to the big leagues, won Rookie of the Year honors, and, most important, my son Lou Jr. was born.

I was sorry to see Gordon go—particularly so after meeting his successor, Charlie Metro, who'd previously been the Royals' director of scouting and conditioning. Before that, Metro had been a fairly successful minor-league manager for seventeen seasons in the Orioles, Tigers, and Cardinals organizations, but as he soon demonstrated to us, he had *too much* minor league in him and didn't know how to handle major leaguers. Metro was a conditioning fanatic and a stickler for rules.

In his first (and thankfully only) spring training, in 1970, he brought in Bill Easton, the former track coach at University of Kansas, and Wes Santee, the great Kansas 1,500-meter runner, and put us on a specialized running program every day in which he'd have us run all around this double field we had, then open the gates and continue the run through the streets and alleys around the ballpark in Fort Myers. Picture the running of the bulls in Pamplona. The media loved it, calling it a great innovation. Then, three days into it, three players got attacked by big dogs in one of the alleys and that was the end of it.

Among the strict rules Metro had was that, after games we lost, we were required to sit at our lockers and ruminate for forty minutes, presumably to rerun the games in our minds, during which time we were not allowed to shave, shower, or eat a meal. None of us had ever seen anything like this. Metro also had a special uniform made up for himself in which he could fit a stopwatch in his pocket. All the goodwill Gordon had built up with the players dissipated quickly, and our play in the field bore that out: from April 21 to May 7, we lost 12 out of 14, and on June 7, with our record 19–33, Metro was fired and replaced by Bob Lemon, who had been our pitching coach. Before that, Lemon had been the manager of three different teams in the Pacific Coast League as well as the pitching coach with the California Angels in 1967 when Cedric Tallis worked there as business manager.

The move was another prime example of Cedric's baseball acumen, as Lemon proved to be the perfect antidote to Metro. A tested baseball man who broke into the game as an outfielder and then went on to have a Hall of Fame career as a pitcher, Lemon knew all the aspects of the game. He also knew how to handle players and, by his calm but firm demeanor, gained our immediate respect. As for me, I had gone into the 1970 season determined not to fall victim to the so-called sophomore jinx—which is what all players who have good rookie seasons ever hear about. I thought about it all winter but got off to a great start—I was hitting .350 after the first two months of the season—and finished at .301 with 11 homers and 88 RBI. I was now fully confident that I belonged in the major leagues.

At the same time, Lemon was able to right the ship after replacing Metro and guided us back to another fourth-place finish. The following year he won Manager of the Year honors after we became the second-fastest expansion team to a winning record, finishing second with 85 victories. Nineteen seventy-one was also the year in which Amos Otis, whom Cedric had stolen from the Mets for the third baseman Joe Foy (whose skills mysteriously deteriorated as soon as he left us), emerged as a potential superstar, hitting .301 with 15 homers and 79 RBI, stealing a league-leading 52 bases, and playing Gold

Glove defense in center field. I was a popular player in Kansas City, mainly because I was looked upon as a blue-collar guy who made the most of my ability, but I could see right away Otis was much more talented than I was. Though he never quite equaled that '71 season, he was a fixture in center field for fourteen seasons in Kansas City, a five-time All-Star, and one of the all-time great Royals players.

My own big breakout season came in 1972, when I hit a career-high .312 with 11 homers, 72 RBI, and a league-leading 33 doubles, and lost the batting title to the Twins' Rod Carew by five points. I also made the All-Star team for the one and only time in my career, but it was just my luck that the manager of the American League team was Earl Weaver. When I ran into Weaver in the hotel lobby, he told me, "Don't bother bringing your glove to the ballpark." I was offended but what the hell, it was Weaver. I guess he remembered me from Elmira. He did get me one pinch hit at-bat in the game, against Tug McGraw, the Mets' closer with the devastating screwball. I was nervous and swung at the first pitch, grounding out to short. Afterward, my mom called me from Tampa and said, "Why didn't you take more pitches so I could see you longer?" Wise lady.

The Royals as a team, however, regressed that year, and after a 13–24 start, we were pretty much out of the race by Memorial Day. We played much better in the second half, but with three games to go in the season, my batting average down to .306 and Carew 11 points ahead of me at .317, Lemon came to me and asked if I wanted to sit them out and preserve my .300 average. I told him, "No way, I want to play" and went 7 for 11 in those last three games. He never said as much, but I know Lem really appreciated that.

Shortly after the '72 season, Lemon was home in California and did an interview with a columnist with the *Los Angeles Times* in which he talked about being a couple of years away from retirement and how he and his wife were looking forward to settling in Hawaii.

Ewing Kauffman, the owner of the Royals, apparently got upset with that, and even though Lem was only fifty-two, he used it as an excuse to fire him. Mr. Kauffman even admitted that he had wanted a younger man to manage the team—in this case, Jack McKeon, who was forty-two and had managed the Royals' Triple-A farm team in Omaha for four years—which, today, I think, would have given Lem quite an age-discrimination lawsuit. I liked Mr. Kauffman, but in this case I felt he'd made a terrible mistake.

Lem had been a terrific manager, and he also did something else that proved to be transformative for the organization: he brought in Charlie Lau as hitting coach in 1971. It is not an exaggeration to say Charlie knew more about hitting and hitting mechanics than anyone I have ever known. He helped turn George Brett from a .280 singles hitter into a Hall of Famer who won three batting titles (including .390 in 1980) and slugged 317 homers. Charlie's gift was that he could spot things in our swings or our approaches and then quietly communicate them and instill confidence. He taught rhythm and movement in the swing, weight shift, hitting through the ball, having the bat in the launching position as soon as the front foot is down. He made me the hitter I was, and I was grateful when, a few years later after I'd moved on to New York, we were able to get him over to the Yankees in 1978.

Later that winter, my contract negotiation with Cedric wasn't going too well and when I held out from going to spring training, Mr. Kauffman called me to his house in Mission Hills to discuss it. I was looking to get a raise to $50,000, and the Royals had been holding firm at $45,000. I told my wife if I didn't get $50,000, I wasn't going to report. But Mr. Kauffman, who founded Marion Laboratories, a billion-dollar pharmaceutical company in Kansas City, was very smart. As soon as I got to the house, he offered me a nice glass of brandy and then proceeded to let me win four or five hands of liar's poker, and before you know it, he'd gotten me to agree to play for the forty-five grand. I'd won about $500 in the liar's poker game, but there was no way I could beat Mr. Kauffman in liar's poker, because he was a mathematical genius. So basically he was just greasing my pockets. Mr. Kauffman had been very good to me—my first year he raised me from $10,000 to $12,500, then raised me to $25,000 after I won the Rookie of the Year, and, despite my breaking my thumb when I was hit by a pitch and missing forty games in '71, he raised me from $33,000 to $36,000. So I just figured after hitting .312 in '72, I should get a bump to $50,000. But the team wouldn't budge.

The first day I showed up for spring training, which was two weeks late, I was already off on a bad foot with McKeon, who called me into his office and said, "I'm not happy that you held out. This is my first year here and we needed you here to be part of this program. At the same time, I expect you to be one of the leaders on this team."

I didn't take that well, only because I had signed for $5,000 less than I felt I should have had. I also had really enjoyed playing for Lem and I felt McKeon had undermined him with Mr. Kauffman. McKeon was a whole different type of guy. He was a talker and he had this big chaw of tobacco. The writers all liked him because every day he would regale them with stories of his exploits in the minor leagues, always keeping their notebooks filled. McKeon had the bull-shit. Now he was asking me to be a leader when I wasn't happy with my contract. It was not a good beginning for either of us.

Then, to compound everything, we had moved from Municipal Stadium to the new Royals Stadium, which had artificial turf, and I didn't adjust to that at all. My legs bothered me all year, my ankles were sore, my knees were sore, and the field was really, really, really hot. In fact, we had this ice trough in the dugout, and you'd come in from the outfield and you'd just dip your feet into it, almost to your midcalf. But by the time you got back to the outfield, your feet were dry and just as hot and you had to do it over and over. At the same time, the infielders on Astroturf could play me a little deeper, so they took base hits away from me and I had a bad year. I hit .250, by far the lowest of my career, except for 1975, when I missed half the season with an inner ear infection. The Royals as a team had a real good year under McKeon, winning 88 games and finishing second, but I didn't have a whole lot to do with it. It all came to a head in the next-to-last series of the season, when we were facing the White Sox for three games—in which two of their starting pitchers, Jim Kaat and Terry Forster, were lefties—and McKeon benched me all three games.

The next day, we were playing Texas with Jim Bibby, a 6'5", 240-pound, very intimidating, hard-throwing right-hander, and I was more than a little surprised to see that McKeon, after benching me against the two White Sox lefties, had me in the lineup again. I went in to see him to ask what was going on and he explained to me that Otis had told him that he was a little scared of Bibby because he threw so hard and had once almost hit him with a pitch. I forget what I said to McKeon, other than I thought this was bullshit and that I suddenly didn't feel so well myself. That didn't go over so well with him. He kept me on the bench for the final three games and I had a sense I wouldn't be playing any more for Jack McKeon.

I really liked Kansas City. By this time, Anita and I had bought a beautiful home there in Leawood, and on Christmas Day 1971, our second child, my beautiful daughter, Kristi, was born. The first time I saw her, she was presented to us in a Christmas stocking. That was the best Christmas present I ever got. Over the winters, I'd worked for a local financial firm selling muni bonds for the new Royals stadium. We had our first son and our daughter there, and I had met a wonderful, wonderful lifelong friend, Walt Coffey, with whom I bought a Honda motorcycle dealership and opened up a bunch of restaurants in the Kansas City area, including the Long Branch Saloon on the Plaza. All of them were successful ventures, and to tell you something about the kind of friend Walt was, we wrote up the agreement for all those ventures on a paper napkin—that was all we had between us, no contract, no lawyers—and we never once had a disagreement! Life was good. But after that '73 season I had a pretty good idea it was over in Kansas City.

On December 7—D-day—I got a call at home from Cedric, and when he started off telling me how much he appreciated all I had done for him, I knew I had been traded. Initially I was sad, but when he mentioned it was to the Yankees, I have to say, even though they weren't that good at the time, I was really excited. The New York Yankees and all their tradition. The city of New York. I asked him who I'd been traded for and he told me Lindy McDaniel, who'd been the Yankees' closer, with 12 wins and 10 saves in '73, and it was flattering knowing they'd gotten a substantial player for me.

My last souvenir of Kansas City was the banged-up watercooler I took home to Tampa with me. I had destroyed it with my bat in one of my tantrums, and as long as the Royals made me pay for it, I figured I'd keep it as a souvenir. I actually hooked it up with new plumbing in my garage, but it eventually went to the junkyard after I came home too many times from a bad day on the golf course and took a golf club to it for old times' sake.

CHAPTER 4

Pinstripes

Having reached the age of thirty and looking back on my winding road of twelve years in professional baseball, I saw one thing clearly: I was destined to be a Yankee. Too many signposts, too many ex-Yankees intersecting with my life, including Lee MacPhail twice, and, so, after my wife, Anita, and I had a good cry about leaving Kansas City—a place we'd gotten to love, fostering deep community ties—the Yankees and the big-city lights of New York loomed as a great new adventure for us that we somehow almost expected.

Growing up in Tampa in the '50s and '60s, I had never been a great fan of the Yankees, who seemed to win monotonously year after year, but you certainly had to respect their legacy of great players, from Babe Ruth, Lou Gehrig, Joe DiMaggio, Mickey Mantle, Yogi Berra, Whitey Ford, Phil Rizzuto, Tony Lazzeri, and on and on, and the thought of just dressing in the same clubhouse and playing on the same field as all of them was exciting.

Except that would have to wait for two years.

The Yankees team I joined in 1974 was slowly trying to emerge from the darkest era in their history—five losing seasons since their last trip to the World Series in 1964, including the previous one, in which they'd gone 80–82. Not only that, Yankee Stadium was undergoing a

$160 million renovation, and for the next two seasons the Yankees would be sharing the Mets' Shea Stadium for their home games. As usual, my first order of business upon joining the Yankees was my contract. I was still disgruntled about settling for $45,000 from the Royals in '73 and even though I'd had a bad year, I felt I was at least entitled to a cost-of-living raise moving to New York. This was also the first year of salary arbitration—a wonderful development for the players won by our union chief, Marvin Miller—and instead of being told by ownership, "This is the offer, take it or leave it," players could now name their own figure and put it in the hands of the arbitrator.

I was hoping not to have to go to arbitration, but when Gabe Paul, the Yankees' general manager, sent me a contract for the same $45,000, I knew things were going to be no different with the Yankees. I sent the contract back to Paul and told him I was looking for $57,500 and then braced myself for a call from him inviting me to his office to play a few rounds of liar's poker! I didn't know it, but Gabe Paul was possibly the most tightfisted baseball executive in history, and here I was already starting off with him with a $12,500 difference of opinion on my worth. After weeks of stalemate, we both resigned to go to arbitration, with Gabe having hiked his offer to $52,500 and me holding firm. When I arrived in New York for the hearing, Gabe invited me out to lunch at a little Chinese restaurant in Queens, not far from Shea Stadium. Over lunch Gabe began making his pitch.

"Oh, Lou, you don't really want to go to arbitration. It's a distasteful process, requiring us to say a lot of disparaging things about you and the season you had last year. This is no way to get off on the right foot with each other. Think about it, we're willing to give you this nice raise and you really need to get to spring training . . ."

By the end of the lunch, Gabe—along with a few cocktails—had worn me down, and I said what the hell and decided to take the $52,500 and get started with my Yankees career. That was when

Gabe told the waiter to bring over some fortune cookies. I couldn't help noticing the sly smile on his face when I opened mine and the little message said, "Be happy with what you get."

I should point out here that George Steinbrenner had bought the Yankees the year before but was almost immediately served with a two-year suspension from baseball after pleading guilty to making illegal campaign donations to President Nixon. So we didn't know a whole lot about the new Yankees owner and didn't see him except when he was in the stands watching our spring training games.

That first spring in Fort Lauderdale with the Yankees was a getting-to-know-you process for more than just me. We had a new manager in Bill Virdon, who we quickly came to discover was a stern taskmaster. Virdon was like a marine drill instructor. All that was missing was the combat fatigues. He never smiled, said little, and was all business, a stickler for physical fitness and fundamentals. One of my first days of camp, Virdon, a Gold Glove outfielder with the Pirates in the '60s and acclaimed as one of the best defensive center fielders ever, came up to me and said, "If there's one thing I know about this game it's that you can't win unless you have a good outfield." He then proceeded to make his point by putting me and all the other outfielders through the most extensive and grueling drills I ever experienced. Every day, during the workout, Virdon would grab these two fungo bats—a long one for flies to the outfield and a shorter one to hit line drives and grounders forty to sixty feet—and he'd start hitting to us, long flies from right field, to left field, to right field, to left field. Then he'd bring us in close and hit line shots and one-hoppers. It was exhausting for everyone but him. He worked our butts off, but looking back at it now, I can see that he turned us all into good outfielders. I had 16 outfield assists in 1974, the most in my career.

After the workout, he put us through this running drill in which we had to run home to first, then home to second, then home to third, and finally all the way around the bases. All the while, Virdon stood at home plate, and as we crossed the plate, he'd give us either a thumbs-up sign to go to the clubhouse or a thumbs-down, meaning you had to take another lap. The first couple of weeks I ran with the outfielders, all of whom were much faster than I was and opened up distance on me. I finally said, "I've got to get smart here," and began running with the catchers. In particular, I began running alongside Duke Sims, a big (6'2", 200 pounds) lumbering guy who was about at the end of his career. This one day I stayed right with Duke until we got to home plate, then ducked behind him—for a place and a photo finish—as Virdon gave him the thumbs-up. Duke and I then both dashed into the clubhouse, but as I was lathering up in the shower, I saw Virdon coming my way.

"Smart guy," he said. "When you finish that shower, you can put your uniform back on and come back to the field and start running again until I give you a thumbs-up."

About the only guy who was able to penetrate Virdon's stern veneer was Sparky Lyle, our irrepressible resident court jester whose clubhouse levity kept everybody loose and was a welcome balance to the frequent turmoil. A prime example of that was an incident in 1974 when our utility infielder "Chicken" Stanley, another truly funny guy, decided to make a bar in his home out of a coffin and for some reason had the coffin delivered to the clubhouse. This was something Sparky couldn't resist, and when everyone was out on the field, he sneaked back to the clubhouse, covered the rims of his eyes with lampblack, and pulled a surgical mask over his head so he looked like a mummy, then climbed into the coffin and shut the lid. A while later, when everyone came off the field, Virdon held a clubhouse meeting. As he was speaking, the lid of the coffin suddenly cracked open and slowly rose Sparky, who said in this deep ghoulish voice, "Who here knows how to pitch to Brooks Robinson?" Everybody cracked up, and even Virdon forced a smile before ordering Sparky back into the coffin.

But tough as he was and hard as he was to get to know, I learned a lot from Virdon, knowledge that became invaluable to me years later when I became a manager myself: the importance of fundamentals and conditioning. I incorporated a lot of his drills with my own clubs—although I was a little gentler in the quantity of the work as opposed to the quality.

I wasn't quite sure where I was going to fit in the Yankees' outfield in 1974, especially after the team acquired Elliott Maddox from the Texas Rangers late in the spring to join the fixtures Bobby Murcer and Roy White. Maddox was reputed to be one of the better defensive center fielders in baseball, and Virdon sent shock waves through the camp when he announced he was installing Maddox in center and moving Murcer, who'd been a mainstay there since 1969, to right—which is where I thought I'd be playing. Ultimately the move made us a better team, but Bobby was devastated by it and never forgave Virdon. Through the '60s lean years Bobby had been the Yankees' lone star, an Oklahoma kid who, because he moved from shortstop to center field like his idol and fellow Oklahoman Mickey Mantle, was automatically stamped with the unwanted label as the next Mick. Bobby always said he considered that an honor, but I wonder if it wasn't really a burden.

I was able to become quick friends with my new teammates Bobby, Thurman, and Roy White, all of whom enjoyed going to the racetrack. Bobby and I became particularly close, perhaps because we were kindred spirits in Virdon's grueling outfield drills. Little did I know 1974 would be Bobby's last year with the Yankees—at least for a while. I remember one of my great pleasures was coming to Yankee Stadium with the Royals and watching Bobby take batting practice, with that smooth, compact left-handed swing of his, smacking ball after ball over that short right field wall and into the right field bleachers. Yankee Stadium was made for him—he'd averaged over 25 homers a year the previous five seasons. But now we were moving over to Shea Stadium with its vast outfield fences, constant winds off Flushing Bay, and all the noise from those jets landing and taking off from LaGuardia. None of us liked it, but for Bobby it was absolute hell. His batting average fell from .304 to .274 and his homers from 22 to 10—all of them hit on the road. He hated Shea Stadium, hated Virdon, and hated what the fates had done to his career. I felt terrible for him.

One thing that stood out to me was the fact that Thurman was the leader in that clubhouse. He was a few years away from being named only the second Yankee captain—after Lou Gehrig—but just by his manner he had already assumed the part. Being a catcher, that was fairly natural. Nothing happens in a game until the catcher puts his fingers down.

My last year in Kansas City, the team had gotten much younger, but this Yankee group was all around my same age and they made it easy for me to fit in, especially Thurman. We had something in common right away—I won the Rookie of the Year in 1969 and he won it in 1970—and we talked about that a lot. Soon our wives became good friends and usually sat together in the family section at Shea Stadium for our games. I liked Thurman's brashness, his toughness, his inner confidence, and his knowledge of the game. It seemed there was a mutual respect right away. One of the things I really loved was how, after the games, we'd hang around the clubhouse and talk baseball over beers—stuff like which pitchers were the hardest to hit, how to handle certain pitchers. Thurman also liked going to the track, and during the season on the road we'd go to play the ponies or dogs on the off-days. It was a close-knit group, but it didn't take long for Thurman, Bobby, and me to become particularly close.

I had a pretty good spring and thought I'd shown Virdon I was a more than decent outfielder, but when we opened the season at Yankee Stadium I found myself on the bench for those first three games against Cleveland. We then went on the road to Detroit where, happily, Virdon had me starting in left field and hitting fifth. My first at-bat as a Yankee I hit a two-out, two-run single to left against Mickey Lolich, the tough, durable Tigers lefty. I went 2-for-3 on the day, and at dinner that night, Virdon came up to my table and said, "Good game, young man," and he had a smile on his face. Now that really made me feel good.

Under Virdon, I had one of my best seasons in 1974, hitting .305 with 9 homers and 70 RBI, and the team, even after losing our top pitcher and staff leader, Mel Stottlemyre, for half the season with a torn rotator cuff in his shoulder, improved to 89–73, just two games behind Earl Weaver's Orioles. We were in the race right up until the next-to-last day, when fate stepped in and handed me a pair of season-ending goat horns.

After beating the tar out of the Indians, 10–0, in the last game in September—a game in which I went 3-for-4 with 2 RBI—we flew to Milwaukee for the final two games of the season, still just a game behind the Orioles. But the flight was delayed by thunderstorms, allowing extra time for the players to get lubricated. During the flight our two backup catchers, Rick Dempsey and Bill Sudakis, started needling each other. The needling accelerated on the bus ride to the Pfister Hotel in Milwaukee and immediately escalated into a full-fledged fight when we got to the hotel lobby. As our traveling secretary Bill "Killer" Kane later recounted, it was "like an old-fashioned furniture fight that you used to see in the westerns—players leaping over couches, lamps tipping over"—and in the middle of the melee, Murcer, attempting to separate Dempsey and Sudakis, got his hand stepped on and suffered a broken finger. Fights like that, especially among teammates, were not commonplace, even among the "Bronx Zoo" '70s Yankees, although I have to say this particular one was a doozy.

With a right-hander, Kevin Kobel, pitching for the Brewers in the next-to-last game, I figured that Murcer would be starting in right field and not me, but Bobby's season was over and I was now his replacement. We went into the bottom of the eighth inning winning 2–0 behind some really artful pitching by Doc Medich. That's when disaster struck. With one out, Bob Hansen, a pinch hitter, tripled for the Brewers, and then Don Money hit a slicing fly ball to right center between myself and Elliott Maddox. Conceivably, Bobby might have been able to catch it, but I got a bad read on the ball, then switched directions trying to catch up to it. At the same time, Maddox rushed over and made a desperate effort to catch it, but the ball landed between us and skipped all the way to the wall for another triple. An ensuing sac fly scored Money to tie the game and the Brewers won it in the tenth off Medich on a double, a sacrifice, and an RBI single by George Scott. The Orioles, who finished the year with nine straight wins, had won earlier in the day, so that was it for our season.

It was a terrible disappointment, but it was tempered by the appearance of Mr. Steinbrenner in our clubhouse in an apparent violation of his suspension. He was wearing a "Yes We Can" button on his lapel, and as the writers all gathered around him, he lavished praise on us: "They did themselves proud. They should be heroes in New York. They made a dull city exciting all summer and fall."

That was my first in-person encounter with the man who would have the most profound influence of anyone, even my parents, on my life.

Over the winter, still in exile, Mr. Steinbrenner made his mark as a force to be reckoned with in baseball when, with Gabe Paul doing all the legwork, the Yankees won the sweepstakes for Catfish Hunter, who had been declared baseball's first modern-day free agent due to a breach of his contract by the Oakland A's owner, Charlie Finley. After a madcap bidding war for Catfish's services against a dozen other teams, the Yankees were able to sign him with a five-year contract for an unheard-of (at that time) $3.35 million. Much as we were thrilled to be getting Catfish, one of the premier pitchers in baseball, there were decidedly mixed feelings about Paul's other big splash that winter—the trade of Murcer to the Giants for Bobby Bonds. Although Bonds was an acknowledged superstar—only the third player in history to hit 30 homers and steal 30 bases in the same season—Murcer was part of our team fabric, popular with all of us. In that respect, the trade was shocking. Bobby later said that it was the worst day of his life.

Nevertheless, in Fort Lauderdale the following February, there was an air of excitement and much optimism; Catfish and Bonds were drawing crowds of visiting media at their lockers every day, and for the first time in over a decade a lot of the writers were talking us up as a potential World Series team. Apparently Mr. Steinbrenner, who was still on suspension, was convinced of that as well. Before the first exhibition game, he summoned Virdon over to his seat in the stands right next to the Yankees' dugout and handed him what looked like a little tape recorder. When Virdon got back to the clubhouse, he gathered us around the table in the middle of the room, set the tape recorder down, and said brusquely, "I've been asked to play this." With that, he pressed the button and walked away.

On the tape was Mr. Steinbrenner, sounding like General MacArthur, delivering this rousing pep talk about there being no substitute for winning and everyone needing to give 100 percent effort, with no excuses, and how he did his part and now it was time for us to do ours. Then, at the end of the speech, he took a page out of *Mission*

Impossible, saying, "This tape will self-destruct in thirty seconds," which brought a laugh from everyone—except Virdon.

As for me, once again I'd had a frustrating contract negotiation. Gabe Paul lived in Tampa, and a couple of weeks before camp, he had asked me over to this beautiful apartment he had on Tampa Bay. We talked and talked, with Gabe never getting around to a number, and then as I was about to leave, he said, "I'll send your contract over in the morning. Don't worry. It's not the hole in the doughnut that counts, it's the whole doughnut."

I drove home shaking my head, and when I told Anita what Gabe had said and asked her what she thought he meant, she said, "It means you're probably getting a minimal raise."

She was right.

Gabe was both cunning and cruel, as he showed at the end of the spring when he released Mel Stottlemyre—whom he'd told to take all the time he needed to rehab his shoulder—one day before the deadline that obligated the Yankees to pay only one-sixth of his contract. The players were furious when we heard this. Mel was loved and respected by all of us. He was a team leader, the ace of the pitching staff since 1964, and for him to be treated by the club that way was just horrible. It cast a pall over the clubhouse, which up until then had been brimming with optimism.

One of our final trips that spring was to Puerto Rico to play the Roberto Clemente charity game, and it gave me the opportunity to get in some bodysurfing, except there was a tropical depression out in the ocean and I wound up getting thrown around pretty good by the big waves. Not long after, I started feeling dizzy and experiencing a loss of balance all the time. I started getting vertigo, especially on plane trips. There'd be times I'd be walking down the street, bumping into buildings like a drunk. During the games, I started seeing two baseballs. I didn't know what was wrong, only that I couldn't hit. The team doctors couldn't find what the problem was and I was really getting scared. Finally, a specialist in New York determined I had an inner ear infection that required surgery. After that, I was told to drink a lot of juices along with amphetamines to restore my energy. But I never felt right the rest of the season, and I missed most of the road games because I was unable to fly. I ended up playing only 74 games, hitting .196.

But I was not the only Yankees casualty in 1975. Because of some crucial injuries to Bonds and Maddox, by August 1, we were in third place, at 53–51, ten games behind. Throughout the season, we'd heard rumblings about Mr. Steinbrenner's dismay behind the scenes, and they finally came to fruition when Virdon was fired and replaced by Billy Martin.

We liked Virdon and felt bad for him. However, we were excited about getting Billy Martin, who'd been a mainstay Yankees second baseman on all those 1950s World Series teams and had a proven record of turning around losing teams in his three previous managing jobs with Minnesota, Detroit, and Texas. Billy was the antithesis of Virdon. He was very animated, talkative, and you could have fun with him, but you also had to be careful not to piss him off. At the end of the year, he called me aside and said, "Don't worry about your condition. Go home, take it easy this winter, and then when you come back next spring, be ready to play, because we're gonna win next year."

He was right. Over the winter, Gabe Paul, with the help of his thirty-two-year-old assistant, an already highly regarded talent evaluator named Pat Gillick—who would later play an important part in my baseball career—executed a pair of trades that laid the foundation for a mini–Yankees dynasty that produced four pennants, two world championships, and five division titles from 1976 to 1981. Their first move was to trade Bonds, our leading home run man in

1975, to the California Angels for right-handed starter Ed Figueroa and center fielder–leadoff man Mickey Rivers. Next they traded Doc Medich, whose 16 wins in '75 were second on the team behind Catfish, to the Pirates for two starting pitchers—a talented but somewhat unstable right-hander, Dock Ellis, and the lefty Ken Brett—plus a rookie second baseman, Willie Randolph. (Gillick had personally scouted Randolph, playing for the Pirates' Triple-A team in Charleston, West Virginia, in '75, and Willie went on to become a six-time All-Star and a fixture at second base for the Yankees through 1988.)

As we began spring training, Virdon and his outfield drills were gone, but there was one new wrinkle in Fort Lauderdale that a lot of the players found somewhat disconcerting. On March 1, Mr. Steinbrenner was reinstated from his suspension by commissioner Bowie Kuhn, and a day or two later a notice, signed by him and Billy, appeared on the clubhouse wall announcing a new club hair policy in which, from here on out, we were forbidden to wear beards or long mustaches and our hair could not exceed over the collar. Poor Oscar Gamble had to shear his then-famous Afro, and guys like myself, Thurman, and Sparky had to trim our locks above the collar. With Steinbrenner's Yankees anyway, the hippie '70s were officially over. And as I learned quickly the following year, the Yankees' "no facial hair" policy was here to stay. When I arrived in camp, I hadn't had a haircut in about two months; my hair was way over the collar, almost shoulder length, and Pete Sheehy, the Yankees' longtime clubhouse man, informed me he could not issue me a uniform until I went over to the office trailer and saw Mr. Steinbrenner.

When I went in to Mr. Steinbrenner's office, he immediately pointed at my hair and said, "Get it cut, Lou. I will not have my players on the field looking like that. You know the rules."

"I don't understand, Mr. Steinbrenner, what long hair has to do with your ability to play baseball," I protested. "I'm a Christian and

Our Lord and Savior Jesus Christ had hair down to the middle of his back and it didn't affect the way he went about his work."

Steinbrenner jumped from his chair. "Oh really," he said. "Well you just come with me."

With that, he led me out beyond the left field wall where there was this big pond. "You see that pond, Lou?" he said. "It's about seven to eight feet deep. If you can walk across it, you can wear your hair as long as you want and I won't say a thing about it! How's that?"

Every day in that spring of '76, Mr. Steinbrenner would stand stoically behind the batting cage wearing his aviator sunglasses, giving hint to the dominating presence he was going to be. It wasn't until the June 15 trading deadline—and a huge ten-player deal with the Orioles in which two of our best young pitchers, Scotty McGregor and Tippy Martinez, and the backup catcher Rick Dempsey were sent to the Orioles for the veteran starters Doyle Alexander and Ken Holtzman—that we began to suspect Mr. Steinbrenner, behind the scenes, was really injecting himself into the daily operations of the team. Billy made it clear to everyone he was opposed to the trade, and he and Holtzman didn't get along right from the beginning.

Despite the daily scrutiny from our hands-on owner, we played relaxed that whole year, with a new sense of confidence, even though most of us, other than Catfish, had never won before. Most of that confidence came from Billy, who was sharp, knew how to maneuver his players, and was the master of the unexpected. In only the second game of the season, Billy shocked us with his genius when he was able to get what appeared to be a ninth-inning, game-winning grand slam home run by the Brewers' Don Money nullified in Milwaukee. As soon as the ball was hit, Billy came charging out of the dugout as Dave Pagan, our pitcher, began fleeing from the mound in terror. But Billy wasn't coming after Pagan, he was screaming to the umpires that time had been called by Chris Chambliss at first base,

right before the pitch to Money. To our amazement, the umpires con-
curred, risking a riot by the Milwaukee fans, and we wound up winning the game, 9–7. I had never seen a home run reversed like that.

My vertigo situation cleared up gradually through spring training
and it was a great relief to feel normal again. I wasn't sure whether
Billy liked me or not—he didn't play me regularly that season—but I
hit .281 in 100 games in what I felt was a nice rebound from the rock
bottom of the year before. My season might have been even better
had I not allowed my temper to get the better of me once again. After
a particularly bad game on July 10, in which I went 0-for-4 to drop
my average down to .268 (from a high of .303 three weeks earlier), I
was so pissed off I heaved my bat in disgust into my locker. But as
I did, my hand hit the divider between lockers and I badly jammed
my wrist. Afterward, I couldn't even open my car door. There was a
knot on my wrist, which I still have, and it bothered me the rest of
the season. Another lesson learned about losing your temper.

One of the things I especially loved watching back in the '70s was
Billy managing against Weaver. The two of them hated each other
and managed every game against each other like it was the seventh
game of the World Series. (I have to confess, years later when I became a manager, I felt—and managed—the same way when it came
to Weaver.) One game in 1976 that stands out for me was July 27—a
makeup game against the Orioles in Baltimore. Dock Ellis and Jim
Palmer were facing off against each other, and I guess Palmer had
been brushing a lot of our guys back, prompting Dock to start mouth-
ing off a bunch of stuff at the Orioles' bench after giving up a homer
to Al Bumbry in the seventh inning. That was when Reggie Jackson,
who had been traded from Oakland to Baltimore at the start of the
season, got up on the top step of the dugout and shouted back to
Dock, "You wanna hit somebody? Go ahead mother——. Hit me!"

I don't know if Reggie had bothered to look that far ahead, but he was the Orioles' leadoff hitter the next inning, and Dock was only too eager to oblige him by hitting him squarely in the back with a fastball. Billy loved guys like that. Of course, you do that today and you're out of the game, for as we know, with all the new rules, there is no retribution in baseball.

While we didn't get into a brawl with the Orioles in that game, earlier in the season we had gotten into one of the wildest brawls in baseball history with our archrivals, the Red Sox. When the schedule came out every year, the first thing we looked at was when we were playing the Red Sox, and we circled those games. When people talk about the Yankees–Red Sox rivalry, I can say here unequivocally it was real. We didn't like them and they didn't like us. Both teams were very talented—we both had stars—and we competed every year for the American League East title. It didn't hurt either that Mr. Steinbrenner put special emphasis on beating the Red Sox, and in the days leading up to a Red Sox series he'd come through the clubhouse reminding everyone to stay focused on the games ahead with Boston. The only team he hated more than the Red Sox was the Mets. There's no question that we played with a little more intensity against the Red Sox.

That was never more evident than on the night of May 20, 1976, and that aforementioned huge brawl. I'd slid home, hard, right into Carlton Fisk, which started the whole thing. I had tried to score from second base on Otto Velez's single to right—despite the fact that the Red Sox's right fielder Dwight Evans had one of the strongest throwing arms in the game. I was actually a little surprised that our third base coach, Dick Howser, waved me in, and I was fifteen feet from home when Fisk already had the ball. I had no choice but to try and run him over. Fisk was a big, strong guy, but I hit him pretty good and, to his credit, he held on to the ball. As we tumbled to the ground he stuck the ball right in my eye, and after getting tangled up with him, I came up swinging. Then all hell broke loose.

"Spaceman" Bill Lee, the Red Sox's pitcher, came charging in off the mound only to be intercepted by Nettles, who slammed him to the ground. Lee tore a shoulder ligament that sidelined him for a couple of months, but he wasn't done fighting, and when he later confronted Nettles again, Graig got off another punch that blackened his eye. Lee was looking for trouble and turned out to be the only guy who got hurt. In the years since, Carlton and I have had many chances to revisit the fight, and like two old, retired gladiators, we're able to laugh about it now.

I'd like to add that the brawl, which went on for about ten minutes, would have never happened today with the new rules preventing the catcher from blocking the plate. I understand you don't want players getting hurt, but at the same time you're out there trying to compete, and the idea is to try and score while the other team, in particular the catcher, is trying to prevent you from scoring. How's he going to do that if he can't block the plate?

Fights and squabbles aside, the '76 Yankees meant business from the start. Rivers hit .312 with 43 stolen bases, becoming the top-of-the-order catalyst the Yankees hadn't had in ages. Figueroa and Ellis combined for 36 wins, while Thurman (.302/105 RBI) won American League MVP honors. Graig Nettles led the league in homers with 32, Roy White led the league with 104 runs, and Sparky and Dick Tidrow combined for 33 saves out of the bullpen. And of course, the team was now back home in the refurbished Yankee Stadium. All this combined to take us from last to second in runs scored, as we led the American League East for nearly the entire season, winning the division by ten games over the Orioles.

In the '76 American League Championship Series, we faced off against my old Kansas City Royals teammates of George Brett, Hal McRae, and Co. and it was a beauty of a series that wasn't decided until the last pitch of the deciding fifth game. With the game tied 6–6 (thanks to a stunning three-run homer by Brett in the eighth), Chris Chambliss led off the bottom of the ninth and hit the first pitch, a high fastball, from the Royals' reliever Mark Littell on a high drive to right-center field. We all jumped from our seats in the dugout, unsure if it was going to be long enough to get out, and then I saw Al Cowens, the Royals' center fielder, jump at the wall and come down empty handed, and Yankee Stadium erupted in joyous bedlam, with thousands of fans pouring down onto the field as Chris tried to make his way around the bases. It had been twelve long years since Yankees fans had experienced a World Series, and I had never seen such joy.

Chris later said the whole thing was a chain reaction. "I just kind of reacted like I always did. I wasn't trying to hit a home run. Sometimes when you react to a high fastball it works out that way. Then, when I was running around the bases, fans were coming at me from everywhere, grabbing me, pounding me on the back. I was just trying to get around the bases and into the dugout—I ran at least one guy over—but I never made it to home plate. Later, after I got to the clubhouse, Nettles said I should return to the field and touch home plate, just to make it official. But when we got back out there, home plate and all the other bases were gone, stripped from their moorings and confiscated by the delirious Yankee fans."

Unfortunately, that was to be our final hurrah for 1976. When we got to the World Series we found, in the defending world champion "Big Red Machine" Cincinnati Reds, a whole different animal. We partied all night after beating the Royals and arrived in Cincinnati for the workout the next day tired and hungover. But Billy thought he could surprise and ambush the Reds, and you had to admire his brashness, confidence, and belief in his players. Unfortunately, we were swept in four games. The Reds just had more talent.

Adding insult to the loss was the disparaging remark that the Reds' manager, Sparky Anderson, made about Thurman in the interview room after game 4. Johnny Bench had been the hero for the Reds, batting .533 with 2 homers and 6 RBI, but Thurman had hit .529 for us. When asked to discuss the two great catchers, Sparky replied, "Gentlemen, don't ever embarrass a man by comparing him with Johnny Bench." As he spoke, Thurman was standing right there, off to the side, seething.

Sparky later apologized to Thurman, but I know that really hurt him. Thurman was intensely proud of his career and his accomplishments and didn't think he should take a backseat to any catcher in baseball, which is why, around All-Star time every year, he was particularly conscious about any media hype surrounding the Red Sox's Fisk. The Thurman-Fisk rivalry was at the center of the Yankees–Red Sox rivalry, and in my opinion, in the eight years they faced off against each other, from 1972 to 1979, Thurman was every bit the Hall of Famer Fisk was; his career just wasn't long enough.

Nobody was more disappointed about our World Series sweep at the hands of the Reds than Mr. Steinbrenner, who wasted no time in reloading for 1977 by taking full advantage of baseball's new free agency system. This was the other monumental gain won for the players by Marvin Miller—the right to become free agents after six years of service—and unlike most of the other owners, who viewed it as a death knell for baseball, Mr. Steinbrenner was a visionary insofar as using it to fast-track a world championship to Yankee Stadium. The biggest prize of the first free-agent class—which was filled with All-Star-caliber talent such as Don Baylor, Bobby Grich, Bert Campaneris, Sal Bando, Joe Rudi, Rollie Fingers, and Don Gullett— was Reggie Jackson, and over Billy Martin's staunch objections,

Mr. Steinbrenner put a full-court press on Reggie and signed him to a five-year contract for $2.96 million. In addition, Mr. Steinbrenner made certain the Reds would not be standing in his way again to a world championship by swooping Gullett away from them with a six-year, $2 million deal. (It sure didn't take long for free agency to have a profound effect on players' salaries!)

We were obviously delighted and excited with these signings, knowing we had an owner who was going to spare no cost in an effort to win. Billy, on the other hand, was particularly upset over the Reggie signing. For one thing, Billy wanted autonomy when it came to putting the team together. Billy was also used to being the star on all his teams. But while Billy had great baseball sense, Mr. Steinbrenner had great business sense and recognized the value of star quality. It was going to be up to Billy, who argued fruitlessly that the Yankees had a perfectly good cleanup hitter in Chambliss, to make it work with Reggie.

From the get-go that wasn't happening.

In spring training, Reggie didn't go out of his way to endear himself to a close-knit team that had just been to the World Series, making statements to the press about how important he was. And then there was the "I'm the straw that stirs the drink" article in *Sport* magazine in which he was quoted disparaging Thurman, our captain and leader. When in 1976 spring training Mr. Steinbrenner made Thurman the first Yankee captain since Lou Gehrig, we were all in full accordance. It was no coincidence either that Thurman went on to have his best season and won MVP honors. Thurman epitomized what a captain should be, with his intensity, his way of handling the pitching staff, and his clubhouse leadership. Everyone on the team respected him and looked up to him, and Mr. Steinbrenner recognized that. We also liked the way he was so gruff with the media. Made it easier on all of us. Making him captain was one of Mr. Steinbrenner's best moves.

The rift between Reggie and the team lasted quite a while and was further fueled by Billy's continuing refusal to bat Reggie in his accustomed cleanup spot. It also didn't help Billy's stability with Mr. Steinbrenner that, despite these splashy, expensive new additions—plus the acquisition of Bucky Dent from the White Sox to shore up shortstop right before the start of the season—we got off to a slow (2–7) start and were in third place in the AL East as late as mid-August.

All the while Billy and Reggie were feuding, players were griping about the constant turmoil, and Mr. Steinbrenner was losing his patience. The problem was that both Reggie and Billy liked the headlines and at times they tried to outdo each other. Compounding it was Ken Holtzman, who'd been Reggie's teammate on the 1972–74 A's championship teams and who really hated Billy. Holtzman was miserable in New York and never hid his desire to be traded. Even Thurman talked about wanting to be traded to Cleveland so he could be closer to his family in Canton. And Thurman was upset not with Billy but rather with Mr. Steinbrenner after he found out the Boss was paying Reggie more than him.

Things first came to a head in a Saturday TV *Game of the Week* on June 18 in Boston, when Reggie misjudged a fly ball in right field and was slow to retrieve it. I was on the bench and momentarily stunned at Billy's rage as he screamed over to Paul Blair to go out to right field and replace Reggie. Then we braced ourselves for the confrontation. Sparky Lyle, who particularly didn't like Reggie, was on the mound for us, and as Paulie ran by him on the way out to right field, we heard him shout, "Wooo-boy! I can't wait to see this!" As soon as Reggie got back to the dugout, he and Billy started screaming and charging at each other and had it not been for our coaches Yogi Berra and Elston Howard grabbing Billy and getting in between, it might have really been ugly. As it was, the whole scene was captured by the national TV cameras. In the clubhouse, Reggie was still agitated and said he was going to have it out with Billy. That's when I said to him, "Get changed and go back to the hotel, Reggie. You don't need any more problems and neither do we."

Mr. Steinbrenner was watching the game on TV from Florida, and after we were swept by the Red Sox, he flew to Detroit, our next stop, amid reports he was going to fire Billy. That was only averted when Reggie, realizing the fans would blame him as the villain if Billy were fired, convinced Mr. Steinbrenner the season would be lost with any more upheaval.

Unfortunately, the inner turmoil with Reggie and Billy continued and things came to a head again during an awful road trip in July in which we lost seven of ten to the Orioles, Brewers, and Royals. We were in Milwaukee, and Thurman and I were having a drink at the Pfister Hotel bar, discussing the whole situation with Billy and Reggie. Thurman said Mr. Steinbrenner was coming to town the next day and suggested we have a meeting with him. Initially, I was reluctant, citing the fact that he was the captain and it was appropriate that only he should be meeting with the owner on a team matter. But I guess he felt I was one of Mr. Steinbrenner's favorites and wanted reinforcement. Despite his strained relationship with Reggie, Thurman felt that, for the good of the team, Reggie should hit cleanup, where he was most comfortable.

The next night we went up to the Boss's suite. He was in his robe and he'd set up a blackboard with all these different lineups on it. He was also armed with a bunch of statistics about Reggie's batting average in the third, fourth, and fifth spots in the lineup. I don't think he had an opinion either way, but he made sure he was prepared.

"So what do you guys think we should do?" he asked.

"This is a little uncomfortable for us, going behind Billy's back like this," Thurman said, "but we only want what's best for the team and we're tired of the constant problems. If Reggie wants to hit fourth, let him hit fourth. He signed here with the idea he was going to hit fourth like he always had. Make him happy."

"What do you think?" Mr. Steinbrenner asked me.

"I agree with Thurman, sir. None of the rest of us care where we hit. It's a simple thing to do. I don't understand why Billy has been so stubborn about this."

We told him we understood the manager had every right to make out the lineup as he saw fit, but Reggie's ego was such that he couldn't perform to his utmost unless he batted cleanup. Suddenly, there was a knock on the door and outside was Billy, who had heard the conversation and demanded to be let in.

"I'll take care of this," Mr. Steinbrenner said, and sent us into the bathroom before letting Billy in.

"What the hell is going on here?" Billy screamed. "Who else is in here?"

He was clearly agitated and Mr. Steinbrenner called to us to come out of the bathroom.

"What are you guys doing here?" Billy demanded.

Before we could answer, Mr. Steinbrenner attempted to calm Billy down, explaining to him that we only wanted to relieve the turmoil on the club by trying to resolve this issue with Reggie and the cleanup spot. Mr. Steinbrenner suggested to Billy that maybe he ought to consider this.

"All we're trying to accomplish," Thurman said, "is to eliminate all this turmoil and distraction and get back to winning."

Billy said he'd think about it.

But it was a very uncomfortable situation. Billy was his own man and took great pride in being the bona fide leader and that whatever he said, went. Thurman and I felt very sheepish and embarrassed. We both liked Billy and here we were going behind his back to the

Boss—over Reggie! Even though Billy kept his cool, it was a very un-comfortable half hour in the Boss's suite. I managed for twenty-three years, and I know if one of my players went behind my back to the owner, I wouldn't be very happy. The next day Thurman and I had lunch and wondered if Reggie would be batting fourth that night. He wasn't.

Instead, the stalemate between Billy and Reggie continued on for another three and a half weeks, and after we were soundly beaten, 9–2, by the Mariners in Seattle on August 6—our fourth loss in five games, which dropped us five games back, in third place—I couldn't take it any longer. We were the defending American League champions and we were seemingly fraught with griping and dissension. After that game I went on a tirade in front of all the writers, basically calling out my teammates to either put up or shut up.

"The team had been struggling and, in the manner of the Yankees of that era, making the worst of a bad situation," said Moss Klein, the Yankees beat writer for the Newark *Star-Ledger*:

Everyone seemed to have a gripe. Munson wanted out, pushing for a hometown trade to Cleveland. Rivers was having bad days at the racetrack and wanted to be traded too. Bucky Dent was upset with Billy pinch-hitting for him all the time. Holtzman and Ed Figueroa were asking to be traded. Reggie was being Reggie. There was tension in the clubhouse and it was carrying over to the field. Sitting at his locker as the writers entered the silent clubhouse minutes after the Saturday-night game in Seattle, Lou launched into this stunning rebuke of the team: "The writers are all here. Why doesn't everyone speak up now? Now's the damn time. Everyone wants to get traded? Talk about it now after you get beat nine to f-ing two by a f-ing last-place team! How come nobody's saying anything now?" It went on

for three to four minutes as everyone, players and writers alike,
looked on in stunned and uneasy silence. But the next day, in
the series finale in Seattle, the clubhouse was noticeably lighter.
Lou had cleaned out the tension, and when the team got back
home, Billy started hitting Reggie cleanup and the team took off.
That was the turning point of the season.

I'm not sure what prompted that outburst by me, other than the
fact that we just didn't play well in the Kingdome and I was sick and
tired of getting our asses beat there by bad Mariner teams. There's no
question that 9–2 loss in Seattle was the low point of the '77 season
and, coincidence or not, when Billy started hitting Reggie cleanup
in the first game home against Oakland, August 10, we continued on
a streak of 24 wins in 27 games to surge into first place and never
look back. Once again our opponents in the ALCS were the Royals,
and though we were also again able to beat them, this was one hard-
fought five-game series, punctuated by the yeoman, truly heroic relief work of our closer, Mr. Sparky Lyle. The Royals won two of the
first three games, and when they knocked out Figueroa in the fourth
inning of game 4 to cut our early lead to 5–4, Billy did something extraordinary, for which today he'd be criticized to the heavens in the
broadcast booth and on Twitter: he brought in Sparky to preserve the
tenuous lead—in the fourth inning—with the Royals at second and
first and George Brett coming to the plate. That was the way Billy
managed—for the moment, for the game at hand, and to hell with
tomorrow. He knew the game was on the line right there, and Sparky
responded by retiring Brett on a liner to me in left and pitching 5⅓
innings of two-hit shutout relief to get us to game 5. We kept wondering: How long could Sparky go? But if anyone thought Sparky's work
for the series was done, having pitched in three straight games, he
would soon prove to be mistaken.

Even we assumed Billy couldn't use Sparky again after his longest outing of the year. What could he possibly have left? What he had was a huge pair of balls and an unwavering will to win. So there we were, down 3–2 in the eighth inning of game 5, when Billy once again called on Sparky, and he pitched another 1⅓ scoreless innings while we scored three runs in the ninth to win it.

Sparky's workhorse, shut-the-door relief work in the ALCS was typical of what he'd done all season for us. Six times he appeared in three or more consecutive games, and in June he recorded five saves in five straight appearances. In September as we blew past the Red Sox into first place, he had four wins and seven saves in thirteen appearances. It was no wonder in 1977 he became the first reliever to win the American League Cy Young Award—he led the league in appearances (72) and games finished (60), with 26 saves and a 2.17 ERA for 137 relief innings. You have to remember, in those days we all played on one-year contracts, but Sparky always wanted to be responsible to his teammates. As I said, he was the ultimate competitor. The tougher the situation, the better he performed—and he always took the ball. When Thurman caught Sparky, he never gave him a sign. He just let Sparky throw.

Kansas City gave us all we wanted in the '77 ALCS, right up to the 45th inning, and after it was over, we were drained physically. But we gutted it out for 12 innings—the last 3⅔ pitched by Sparky—to beat the Dodgers in game 1 of the World Series, and after losing the next game, we went to LA and took control of the series. Los Angeles was quite a different atmosphere, with Sinatra, Don Rickles, Kirk Douglas, and all these Hollywood celebrities around everywhere. It was fun to see all the stars, but we had business to attend to out there, and after winning two out of three at Chavez Ravine, we came home on the brink of winning the first Yankees world championship since 1962.

It was then, of course, that Reggie had his finest moment—and to his credit, he had a lot of them—hitting three home runs, each better than the other, to tie Babe Ruth's World Series record and complete the job. With three majestic swings, Reggie erased all the bullshit that had surrounded him his first year as a Yankee. Truthfully, we were all very happy for him. It brought us closer together as a team and it was especially great to see Reggie and Thurman hugging. As the season wore on, Thurman had started to come to the realization that Reggie was a winner and, as such, gained more respect for him. Reggie had said some stupid things but he was basically a good guy. At the same time, Reggie respected Thurman as the legitimate leader of the team and cultivated Thurman's friendship so he would be more accepted by the rest of the team. In a lot of ways, that mutual respect steeled us for more adversity that was to come in 1978.

CHAPTER 5

Death of a Captain and a Dynasty Detoured

I needed the full three and a half months of winter to recover from my first world championship.

If that sounds a little strange, it's only because, upon reflection, I realized it shouldn't have been so hard. We were a team that had learned how to win, with a core of hard-edge veteran players: Thurman, Reggie, Nettles, Roy White, Chris Chambliss, Rivers, Bucky, Sparky, players who didn't buckle under pressure. And yet it seemed as if we spent nearly the entire season on the precipice, dealing with our own self-inflicted wounds. Much of this had to do with Billy and his inability to get along with Reggie.

As I've said earlier, Billy, in my opinion, was a managerial genius, a brilliant in-game strategist, both fearless and cunning. At the same time, I came to see during the course of the 1977 season just why Billy, after always achieving instant success, had been subsequently fired so quickly in his three previous managing jobs. Think about it: in his first full season as the Yankees manager he'd taken the team to its first World Series in twelve years. He was the unquestioned toast of the town, and yet, in 1977, he was on the brink of being fired at least three times. How does that happen? We all rejoiced in that triumphant clubhouse celebration after the World Series; Billy right in the middle of it, pouring champagne over Mr. Steinbrenner's head while wrapping his arm around Reggie and heaping praise on him for his three-home-run night. It was probably the happiest moment of Billy's entire life.

But after thinking back on all that had gone down in 1977, I knew it wouldn't take much in '78 for Billy and Reggie to renew their hostilities, and I worried that the mix of Billy, Reggie, Mr. Steinbrenner, and a new team president in Al Rosen was just going to be too combustible.

You could see this coming when Gabe Paul resigned as the Yankees' general manager after the '77 season and Mr. Steinbrenner wasted no time in replacing him with Al Rosen, his longtime friend and a former American League MVP with the Indians whom he'd idolized as a kid growing up in Cleveland. On his way out the door, Gabe said: "I'm going to miss New York, but I'm especially going to miss the excitement of Billy Martin. I know people think he's tough to get along with, but I didn't find that at all. We got along a lot better than people think we did, especially at the end."

That was true. Gabe was Billy's one ally in the front office, who many times had served as a sounding board for Billy, as well as a buffer between him and Mr. Steinbrenner, and the peacemaker between Billy and Reggie. I should say here also that Gabe was the one Yankee executive who could restrain Mr. Steinbrenner from making impulsive deals, which would become an issue in the years to come.

So when the '78 season began unraveling, us falling fourteen games behind as late as July 19, there was no one to intervene for Billy when he went on that drunken rage about Reggie and (by association) Mr. Steinbrenner at O'Hare Airport in Chicago four days later. Instead of trying to save Billy, as Gabe had done so many times,

Rosen told Mr. Steinbrenner the only way to calm things down would be to get rid of Billy and allow him to bring in his man, Bob Lemon. Rosen and Billy had no use for each other, going all the way back to their '50s playing days as mutually hotheaded principals in the fierce Yankees-Indians rivalry.

A few words here about Bob Lemon: While on the exterior he came across as calm and easygoing, you did not want to cross him. Because if you did, he would not hesitate to confront you, even with his fists. He was from the old school. When I was playing for Lem in Kansas City, I remember having this particular shirt, a flowery thing with a big collar and ruffled cuffs like Elvis used to wear, and he didn't like it. Combined with the fact that my hair was always too long for him, he told me I "looked like a hippie with that foo-foo shirt" and ordered me not to wear it anymore. A couple of weeks later, we were going on a road trip and I *wore* the shirt under my sport jacket to try and hide it, but Lem saw it, came up to me, and ripped the buttons off! Like I said, you didn't defy him.

He also liked to have his cocktails, a telltale sign of his drinking being his very pronounced, bulbous nose, for which he took a lot of good-natured kidding. One time we were on the team bus going to a spring training game and made an unexpected stop at a gas station. Everyone was wondering what was going on, and Nettles yells out from the back of the bus, "We have to stop to get batteries for Lem's nose!" Lem had a saying: "I never bring bad losses home with me. I always leave 'em in a bar somewhere along the way."

Lem was the antithesis of Billy's high-strung persona, and with the help of the New York newspaper strike, we played relaxed, confident baseball the rest of the '78 season. After beating the Red Sox in the playoff game, it continued that way in the postseason against the Royals (again!) and the Dodgers.

In 1977, the Royals had taken us the full five games in the ALCS, with Sparky having to pitch a total of 9⅓ innings of one-run relief over four of them. This time, we knew we were the better team. After splitting the first two games in Kansas City, we broke their backs in game 3 at Yankee Stadium when George Brett hit three home runs (all solo shots) off Catfish and we came back to win the game, 6–5, on Thurman's two-run homer off Doug Bird in the eighth inning; a homer which can only be described as a howitzer shot, over 400 feet into the left-center-field monuments. It was Thurman's first home run in 54 games and probably the longest of his career. Afterward, even the Royals' manager, Whitey Herzog, couldn't contain his admiration, telling the writers, "That darn Thurman sure did hit it, didn't he?"

We closed it out the next day, Guidry and Gossage combining to outpitch the Royals' ace, Dennis Leonard, 2–1, and it was on to Los Angeles for a second straight World Series matchup against Tommy Lasorda's Dodgers. After losing the first two games in LA, we came back to New York and won all three in Yankee Stadium to take command of the series. I would be remiss if I didn't mention that in game 3, Nettles put on one of the most spectacular displays of fielding artistry in World Series history, robbing the Dodgers of extra-base hits in the fifth and sixth and ending bases-loaded rallies with diving stops of balls in the hole. In all, Nettles saved at least five runs behind Guidry.

The next night we went ten innings before winning, 4–3. I don't know why it was, but I felt particularly cocky when I came to the plate with two out, White on second, and Reggie at first in the tenth. I just remember saying to Jerry Grote, the Dodgers' catcher, "You can tell Lasorda this game is over," before lining an RBI single off Bob Welch into right-center field.

That was the backbreaker for the Dodgers. We beat them handily the next two games, 12–2 and 7–2, and what made it especially satisfying was Catfish limiting the Dodgers to two runs over seven innings to win the final game of the 1978 World Series.

On the joyous flight back to New York, I thought about something Mike Lupica of the New York *Daily News* said to me after the playoff game in Boston, about my play off Remy and Bucky's homer being the capper on this "miracle" comeback season. Miracle my ass.

As I told Mike, my play against Remy, Bucky's homer—or Reggie's homer and Goose gutting it out for the final 2⅔ innings—were merely products of a team that knew how to win. Just like in the postseason afterward, Thurman nullifying Brett's three homers in game 3 of the ALCS against Kansas City; Catfish shrugging off his loss to the Indians that forced the playoff game by winning the final World Series game against the Dodgers; or Nettles making those game-saving plays in game 3 of the World Series. If we'd spent '77 learning how to win, we spent the second half of '78 proving it.

We were all in our prime, with an owner who would spare no expense when it came to replenishing the team with talent, and there was every reason to believe that the consecutive world championships in 1977 and '78, hard as they were to achieve, were the beginning of a new Yankees dynasty.

Still, there were always going to be postseason changes. Although he handled it with typical unselfish class, Sparky was extremely unhappy at being supplanted by Goose as the team's closer a year after winning the Cy Young Award, and Mr. Steinbrenner acceded to his demand for a trade a month after the '78 season, sending him to Texas for a package of players that included a nineteen-year-old left-handed pitching prospect named Dave Righetti. It was a trade that would eventually pay huge dividends for the Yankees as Righetti went on to become first a dominant starter who pitched a July 4 no-hitter against the Red Sox in 1983, and later an equally dominant closer who saved 223 games for the Yankees from 1984 to 1990.

But initially the trade had huge repercussions at the start of the 1979 season in the wake of a shower room scuffle on April 19 between Goose and Cliff Johnson, the big, lumbering first baseman and DH. As the two tussled, Goose slipped to the floor, and tore ligaments in his right thumb. He was out nearly three months and, with Sparky gone, there was no one to adequately replace him. We had a particularly bad road trip in mid-June, losing five out of six in Minnesota and Texas to fall to 33–30, and that's when Mr. Steinbrenner decided we needed a "reverse" personality change with managers and fired Lemon in favor of bringing back Billy. By the time Goose got back, July 12, we were in fourth place, nine and a half games behind.

Two days earlier, I had managed to get myself embroiled in one of the silliest tantrums of my career when I went at it with Ted Giannoulas, the famous San Diego Chicken. We were playing the Mariners in Seattle and I was in a bad mood anyway because we never played well in the Kingdome. As I was trotting out to left field in the bottom of the fourth inning, the Chicken was standing in the infield, doing his thing, waving his hands as if to cast a hex on Ron Guidry, who was throwing his warm-up pitches. I didn't see any need for this sort of shenanigans so I started chasing the Chicken off the field, and when I couldn't catch up to him, I threw my glove at him. I'll say this: he was genuinely startled.

When I got out to left field, he followed me out there, waving a white flag of surrender, and tried to shake hands with me. I just waved him off and screamed at him to get the hell out of there. Later I told the writers he didn't belong on the field, clowning around out there where players are making a living. Bucky Dent said afterward that it was the funniest thing he ever saw at the ballpark. I was just sick and tired of losing all the time in the Kingdome. Giannoulas, for his part, said he couldn't understand my being upset, adding, "And to think I voted for him for the All-Star team." I did feel bad about it later and when I saw him a couple of years after, I apologized to him.

I took pride in competing. I used my temper to give me a second gear to get me to perform better. It was probably a lot of wasted energy, but it wasn't a show, especially when I was a player. I was really pissed. Maybe in this instance, with the Chicken, I might have been more restrained if it had been anywhere else but in the Kingdome. In retrospect, it was stupidity on my part. I should have just ignored him.

There was one good thing to come of the Chicken flap: I later found out my dustup with the Chicken served to put the kibosh on plans the Yankees had for their own mascot. Earlier that year it seemed one of the creators of *The Muppet Show* had come to the Yankees about creating a mascot for the team—a pear shaped "Yankee blue" creature named "Dandy"—to parade around the park and in the stands as an added attraction for young fans. The Yankees had quietly signed a $30,000 deal to lease "Dandy" for three years with plans to unveil him in late July. But after my blowup with the Chicken and reading my quotes about mascots having no place on the field, Mr. Steinbrenner agreed with me and canceled the deal. "Dandy" never saw the light of Yankee Stadium, unconditionally released before he ever set foot on the field.

About the only good thing that happened during Goose's absence in '79 was the trade with the Cubs that brought Bobby Murcer, my old running mate, back to the Yankees after a four-year absence. I was glad to have Bobby back but at the same time I felt sad that he had missed out on those three American League pennants and two world championships.

Even after Goose's return we didn't play much better and had fallen to fourteen games behind when we swept a three-game series from the White Sox in Chicago at the end of July. During that series, Thurman and I stayed with Bobby at the apartment Bobby had rented there in Arlington Heights during his stay with the Cubs—and for those couple of days it was once again the best of times for three close friends. On Tuesday night after the second game, we stayed up late, till 3:00 or 4:00 a.m., talking about old times. Thurman and I were so glad to have Bobby back with us and Bobby was so glad to be back. But he couldn't get past missing out on those two championships. For that he hated Gabe Paul, and we all cut up Gabe pretty good that night. At one point we started talking about the season at hand.

"You know," Thurman said, "we were at a very similar deficit this time last year. I think we can do it again. It's not too late! Tell you what, I'm gonna dedicate myself to that. We can do this!"

"I'm with you, Thurm," said Bobby. "I wasn't here last year but this team is too good to be this far out."

That night we all made a pact to make a concerted effort to pull off another great comeback, just as we'd done in '78. For Bobby it was especially important. He couldn't stop talking about how much he resented Gabe Paul for trading him away from the Yankees. He was thirty-three now and he didn't know how many more chances he would get. We talked and laughed into the night, dreaming, if you will, about more glory together.

During the course of that late-night bull session, Thurman talked about his new plane, a Cessna Citation 501 jet, which was considerably more powerful than the Beechcraft prop jet he'd been piloting the previous couple of years. I'd flown a few times with Thurman on the Beechcraft—to the Bahamas during spring training for fishing trips (which prompted Mr. Steinbrenner to remark one time, "Damn, you guy guys play quick spring training games!"), and on short road trips from Baltimore to New York. It was very comfortable and Thurman was a good pilot. But this plane was a lot sleeker and bigger. It looked like a huge bullet, with much more horsepower, and it was much more difficult to maneuver. Because of that, both Bobby and I didn't feel comfortable going up with Thurman in this plane. As Thurman went on about what a great plane it was, we tried our darndest to convince him to sell it. He had two other planes as well and it was getting a little difficult financially for him. But he kept talking about his love for flying, and I knew our pleas were falling on deaf ears.

That was the last conversation I ever had with him.

After we completed the sweep of the White Sox on Wednesday night, August 1, Thurman flew his plane home to Canton, Ohio— Bobby actually accompanied him to this small airport on the out- skirts of Chicago and watched him take off. The next day was an off-day and I was enjoying it in the pool with my kids at my home in Allendale, New Jersey, when Anita called me to the phone. It was Mr. Steinbrenner, she said, and he sounded very upset. When I got on the phone, Mr. Steinbrenner was all broken up and I could barely understand him—not to mention *comprehend* what he was saying.

Thurman was dead . . . plane crash attempting to land his plane at the Canton-Akron airport . . . didn't get out alive. I couldn't be- lieve what I was hearing. My first reaction was anger. I was mad at Thurman for that big airplane, mad that he wouldn't listen to Bobby and me. Then I just began crying, uncontrollably, as my mind be- gan racing with all those great memories: the 460-foot home run off Doug Bird that won game 3 of the '78 ALCS against Kansas City; the image of him shuffling around the clubhouse with that lumpy body and those scruffy whiskers that perpetually pushed the envelope on Mr. Steinbrenner's facial hair code. Catfish used to say Thurman was the only guy he ever knew who could make a $500 suit look like $150.

He had this gruff exterior that was intentionally intimidating to most of the writers, but underneath that facade he was a teddy bear, a devout family man who, because of his own father's long absences from the home during his childhood, doted on his kids, quietly visited sick kids in hospitals on the road, and took up flying so he could get back to his family in Canton every chance he could during the season. I remember one time we were on the road and Thurman sneaked off one morning to visit a hospital for kids with cancer. Somehow his wife, Diane, found out about it, and when he got home she asked him why he didn't tell even her about it. "Because you would've told the writers," Thurman replied.

Thurman was the consummate warrior, who played through pain and would never let on. He was a real clutch hitter, who loved being up there with the game on the line, and he reminded me a lot of myself. We were similar right-handed gap hitters, and I'm quite certain we'd have both hit a lot more homers if we'd played in Fenway Park instead of Yankee Stadium. Behind the plate, he took charge of our pitchers and had that unorthodox slingshot throwing style that was nevertheless very accurate. He was the captain. Our spiritual leader. If he'd stayed alive, I have no doubt he'd be in the Hall of Fame and, if he'd wanted, would have been a helluva manager.

Now, just like that, he was gone. August 2. My wife's birthday. And so every year I am reminded of my dear friend.

Those next few days were a blur. We opened up a four-game wraparound weekend series with the Orioles at Yankee Stadium the next day, and all I remember is the overwhelming grief I felt in left field as they played the National Anthem while, on Mr. Steinbrenner's orders, no one stood in the catcher's box. The other jolt to reality had been seeing Thurman's locker when we came into the clubhouse; also on Mr. Steinbrenner's orders, the locker had been emptied except for his catching gear, with his nameplate on top replaced with his number, 15. I have no memory of the game that night, other than we were shut out, 1–0, by our former Yankee teammates Scotty McGregor and Tippy Martinez. Before and after the game, Mr. Steinbrenner was in the clubhouse, just kind of walking around in a daze, patting guys on the back. You thought of him as the tough general but here he was breaking down, his eyes watery and red, unable to conceal his distress.

Mr. Steinbrenner really respected Thurman. He loved his toughness, loved the way he left everything on the field. He admired his baseball acumen and he was impressed with what a good family man Thurman was. He'd become very close to him. Probably the biggest measure of his respect for Thurman was the fact that he almost never took a shot at him in the papers like he regularly did with the rest of us. The only other one whom he never dared touch up was Catfish.

On Monday morning, with one more game to go in the Orioles series, we boarded a plane for Canton to bury Thurman. The airport there is only a short distance from Thurman's house, but I remember that the bus ride felt like forever. We got to the house, and seeing Diane and Thurman's kids made it even more difficult. But Diane was strong. She had always been a rock of stability for Thurman. We went from there to the funeral at the Canton Civic Center, which was packed, and Bobby and I both delivered eulogies. The rest of the day and the game back in New York that night also remain a blur. I just know that Bobby lifted everyone's spirits by driving in all five runs of our 5–4 win over the Orioles, including a three-run homer off Dennis Martinez in the seventh inning. There couldn't have been a finer tribute to his best friend, and afterward Bobby gave his bat to Diane. The only Yankees uniform I still have is the one I wore the rest of 1979 with the black armband and the "15" patch for Thurman. It's not for sale. Ever.

With Thurman taken from us so suddenly, it was hard to imagine how we were going to get through the rest of the season. You're professional ballplayers and you've got a job to do, but it's hard to do it when your heart and mind are elsewhere. That's why the now-famous "girl on the bus" caper, juvenile and raunchy as it may have been, turned out to be a welcome diversion for all of us—even, I think, Mr. Steinbrenner.

It seemed that after the last game in Chicago, a young girl in short-shorts managed to break through the crowd at the visiting-team gate and make her way onto our bus, whereupon she produced a magic marker, pulled down her shorts, and began asking for autographs—on her bare behind! It wasn't until Billy and our traveling secretary Bill "Killer" Kane—who had been upstairs in the press-room bar having drinks with White Sox owner, Bill Veeck—arrived and saw the girl and had her hastily ejected off the bus by the security guards. Everyone had a good laugh about it, and it was, we thought, quickly forgotten in the ensuing days of Thurman's death and funeral.

Unfortunately, it was anything but forgotten in Chicago after Mike Royko, the columnist for the *Chicago Sun-Times* got ahold of the story from a woman in the crowd whose son had been waiting by the bus for an autograph only to be pushed aside by the girl. Royko's column about Yankees players blowing off young kids to sign autographs on a girl's naked butt was front-page news in Chicago and back-page news in New York right after Thurman's funeral. It was such big news that Bowie Kuhn, the commissioner of baseball, announced he was conducting an investigation of the incident. The day the story broke in the New York papers, Mr. Steinbrenner came down to the clubhouse and was furious. "How could you guys do this?" he screamed. "You've embarrassed the Yankees and embarrassed me and now I've got the goddamned commissioner coming down on us!"

I listened to him going on, and in light of all the grief we had all been feeling, the absurdity of this whole thing made me start to laugh. I don't know why, I don't know what made me say it, I was still so mad about Thurman, I just blurted out, "Oh, c'mon, George. If you'd have been on the bus you would have given her your autograph too—and it's a lot longer than ours! C'mon, it was all in fun." For a moment, everyone was silent. George looked at me, at first, I think, disbelieving at what I had just said, then he smiled and waved his arms, saying, "I give up!" and walked out of the room. That's when we all had a welcome laugh, and it was the last we ever heard about it.

I have little memory of the rest of the '79 season other than the fact that Mr. Steinbrenner's managerial "reverse" of Billy for Lemon did not have the same desirable effect as the one of 1978. We never got out of fourth place, finishing 13½ games behind, and at the end of the year we lost our other cornerstone clubhouse leader when Catfish succumbed to the chronic pain in his shoulder and retired. At the same time, we had more internal upheaval. Rosen resigned as team president in midseason, and shortly after the World Series Billy got himself in hot water with Mr. Steinbrenner again by engaging in a barroom fight in Bloomington, Minnesota, with a guy who was described in the papers as a middle-aged marshmallow salesman.

Looking back now on the 1979 season, as far as I'm concerned it could have just as well started and ended on Opening Day—which I missed because of the birth of my son Derek, the happiest moment of that year.

Mr. Steinbrenner took a couple of months to replace Rosen before finally settling on Gene Michael—"the Stick"—as his new GM. After retiring as a player in 1976, Stick was hired by Mr. Steinbrenner as a scout and then, in 1979, managed our Triple-A farm team in Columbus. Looking back, I'm not surprised Mr. Steinbrenner chose to make Stick, who had no front-office experience, his GM. Stick—a rangy, excellent defensive shortstop in his playing days who couldn't hit a breaking ball to save his life—was a guy who knew baseball and was an excellent judge of talent. His evaluations of players, both the ones he managed at Columbus or scouted before that, were most often spot on, and Mr. Steinbrenner recognized that. Something that was not so well known about him was his skill as a gin player, with which he made hundreds of extra dollars during the season from Yankees personnel patsies. I learned early on to avoid those late-night card games on the road in which Stick was one of the participants.

Stick had barely been in the GM job a couple of weeks when Billy had his latest off-the-field imbroglio in Minnesota, and at first Mr. Steinbrenner wanted him to take over as manager. But he was finally able to convince the Boss he should remain as GM and hired Dick Howser, our former third base coach who had left to become the head baseball coach at Florida State, to replace Billy. After that, Stick set about making over the team, post-Thurman and post-Catfish, with a series of inspired trades and free-agent signings. To replace Thurman, he traded Chris Chambliss to the Blue Jays for catcher Rick Cerone and a left-handed starter, Tommy Underwood, and off the free-agent market he signed Bob "the Bull" Watson, for first base, plus lefty Rudy May and the old Red Sox graybeard Luis Tiant for the pitching staff. With Watson hitting .307 with 13 homers as the right-handed platoon first baseman, Cerone hitting a career-high 14 homers behind the plate, and May and Underwood combining for 28 wins, we rebounded by winning 103 games in 1980, beating out Weaver's Orioles by three games for the AL East title.

From a personal standpoint, however, the 1980 season was not as enjoyable as it should have been. Much as I had looked forward to playing for Howser—whom we called "Baby Dome" because of the size of his head—I sensed early on that my playing time was going to be curtailed considerably when I didn't get a whole lot of spring at-bats. Neither did Murcer, and as we bided so much time on the bench when we felt we should be playing, we gave Howser a rough time. It didn't matter that the rest of the players were getting the job done; we were both players in our late thirties, closer to the end of our careers, and we saw it slipping away right before our eyes. Before a long road trip in August, Howser called me into his office and said, "You've given me a hard time all year but you've got experience and I'm going to give you a chance to play if you think you can get it done."

"Damn straight," I said, and from August 15 to September 5, I started almost every game and lifted my average from .261 to .310. But then Howser called me in and said, "You look tired and look like you could use a day off." I agreed, but inexplicably one day off turned out to be just three starts over the better part of three weeks. Things came to a head in a September game in Toronto in which I'd gone in to play left field late in the game. It was a cold and foggy night in old Exhibition Stadium and Yogi was in charge of positioning the outfielders, but I couldn't see him. I could only hear someone yelling, and I finally just gave him a hand wave as if to say "leave me alone." When I got back to the dugout, Howser came up to me and said, "I didn't appreciate the way you showed up Yogi out there." When I protested that I couldn't see anything in the fog and got a little testy with him, he said, "Why don't you just brick it."

We were on the bus to the airport and I was telling Nettles about what transpired with me and Howser and asked him what "brick it" meant. "It means, why don't you just go home," he said.

Now I was really pissed. On the plane ride to Boston, I went up to the front and confronted Howser, who told me to see him later in his suite at the hotel. When I got up to Howser's suite he was sitting there with our pitching coach—Stan "the Steamer" Williams—who also served as his enforcer.

"Just so you know," Howser told me, "from now on I'm gonna platoon you." (I'm thinking, "This is my reward?") "And if you're not happy about that," Howser continued, "I suggest you demand a trade and get the hell out."

Looking back, I can understand why Howser took that stance with me. He was a first-year manager who'd done a heck of a job keeping the team in first place for nearly the entire season despite constant criticism and barbs from Mr. Steinbrenner—and I'm sure he viewed Murcer and myself as Mr. Steinbrenner's boys, who weren't being team players and making his job even more difficult.

The otherwise rejuvenating 1980 season came to a screeching and shocking end when we were swept in the ALCS by the Royals. We were a much better team than Kansas City, but nothing went right for us—most notably the play in the eighth inning of our 3–2 game 2 loss in which Willie Randolph was thrown out at the plate attempting to score on Watson's two-out double only because George Brett was in perfect position to catch Royals' left fielder Willie Wilson's over-throw of the relay man. Not long after, Mr. Steinbrenner took out his wrath by firing our third base coach, Mike Ferraro—which proved to be the last straw for Howser, who resigned as manager a few days later. At the press conference in Mr. Steinbrenner's office in Yankee Stadium, it was announced that Stick would be moving down from the front office to become manager.

Toward the end of the press conference, Howser was asked by the writers if he had any advice for Stick, who was about to become Mr. Steinbrenner's sixth manager—not including Billy twice—in nine years.

"Yeah," he said, "have a strong stomach and a long contract."

Words to remember.

I had always liked Howser when he was a coach. We kidded around a lot and periodically had drinks together on the road. But when he became a manager the relationship changed, and, looking back, I learned something from that. He had his reasons for doing what he did with me, and he won the most games of any Yankee manager since 1963. But when it happens to you, losing playing time for no good reason, you don't like it, and I was thirty-seven then and wondering what was going to happen to me. That's when Mr. Steinbrenner called and told me he wanted me back.

With Stick as the manager—a guy we knew Mr. Steinbrenner liked and respected—and the addition of Dave Winfield, the premier player on the free-agent market, whom Mr. Steinbrenner signed to a monster ten-year, $23 million contract, I had high hopes about the 1981 season. But while we did manage to get back to the World Series, it was another season fraught with turmoil, starting with the two-month players' strike that resulted in the cancellation of 713 games from June 12 to August 9. Once the strike was settled, Baseball Commissioner Bowie Kuhn announced a split-season format to determine the postseason, with all the teams in first place on June 12— one of which was us—automatically qualified for the postseason. That should have put Stick in good stead with Mr. Steinbrenner, but we were a veteran team, and after the long layoff it took some time for us to get on track again. Too much time.

As we struggled out of the second-half gate, losing 10 of our first 16 games in August, Stick was hearing it every day from Mr. Steinbrenner until finally losing it on August 28 in Chicago, when he told the writers he was tired of being threatened. "If George wants to fire me he should just go ahead and do it," he declared. I cringed when I heard that, knowing there was no way out once you challenged the Boss in public, and sure enough, on September 6, Mr. Steinbrenner dropped the ax on Stick and brought old reliable Bob Lemon out of the bullpen to manage the team for the rest of the season.

The split-season format forced baseball to add an extra tier to the playoffs, and when our first-round opponents, the Milwaukee Brewers, won back-to-back games at Yankee Stadium to tie the best-of-five first series, Mr. Steinbrenner came into the clubhouse and started reading us the riot act. After a few minutes of this, Cerone, a tough-as-nails Jersey guy, popped up: "Screw you, George. You don't know what you're talking about. You don't know anything about baseball!"

Everyone kind of froze in silence. Here was Cerone, who'd barely been with us a year and half, having the impudence to tell off the Boss in front of the whole team. You could do that with Mr. Steinbrenner, but you'd better be prepared to back it up—which is precisely what Cerone did, going 2-for-3 with a backbreaking seventh-inning homer the next day that cemented our 7–3 clinching victory. We followed that up by sweeping Billy Martin's Oakland A's in the ALCS—a crushing loss for Billy, who so desperately wanted to show up Mr. Steinbrenner.

After the last game of that series I made a point to go over to the A's clubhouse. When I walked into Billy's office, he was seated at his desk, crying. I went up to him and gave him a hug and, in an effort to console him, said, "Whatever success we've had came from you, Billy. You were the one who taught us how to win, and for that you should be proud."

I know that made him feel good. I knew how hard Billy took losing—that was one trait we had in common—and losing to the Yankees especially hurt him. The Yankees were his life. When he got fired in '78 and then again in '79, I felt bad for him. We'd had kind of an evolving relationship. Early on, when Billy first came to the Yankees, I wasn't one of his favorites, as Nettles, Thurman, Catfish, Chambliss, and Sparky were. I had to prove myself to him. In '75 and '76 he platooned me all the time and I think he looked at me as a platoon outfielder. It wasn't until a game in 1977 in which there was a long rain delay that I finally felt I was one of his guys. I'd gotten a couple of hits before the rain came and just before the game was to resume he came to me and asked, "Do you want to stay in?" That's the way he showed what he thought of you. Of course, I hit .330 that year, so he really had no choice but to keep playing me.

As for the '81 World Series, once again against Lasorda and the Dodgers, about all I can say is it was one big fiasco. We won the first two games in New York and were looking to put a hammerlock on the Dodgers by beating their Mexican phenom, Fernando Valenzuela, in game 3. And it looked hopeful from the outset when a clearly nervous Valenzuela walked Willie Randolph to start off the game and issued a second free pass to Winfield one out later. That brought me up, and with Valenzuela continuing to struggle with his command, I ran the count to 3-1. I knew from all the scouting reports Valenzuela's best pitch was his screwball, but at the same time, I had never hit a World Series homer, and I thought, *If I stand off the plate a little and this guy sneaks a fastball, I can really do some damage.* Instead, he threw me a very hittable screwball and I pulled it right to the shortstop, who turned it into an inning-ending double play.

Of all my at-bats in all the World Series games I played in, that's the one I'll never forget until the day I die. If I'd been thinking as a hitter, I would've gone the opposite way with it. If I'd have held back just a little and driven the ball to the opposite field it would have been good for two runs and we would have been on our way to putting away the Dodgers right there.

Instead, the Dodgers came back to score three runs off Righetti in their half of the first inning, knocking him out in the third inning, and later, in the eighth, Lem kind of lost his mind. We were trailing 5–4 when Aurelio Rodriguez and Larry Milbourne started the eighth with consecutive singles against Valenzuela, bringing up the pitcher's spot in the order. All of a sudden Lem gets up, looks down the bench, and hollers out, "Where's my bunter?" I'm sitting there saying, "What?" When nobody moved, Lem shouted out again, "Where's my bunter?" Again nobody moved, and Lem, in exasperation, shouted again, "Where's my damn *bunter*?" We were all trying to hold back our laughter, especially Murcer, until he realized that the bunter in question Lemon was looking for was *him*!

"Grab a bat, Murcer, and get up there."

Bobby was as stunned as all of us. Here was the one power-hitting threat on our bench, and Lem was ordering him to bunt! He'd probably never been asked to pinch-hit a bunt in his life—which became apparent when he popped up his bunt attempt to Ron Cey in third base foul territory, who alertly threw over to first to double up Milbourne. For the rest of the series, Bobby took such a beating, all of us yelling "Where's my bunter?" at him, and for years afterward it became a running joke. Whenever I saw Bobby in a restaurant or bar, I'd shout out, "Where's my bunter?"

Meanwhile, sometime after the second game in LA, Mr. Steinbrenner got into a fight, allegedly with a couple of drunken, rowdy Dodgers fans, in the elevator of our hotel. We all kind of chuckled when we heard his story of the incident the next day; of how he defended our honor and cleaned the floor with these two ruffians. We always figured what really happened was he got into an argument with his wife and punched a wall. But a World Series that had started off so promising in New York had now quickly descended into a calamity of errors with us getting swept in LA. Game 6 back at Yankee Stadium was the final humiliation, a 9–2 drubbing that got its impetus when, with the score 1–1, Lem pinch-hit for Tommy John in the fourth inning—again with Murcer. This time there were runners on first and second with two out, and obviously, Lem was hoping for a three-run homer that would get us back on track. And darn if Bobby almost delivered on it, hitting a flyout to deep right field. But John was understandably furious at being removed from the game after just four innings. In effect, that was the end of our season right there, as the Dodgers rallied for seven runs in the next two innings against our bullpen.

Right after the last out, on orders from Mr. Steinbrenner, the Yankees' longtime public address announcer, Bob Sheppard, read an apology to the Yankee Stadium fans for us losing the World Series. After beating the Dodgers in both the '77 and '78 World Series, I suppose Mr. Steinbrenner thought we'd have no problem beating them a third time. But this was embarrassing. We'd given it our all, and now he was apologizing for our play? What a way to end the season.

Even though I hit .438 in the '81 World Series, I was once again uncertain about my future. I'd appeared in only sixty games in the strike-shortened season, and with Jerry Mumphrey and Dave Winfield having been brought in as right-handed bats to complement Oscar Gamble and Bobby Murcer in the outfield, I wasn't sure just where I fit in. All these things were going through my mind back home in Tampa when I got a phone call from Mr. Steinbrenner asking me to come over to his office at American Ship. I told Anita, "Don't be surprised if, when I come home, I'm no longer a Yankee."

The meeting started out with Mr. Steinbrenner thanking me for everything I'd done for the Yankees and what a good run we'd had. He asked me what I wanted to do and I told him I still wanted to play even though I knew my role might be diminished. At that point, he said, "Let's talk about it. Have you ever had a long-term contract?" When I said no, he asked, "Well, would you like one?" He caught me completely by surprise.

"Well . . . uh . . . sure," I said.

"Good," he said. "Here's what I'm gonna do. I'm gonna give you a three-year deal for $300,000, $350,000, and $400,000."

I was flabbergasted. I thought I was stealing money. This, I thought, more than made up for all those times I felt I'd cheated myself out of money. I'd be forty-one before this contract was over. The next day, Anita called Mr. Steinbrenner to thank him, and he told her that was the first time he'd ever gotten such a call from a player's wife. But as I was soon to learn, with Mr. Steinbrenner there was always a catch— which in this case was a weight clause that required me to get under 205 pounds or be subject to daily fines of $250. I had never had a weight problem, so I didn't think much of it at the time. But this was George's way of maintaining the upper hand.

Anita and I were enjoying a wonderful relaxing winter, content in the feeling that, for the first time, we had financial security when, in mid-January, who shows up at my door but Hopalong Cassady, the former Ohio State Heisman Trophy–winning running back who worked for Mr. Steinbrenner as the Yankees' minor-league fitness coach. He was dressed in a sweat suit and carried a duffel bag.

"Mr. Steinbrenner has instructed me to start working you out, Lou, in preparation for spring training," Hoppy said, handing me the duffel bag. "Remember what Mr. Steinbrenner said about your weight? We'll I'm here to make sure you get there the right way."

I didn't know what to say. Hoppy informed me he'd gotten permission to use the track at the University of South Florida, where he'd taken the liberty of setting up an obstacle course. After I was done running the course, Hoppy said, we would then go over to the gym, where I'd work the Nautilus machine. The first day, Hoppy got himself a cup of coffee, went up in the stands, and blew his whistle for me to start running my laps around the track. "You're going to need to get under forty minutes," he said.

Well, it took me a little over an hour, and as I came in, Hoppy was shaking his head. "This is embarrassing, Lou," he said. "I'm ten years older than you and I can do this course faster than that."

The second day I did the course there was no improvement and

Hoppy was just as critical of my performance, again maintaining that he could easily run it under forty minutes.

"I'll tell you what, Hoppy," I said. "You know that Spanish brandy you like so much? I'll bet you a bottle of that and two hundred dollars that you can't do this course in under forty minutes."

"You're on," Hoppy said.

The next day, I took the whistle and went up in the stands with a cup of coffee and watched Hoppy huff and puff his way around the track. He couldn't do it either—for three more days he tried—but I gave him the brandy and the $200 anyway. When I got to spring training in Fort Lauderdale a couple of weeks later I weighed in right around 210 pounds, but when Mr. Steinbrenner saw my weight sheet, he confronted me in the parking lot, frowning.

"I can't believe I had my fitness guy pick you up three days a week to get you in shape and you come in here still overweight," he fumed.

I thought he'd laugh when I told him what had happened with Hoppy—it was stupid on my part—because that made him even madder. "That damn Hoppy," he said. "Played too many games with a soft helmet."

Alas, that wasn't the end of it. For the next two weeks Mr. Steinbrenner was relentless in enforcing that weight clause, ordering Lemon to play me in A games and B games without a day off, all the while fining me $250 a day. At one point I had to be restrained from coming to blows with Lem. After playing a night game following a B game in the afternoon, I was so tired and my feet were hurting so much that I pulled off my shoes and heaved them over the right field fence. Lem did not take kindly to that, and after he called me out, I charged at him as the other players got between us.

Calculated on his part or not, the weight clause issue wound up serving a second purpose for Mr. Steinbrenner. After I began complaining to the writers about being treated like "Little Orphan Annie" and he fired back, saying I would be lost if I ever had to go into business instead of playing baseball, it dominated the back pages of the New York tabloids for a week.

Running and fitness were the orders of the day that spring of '82. After our loss to the Dodgers in the World Series, Mr. Steinbrenner, noting the continued success of the Royals and Reds on their artificial turf, determined we needed to go in a new direction—to a speed team—and brought in two of the Reds' fastest players, Ken Griffey Sr. via a trade and Davey Collins as a free agent. When we arrived at camp we were greeted by Harrison Dillard, the 1948 Olympic gold medal hurdler, who had set up a series of running drills for us. For the first week all we did was run in these heavy sweat suits and we weren't allowed to pick up a bat. The writers all thought this was very amusing and began calling us the "Bronx Burners" in their stories, which got Mr. Steinbrenner highly annoyed.

I felt bad for Lem. It was a particularly difficult spring for him. He had all these outfielders—Mr. Steinbrenner had hedged his bets on the speed game by re-signing me and Murcer—and he had no idea what he was supposed to do with them. During the course of the 1982 season, the Yankees went through forty-seven different players, three managers, five pitching coaches, and three hitting instructors. Mr. Steinbrenner was seemingly in a constant state of panic, firing Lemon after just fourteen games, bringing back Stick. That first day on the job, Stick asked me, "What do you think?" I told him, "Stick, you've made a terrible mistake. This is a mess and I don't know how you'll ever be able to sort it out." It turned out that night was the game in which Reggie made his spectacular return to Yankee Stadium with the Angels after Mr. Steinbrenner had decided not to re-sign him, and he hit a monster home run off Guidry. As he circled the bases, the crowd of nearly fifty thousand rose in unison and all started chanting "Steinbrenner sucks!" Watching this from his box,

Mr. Steinbrenner was apoplectic. After the game he summoned Stick and his coaches up to his office. Stick told me when he got to the office, Mr. Steinbrenner was standing in the door and greeted him by saying, "You're killing me, Stick!" His first game! He managed the team for the next three months before Mr. Steinbrenner fired him after we lost both ends of a doubleheader on August 3. For his third manager of the 1982 season, Mr. Steinbrenner turned to Clyde King, his longtime confidant.

At one point, we lost 12 out of 15 games in September, and we finished up 79–83, in fifth place. Despite the glut of outfielders, I was able to get into 102 games—the last time I would play 100 games—and hit a very respectable .307. But it was hardly a satisfactory season for me, as the realization set in how far we had gone astray from the '76–'78 glory years when Thurman was our leader and rock.

Clyde King was a smart man. Even though he looked like a college professor with those horn-rim glasses, he was tough. He was also Mr. Steinbrenner's man and everybody knew it, to the point where we thought a lot of the time George was writing out the lineups for him. As such, we all assumed he'd be back as manager in 1983. But when reports came out the last week of the '82 season that Billy had torn up his office in Oakland after an argument with the A's general manager, Sandy Alderson, all of a sudden, Clyde had no chance.

I wish I could explain the fatal attraction between Mr. Steinbrenner and Billy Martin. When I think about it—hiring and firing a man five times to manage the Yankees—it's incomprehensible. Only George Steinbrenner could contrive something like that. When Billy came back for the third time in 1983, no player on the team had ever experienced anything like that. But Mr. Steinbrenner loved toughness and he also understood that baseball was entertainment—and Billy provided both. Billy was his star and Billy more than anyone else could get him regularly on that coveted back page of the tabloids.

Sadly, with each of his succeeding tours of duty as the Yankees' manager, things with Billy seemed to get crazier and crazier, and even though we bounced back with 91 wins in 1983, the season was punctuated by one tempest after another between Billy and the umpires, Mr. Steinbrenner and the league officials, and Billy and Mr. Steinbrenner. From the Yankees' standpoint it will probably be most remembered for the Pine Tar Game, which dragged on for over a month through the courts of New York after Billy initially succeeded in getting a two-out, two-run, ninth-inning homer by George Brett off Goose Gossage nullified on July 24 at Yankee Stadium.

What happened was, before the game, Graig Nettles had been watching Brett taking batting practice with a bat that had pine tar on it beyond the legal limit of 18 inches up the handle. When he alerted Billy to this, Billy said, "Okay, but we're not going to say anything about it now. Let's wait and see what happens during the game." When Brett hit the homer, Billy raced out of the dugout, screaming to the umpires to check the bat and, upon inspection, they agreed the pine tar on it exceeded the legal limit. That's when Brett went totally crazy, charging the umpires like a wounded bull in a scene that is still replayed on the TV sports networks every July 24. Once again, Billy looked like a genius, although Nettles deserves the credit for being the heady player he was.

But it was short-lived genius for us when the Royals appealed and American League president, Lee MacPhail, citing the "spirit of the rule" (whatever that was), overturned the umpires' decision, restored the home run, and ordered the game picked up in the ninth inning 3½ weeks later. During that time, Mr. Steinbrenner fought MacPhail's decision through the courts and made a public statement that MacPhail, who lived in Manhattan, "might want to go house-hunting in Kansas City." That got him docked with a one-week suspension and a fine of $50,000 from Commissioner Kuhn. On the other hand, Billy was suspended twice during the season by MacPhail for his run-ins with umpires. It was chaos throughout, and after the season none of us were surprised when Mr. Steinbrenner once again fired Billy.

What *was* a surprise was his decision to elevate Yogi from the coaching staff to succeed Billy, if only because Yogi had never openly expressed interest in managing again after he'd been fired twice before—by the Yankees in 1964 and the Mets in 1975, despite having taken both teams to the World Series. In addition to it being another disappointing (third-place) season teamwise, I could see the end coming for me in 1983. I missed most of the last two months with a sore shoulder and dizzy spells, which may have been a recurrence of that inner ear problem I'd suffered in 1975. I hit .291 but in only 53 games, and at the end of the year I was joking with the writers about the "angel of death" circling overhead around me.

That winter, Yogi called and asked me if I would be willing to serve as his hitting coach in addition to being a part-time player. I was making $400,000, I had a small tear in my rotator cuff, which prevented me from taking more than a few swings in batting practice, and, at forty-one, I knew I couldn't produce the way I once had, so I agreed. I'd always had a passion for hitting after having had the good fortune of learning the mechanics of it from the master, Charlie Lau. For the first two and a half months I really enjoyed my new job, working with the hitters but playing infrequently. I was hitting over .300 but in only 80 at-bats when Yogi came to me in mid-June, accompanied by that "angel of death." He needed a roster space, he said, for Brian Dayett, a promising young outfielder who was hitting over .300 at Triple-A Columbus.

"What do you think about becoming a full-time coach?" he said. "Maybe you want to talk it over with Mr. Steinbrenner?"

I knew the time was right, and after calling Mr. Steinbrenner we

agreed that I would retire, with my final game and an official ceremony, on Saturday afternoon, June 16, at Yankee Stadium. But first we
had to go to Boston for a midweek series against the Red Sox, and on
the final game, Thursday, something extraordinary happened to me.

Yogi had put me in the starting lineup, and when I came to the
plate for my first at-bat, leading off the second inning, the Fenway
Park crowd of over 28,000 rose to their feet and gave me a standing
ovation. I was stunned. I had been a bitter rival competing against
the Red Sox, but for the great fans of Boston, time, I guess, had
healed all those old wounds. After the ovation subsided, I hit a single and later came around to score. I later doubled in the fourth and
singled in the sixth, finishing the day 3-for-3 to raise my average to
.321. Afterward, I was thinking to myself, "What did I just do? I can
still hit!"

June 16, 1984, my last day as a player, was almost anticlimactic
after the reception I'd gotten in Boston. There were 37,583 fans at
Yankee Stadium, including Anita, my three kids, my parents, and
two of my uncles, Mac and Manuel, and it was only fitting that we
should be playing the Orioles and the man in the other dugout—
Earl Weaver. When I came to bat for the first time in the second inning, I got goosebumps seeing the crowd on their feet, applauding
and screaming "Louuuu! Louuuu! Louuuu!" In my little speech I
thanked Anita for putting up with me all those years and for the
sacrifices she made, raising the kids while I was away so much, and I
thanked God for the blessings of my career. I only wish I could have
given the crowd the same finish I'd given the Boston fans, but I took
an 0-for-5 against Scotty McGregor, a guy I'd previously had a lot of
success against.

At least I was credited with the game-winning RBI on a bases-
loaded groundout in the third, and I also made a nice throw to catch
Ken Singleton trying to stretch a single into a double in the second.

What was especially touching was Yogi sending Steve Kemp out to replace me in left field in the ninth inning so I could get one last ovation from the crowd. As I trotted in, I couldn't help seeing Anita standing in the box seats behind our dugout crying her eyes out.

My 0-for-5, which was mostly the product of being overanxious all day, was just as well, though. I had no doubts I had made the right decision to retire, with a .302 average for the season and .291 for my career. As I told the writers, "I hope my hitters didn't watch me today. I would have set them back years!"

A part of my life was over and I wasn't sure what lay ahead, other than working with the hitters. I did, however, get a hint later on in the '84 season after I'd been asked to participate in a *Sporting News* cover photo shoot at Yankee Stadium. My friend Barry Halper, one of the Yankees' limited partners, was one of the foremost collectors of baseball memorabilia, and he'd arranged to have a group of Yankees—myself, Rickey Henderson, Don Baylor, Willie Randolph, and John Montefusco—pose in the original uniforms of the all-time great players (Ty Cobb, Cy Young, Honus Wagner, and so forth), and even Mr. Steinbrenner had agreed to be in the picture, posing as the great Yankee owner Jacob Ruppert, in an old three-piece suit and a fake handlebar mustache. But the day of the shoot, I got delayed at home, and Baylor and Randolph also missed it, causing much dismay on the part of Mr. Steinbrenner. When I got to the park, Barry came up to me and warned me that Mr. Steinbrenner was in a fury.

"I was riding up in the elevator with him afterward and he told me Willie better not ever ask for another favor for his wife and that Baylor can forget about any more extra tickets for the players association," Barry told me.

"Oh shit, he really *is* pissed," I said. "What did he say about me?"

"You?" Barry replied. "Oh he said he's gonna *really* fix you, Lou. He said he's gonna make *you* the manager!"

CHAPTER 6

Managing for the Man

Despite all the speculation about Mr. Steinbrenner's plans for me to one day manage the Yankees, I had no illusions of that happening any time soon. Not with Yogi at the helm. Yogi was an iconic Yankee, seemingly untouchable from Mr. Steinbrenner's public criticism and impulsive acts. Or at least so I thought.

In welcoming me to his staff, Yogi made a point of saying I needed to be concerned only with the hitters, especially the young ones coming through the system. It was understood, not so much from Yogi but from Mr. Steinbrenner, that as a coach now, I would be part of all the organization meetings but not in any of the decision making, which was fine with me.

One thing I needed to keep in mind, Yogi told me, was that, as a coach, I had to separate myself from the players. I was part of management now and, so, on the road, I found myself hanging out more with the other coaches, the traveling secretary, "Killer" Kane, and even the writers. Whenever the writers would see me in the hotel bar late at night I would joke that I was the "midnight coach" in charge of curfews. One night in late June—an off-day—we had flown into Kansas City, and, as I was accustomed to doing, I invited all the players and some of the writers down to my restaurant, the Long Branch

Saloon on the Plaza, which I co-owned with my close friend Walt Coffey, and treated them to dinner. It was a popular place where, after dinner, a few of the players would take the liberty of becoming guest bartenders. This one night it got to be about 1:00 a.m., with the place nearly cleared out, when one of the writers joked that I was breaking curfew.

I smiled and pointed to the corner of the bar, where forty-five-year-old Phil Niekro, our starting pitcher the next night, was sitting all alone, nursing a scotch.

"I can't leave here until he does," I said, "and who am I to tell 'Father Time' he has to go to bed?" (For the record, we lost a 3–2 squeaker to the Royals the next night, but Niekro went all the way and gave up only three runs.)

At the time of my retirement in '84, we had been scuffling as a team, six games under .500, and from June 29 to July 6 we lost six out of eight to fall to 25–35. It was then that Mr. Steinbrenner—adhering to his own father's oft-repeated credo, "It's far better to be the hammer than the nail"—began hammering Yogi with regularity. It all came to a head at a meeting in Mr. Steinbrenner's office at Yankee Stadium in early July. The meeting included Mr. Steinbrenner, Clyde King, who had been elevated to general manager at the beginning of the '84 season, Yogi, and all the coaches. The only person to do any speaking, however, was Mr. Steinbrenner, who, for nearly ten minutes, lambasted Yogi for the performance of the team, repeatedly referring to it as Yogi's team. All the while Yogi sat there, seething, until finally he'd had enough.

Rising to his feet, he began shouting at Mr. Steinbrenner. "This is not my f-ing team, it's your f-ing team. You brought all these players in here that nobody else wants. You're not gonna blame me for this. If you want to fire me, go ahead!" With that, he stormed out of the room, but not before flinging a pack of Chesterfields at Mr. Steinbrenner, striking him in the chest.

I had the utmost respect for Yogi. Everyone did. To see him get lambasted like that by Mr. Steinbrenner was embarrassing, and I loved the fact that he didn't take it and fought back. Yogi knew baseball and he knew who could play and who couldn't. His best advice to me was to not get down on myself if the hitters didn't perform, that all a coach can do is impart his advice and work hard every day with the players. He was especially proud of his son, Dale, who joined us that year. With Dale, he told me, "Make sure you give him special attention!" When I became manager in '86, I wanted desperately to hire Yogi as my bench coach, but by then he'd already had his falling-out with Mr. Steinbrenner and told me that as much as he'd love to help me, there was just no way he'd come back to the Yankees.

We were all stunned at Yogi's uncharacteristic and unrestrained rage and sat there, frozen, waiting to see Mr. Steinbrenner's response at just having been told off in front of everyone. Ignoring the pack of Chesterfields, he watched Yogi storm out the door, shook his head, and said softly, "My manager's lost control," before continuing on with the meeting as if nothing ever happened. The whole scene was extraordinary.

But in the days following, Yogi began lobbying Clyde King about infusing the team with some youth, particularly in the infield, where he wanted to give Bobby Meacham a full shot at shortstop and bring up Mike Pagliarulo, a promising left-handed power hitter at Columbus, to play third. King agreed and was able to trade our incumbent third baseman, Roy Smalley, to the White Sox on July 18, opening the door for Pagliarulo. Now, as Yogi told me, it was my job to help make these kids major-league hitters, working with them on their mechanics and approach, and helping them read defenses and study pitchers—as I'd done with Don Mattingly.

I first got to really observe Mattingly during spring training in 1983, and I could see right away he had great hand-eye coordination and didn't swing and miss much. He had more of a left-handed inside-out swing, to left center. But as he was playing a power position—he was alternating between left field and first base that first year—we needed to get him pulling the ball more to take advantage of that short right field porch at Yankee Stadium. So I used the weight shift approach with him, which I learned from Charlie Lau, in which the swing starts at the feet and then uses the lower body to generate more power. We got Mattingly to use his bottom hand to give him full arm extension to get power. We also incorporated a little body movement to improve the quickness in his swing.

Mattingly had about the smallest takeaway I ever saw in a hitter—the only one I could compare it to was Paul Molitor's—where his hand went back, at most, a couple of inches until he was fully cocked. One of the fallacies of hitting is that your head has to stay stationary. In fact, your head should release with your stride. It should be centered over the belly button, which allows you to get to your front side so much easier. The idea is to set that front foot quick and let your legs get to the ball. With Donnie's small takeaway, it made it much easier to work with him.

Years later, Mattingly reaffirmed how those sessions helped in transforming him into a power hitter.

"I was a gap hitter when I first came up, using mostly my top hand," Mattingly said. "Lou taught me how to use the bottom hand and get backspin on the ball, and all of a sudden the power came. Essentially, he taught me how the swing works, how everything causes something else, like a chain reaction. The best advice I got from Lou was, 'Give it a try and if it doesn't work get rid of it, but if it does work, make it yours and it becomes what you are.' The first time he said that to me was in '83, [at] my first major-league spring camp. Lou was watching me from behind the batting cage and he said, 'Put your head back, just a little. Just try it.' I went back to the minor leagues and hit 8 homers in 43 games and I could see the power starting to come. I'd never hit more than 10 homers in my first five seasons in the minor leagues, and I hit 23 in 1984."

Yogi had a great way of simplifying things. He said we needed Donnie to hit for power. Same thing with Pagliarulo. And, with Meacham, we didn't want him hitting fly ball outs, not with his speed.

Mattingly in '84 had the first of six straight Hall of Fame–caliber seasons, beating out Dave Winfield for the batting title, .343 to .340, on the last day of the season while also leading the league with 207 hits and 44 doubles. Pagliarulo had 7 homers and 34 RBI in just 67 games, Meacham hit .253, and two other rookie pitchers, Dennis Rasmussen and Joe Cowley, combined for 18 wins after joining the rotation late. With the infusion of the kids, the Yankees went 51–29 after the All-Star Break—the best record of any team in baseball—and we just assumed Yogi had been exonerated in Mr. Steinbrenner's eyes.

In fact, after acquiring another superstar in Rickey Henderson over the winter, Mr. Steinbrenner made a public promise that Yogi would get "a full season in 1985, win or lose." As it turned out, Yogi's "full season" was all of 18 games, and Rickey was a participant in only six of those, having started the season on the disabled list with a hamstring injury.

Even though we started out sluggishly (6–12), nobody saw this coming, especially Yogi, who, as a result of his firing, went fourteen years without setting foot in Yankee Stadium or speaking to Mr. Steinbrenner. We'd gotten Rickey to be a big part of the offense and he was hurt, and we thought we had plenty of time to turn it around. Everybody loved Yogi. He was a one-of-a-kind individual. It was shocking, but George was developing a pattern with his managers. Almost as shocking was that, to replace Yogi, he was bringing back Billy Martin for the fourth time.

Yogi was fired on Sunday, April 28, in Chicago, and from there the team flew to Texas, where Billy and his agent, Eddie Sapir, were waiting for us in a suite at the hotel, with Mr. Steinbrenner on a speakerphone from Tampa. In explaining the change to the coaching staff, Mr. Steinbrenner said he thought we had better talent than how we were playing. Then he said something that made me very uncomfortable, telling Billy in front of Sapir, "The reason Lou is up there [on the coaching staff] is for you to prepare him to manage at the big-league level." That caught me totally by surprise. Why me? I think maybe Mr. Steinbrenner knew how I got along with all the different factions on the team. I also think he always wanted to have someone who was popular with the fans, ready in the wings, in the (likely) event he would have to fire Billy again.

I'll say this: it was to Billy's credit that he did do everything he could to prepare me. I could talk to him about different strategies during the course of a game or over drinks later. I liked his aggressive style and the fact he wasn't afraid to take chances. The one thing I didn't like about him was that he either liked you or he didn't, and there was no gray area. I also knew how badly he wanted to manage the Yankees.

That was never more apparent than the crazy four days in Cleveland, July 29 to August 1, when Billy was hospitalized in Texas with a punctured lung and I was asked by Mr. Steinbrenner to manage the team in his absence—with one caveat. Billy had come up with an idea in which he would help me manage the team by phone from his hospital room. He would call me before the game with the lineup,

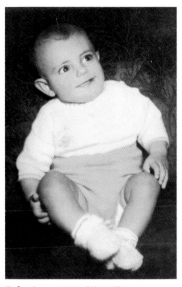

Baby Lou, 1943, West Tampa, Florida.

Three-year-old Lou with father Louis and mother Margaret, 1946, West Tampa, Florida.

Tony LaRussa and I played together on the American Legion Post 248 team, which captured the 1960 championship. In the team banquet photo here, I am on the left, third from the bottom. Tony LaRussa is on the right, first from bottom.

An All-American basketball player at Jesuit High School in Tampa, I attended the University of Tampa for a year, where I played basketball and was an All-American in baseball for the Spartans in 1962.

My lifelong love of fishing began as a boy with my father, Louis. Here we are with our catch in 1959.

In the 1969 season, I was the American League Rookie of the Year. I'm remembered by the Royals' historian (Curt Nelson) as "a man of firsts" in Royals history: first franchise batter, first franchise hit (a double off the first pitch he saw), and first franchise run scored. *Courtesy of the Kansas City Royals*

With some of my Kansas City Royals teammates in 1972 at Kansas City Municipal Stadium at 22nd and Brooklyn. L–R: Amos Otis, Fred Patek, Cookie Rojas, and Lou. *Courtesy of the Kansas City Royals*

With my wife, Anita, on the field at Kansas City Municipal Stadium for the Royals' Family Day.

On April 12, 1967, I married Anita Garcia at St. John's Presbyterian Church in Tampa.

Arguing with umpire Ron Luciano after being called out at home at Yankee Stadium in 1978. *Joe McNally*

My reaction after being called out at home plate in a close play in the fourth inning of the third playoff game between the Yankees and the Royals on Friday, October 6, 1978, in New York at Yankee Stadium. Home plate umpire Ron Luciano had the last word: I was out. *Associated Press*

Going above the fence to rob a home run from Dodger Ron Cey in the fourth inning at Dodger Stadium in Los Angeles on Saturday, October 15, 1977. *Associated Press*

Thurman Munson, already in his catcher's gear for the next half of the inning, runs onto the field where he had to restrain me after my collision with Red Sox catcher Carlton Fisk resulted in a brawl. *The New York Daily News*

NBC sportscaster Joe Garagiola interviewing Anita and me following my final game as a player, on June 16, 1984.

Me, Anita, Lou Jr., and Kristi in 1975 at the Yankees' Family Day.

Family portrait, 1981. L–R: Kristi, Lou Jr., Derek, Lou, Anita.

With Anita in the backyard of our "Yankee home" in Allendale, New Jersey, 1985.

Chatting with then manager Yogi Berra before the start of an exhibition game against the New York Mets in March 1984. *Associated Press/G. Paul Burnett*

George Steinbrenner (center) and Billy Martin (left) were both hugely important to my career in baseball. Here we are in the dugout during spring training in 1988, the year I was general manager for the team. *Associated Press/Bill Cooke*

October 1990. Reds fans celebrate
the team reaching the post-season.
Courtesy of the Cincinnati Reds

Cincinnati Reds owner Marge Schott
looking on as I hug my son Derek at the
news conference announcing my hiring
as Reds manager in 1989.

Friends and rivals since boyhood, Tony La Russa and I were
excited to manage against each other in the 1990 World Series.
Here we are shaking hands before game 1 at Riverfront Stadium
in Cincinnati. *Courtesy of the Cincinnati Reds*

Hoisting the World Series trophy with Marge Schott at a celebration in downtown Cincinnati. *Courtesy of the Cincinnati Reds*

On our twenty-fifth wedding anniversary, Marge Schott presented Anita and me with a pair of handcuffs as an anniversary gift.

October 30, 1990, the World Series champion Cincinnati Reds were honored in the White House Rose Garden by President George H. W. Bush. *Courtesy of the Cincinnati Reds*

Following the Reds' 1990 World Series sweep of the Oakland A's, our Piniella family posed with the World Series trophy. L–R: Lou Jr., Kristi, Derek, me, and Anita.

1992 family portrait. L–R: Anita, me, Kristi, Lou Jr., Derek.

In 1993 I decided to take a chance on a team out west, beginning almost ten years with the Seattle Mariners that would last until 2002. *Courtesy of the Seattle Mariners*

During a game against the Yankees in August 1999, I had to be restrained by my bench coach, John McLaren, while arguing a call with home plate umpire Ted Barrett. The Yankees had the bases loaded with Bernie Williams, Chili Davis, Tino Martinez, and Scott Brosius at bat. *REUTERS/Roger Bacon/Alamy*

After the amazing season we'd had, the 2001 ALCS was one of the most difficult losses I'd faced. Here I am congratulating the Boss following the Yankees' win in game 5. *REUTERS/Alamy/Mike Segar*

Alex Rodriguez and I remained close long after he left Seattle for Texas. Even when we were playing against each other, as here in 2000, neither of us ever forgot how his time in Seattle had shaped him. *Associated Press/LM Otero*

"Daddy's girl" Kristi Piniella with me on her wedding day in 1995.

1999, Lou Jr., Derek, and me at Virginia Tech in Blacksburg, Virginia, where Derek played football in 1998 and 1999.

Kicking my cap after being ejected from a game against the Rangers in September 2002 by umpire C.B. Bucknor. *Mark Harrison/Seattle Times*

A couple of Seattle fans screaming their support for me during my first season as manager of the Tampa Bay Devil Rays in 2003. *REUTERS/Alamy/ Anthony P. Bolante*

While it was great to be home in Tampa Bay, managing the Devil Rays was one of my hardest challenges. *Courtesy of the Tampa Bay Rays*

Signing autographs for Devil Rays fans at spring training in Port Charlotte, Florida. *Courtesy of the Tampa Bay Rays*

With my grandkids. L–R: Kassidy, Anica, and Sophie at Tropicana Field, 2002.

After the announcement that I would be the new manager of the Chicago Cubs on October 17, 2006. *REUTERS/Alamy/Frank Polich*

Arguing with third base umpire Mark Wegner in a game against the Atlanta Braves in 2007. Not only was I ejected by Wegner, but that outburst drew a four-game suspension. *Associated Press/Nam Y. Huh*

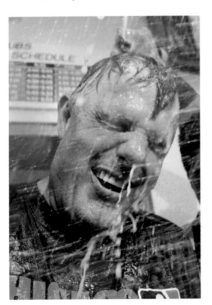

Being doused with champagne after we clinched the National League Central Division in 2008. *REUTERS/Alamy/Nam Y. Huh*

Changing pitchers in 2007. *Steve Green, Chicago Cubs*

A 2007 pregame radio interview with Cubs broadcaster and Hall of Famer Ron Santo. *Steve Green, Chicago Cubs*

With my granddaughter Kassidy at her first horse show in 2003.

Now that I'm retired from managing, Anita and I spend as much time as we can with the family. Here we are with our granddaughters Ava, left, and Mia.

With Anita and our granddaughters on Lake Magdalene in Tampa in 2016. L–R: Kassidy, Anica, Mia, Lou, Anita, Ava, Sophie.

Our family.
Back row L–R: Derek, his wife, Michelle, Kassidy, Janet, Lou Jr., Kristi, Lou.
Front row: Sophie, Ava, Anita, Mia, Anica.

and then, with an open line to the dugout in Cleveland, he would call periodically during the course of the game with strategy decisions and pitching changes. He just didn't want to let go.

It went okay, without incident, for the first two games, which we won, 8–2 and 8–5, but then, in an effort to give Billy the credit, I made the mistake of telling the media what was happening. All of a sudden, the next night we were getting crank calls to the dugout from all over the place—and at the same time, the Indians' president, Peter Bavasi, mischievously directed the stadium's switchboard operator to relay all of Billy's calls to the Indians' dugout. In addition, Billy had apparently left the hospital after the first two games and was now making his calls from a bar. It was absolute chaos. I had assigned Butch Wynegar, our backup catcher, to answer the dugout phone and relay Billy's strategy instructions to me, but at one point, Butch came back to me, crying.

"What's wrong, Butch?" I asked.

"Billy keeps telling me I'm a horseshit catcher who doesn't know how to call a game," Butch said. "I thought he was supposed to be managing this game."

We lost the last three games of the series, the final one 9–1, and by then I had had enough. When I got home that night, I told Anita, "I'm done. I'm not going back to work tomorrow," and despite her urgings to "just do your job and concentrate on your hitting coach job," I was AWOL for the first game of the home stand. Early that evening, Mr. Steinbrenner called me to ask what was going on.

I told him what happened in Cleveland. "I didn't sign up for this, getting caught up in this firestorm for four days in Cleveland. It became a joke and took all the fun out of the game for me."

"Okay, Lou, just calm down," he said. "You're doing a really good job as the hitting coach and Billy needs you back."

Billy called me as well and they were both very charming. But I was hurt and upset. Billy just wanted total control.

Because of Anita, my second "retirement" from baseball lasted just that one day, and we began to play well in August, going 20–7 to climb back into the pennant race with Toronto. Rickey was everything we (if not Yogi) could have hoped for, leading the league with a club-record 80 stolen bases and the most runs scored (146) since Ted Williams in 1949. As late as September 10 we were just 1½ games behind the division-leading Blue Jays. That was when it all, especially Billy, fell apart. After losing three straight to the Blue Jays at Yankee Stadium, Mr. Steinbrenner went on a tirade in the press box, ripping into the team to the writers and sarcastically calling Winfield "Mr. May" in reference to Reggie's "Mr. October." The team reacted by losing five more in a row, and then, on September 21, Billy got into an ugly barroom brawl with our pitcher Ed Whitson at the Cross Keys Inn in Baltimore. I could almost see this coming. Billy and Whitson had no use for each other and Billy had been in a foul mood after losing to Earl Weaver and the Orioles in the first game of the series the night before. As such, even though we won the next day to end an eight-game losing streak, I decided to avoid Billy and the other coaches and went out to dinner Saturday night with "Killer" Kane at Sabatino's in Little Italy. When we got back to the hotel, which was actually in a suburb of Baltimore, there were all these police cars in the parking lot. I saw Willie Horton, one of Billy's top lieutenants on the coaching staff, standing in the lobby, and I asked him what happened.

"Billy got in a fight with Whitson and got beat up pretty good," he said. "He's up in his room. He's been looking for Killer."

We went up to Billy's room, and I have to say he was a pretty pathetic sight. He was standing there in his underwear, his arm in a sling, with scratches and cuts all over his face. But Billy being Billy, he was not about to nurse his wounds and call it a night.

"I want you to go knock on Whitson's door and tell him I want to finish this thing," he told me.

I thought, *The scotch is really lying to him.* I never did go to Whitson's room. The next morning, I was shocked to see Billy at the ballpark, sitting in the visiting team manager's office, making out the lineup. He managed the whole game with his arm still in a sling. After the game he asked me to accompany him in his private limo for the ride back to New York. He was happy about winning the last two games of the series against Weaver, and he even mused about possibly winning manager-of-the-year honors. But he was worried about how Mr. Steinbrenner and the media were going to look on his fight with Whitson.

With all the nonsense and Billy's trials and tribulations, we still wound up winning 97 games in 1985—the final one an 8–0 shutout by "Father Time" Phil Niekro that was his 300th career victory—and I thought that would probably be enough to warrant Billy's coming back. But then a week went by after the season with no word from Mr. Steinbrenner about Billy. He finally broke his silence by declaring that he was going to leave the decision on the manager entirely up to Clyde King and his new assistant general manager, Woody Woodward. "I will have no hand in this whatsoever," he said.

Everybody knew that Clyde, a teetotaler who'd been a pitcher for the Dodgers in the '40s and '50s when they were the Yankees' archenemies, had absolutely no use for Billy. So this was the kiss of death for Billy. After a couple of weeks of Clyde and Woody supposedly going through an interview process for the job, I got a call from Clyde asking me to come to the stadium to talk about becoming the new manager.

I never did ask whether there really had been an actual search, but years later Woody revealed what happened: "Anyone who was around George Steinbrenner knows there were times he didn't want to be the guy to fire someone or hire someone, and in this case, we were told that firing Billy and hiring Lou was what we were going to do. My guess is there was no thorough search on Clyde's part, because he didn't include me in any interviews. The one part that disturbed me about Lou was that he'd had no managerial experience. I did feel he'd learned a whole lot from Billy, who was a great manager when the game started, and I felt he had all the attributes to potentially become a Hall of Fame manager. But we were still talking about hiring a manager with no experience—in New York."

When I got to the stadium, Clyde greeted me warmly in his office and got right to the point.

"Lou, we've decided to make a change with the manager and we want you to take over for Billy," he said. "I trust this is what you want to do and I've already taken the liberty of drawing up this contract. We're prepared to start you off at $150,000."

"A hundred and fifty thousand dollars?" I said. "That's what I was making as a coach, Clyde! I can't manage for that."

"No, no, no," Clyde protested. "You were making $75,000 as a coach. I have your contract right here."

"That's my Yankee contract, Clyde," I said. "You need to call down to Mr. Steinbrenner's office at American Shipbuilding in Tampa and check the separate contract I have with him for an additional $75,000."

Clyde was flustered. He was just now learning about the inner workings of Mr. Steinbrenner and the kind of secret deals he made irrespective of his general managers. We wound up agreeing to $200,000 (and nothing extra from American Ship) and so, befitting my uniform number, I was Mr. Steinbrenner's ninth different manager in fourteen overall changes since he took ownership of the Yankees in 1973.

Even though it happened quicker than I had anticipated, I felt I could handle the job. If I didn't, I would have asked Mr. Steinbrenner for more time. On the other hand, I always thought he'd treat me differently from how he treated all his other managers, that he'd have more patience with me. I also never thought Billy would be coming back all the times he did. I was very naive. I remember how proud I was getting on that plane in Newark for Fort Lauderdale in February 1986 to start my managing career. It was an exciting time.

My first order of business was putting together a coaching staff, and I will be forever grateful for Clyde and Woody bringing in Joe Altobelli to be my bench coach. We all agreed I was going to need a good, sound baseball man to sit beside me, preferably someone who had previously managed in the big leagues, and Altobelli, who'd managed sixteen years in the minor leagues before managing the Giants from 1977 to 1979 and then winning a world championship with the Orioles in 1983 (the year after Weaver retired), fit the bill perfectly. Joe's experience and knowledge were invaluable, as well as his calming influence when Mr. Steinbrenner started getting on me. I still remember his assuring words midway through the '86 season when, on a flight home from a road trip, he said, "Well, young pup, you're ready now."

The team I inherited from Billy was much the same as that of '85, with one notable exception. Over the winter, Mr. Steinbrenner, in an effort to shore up an aged and uncertain starting pitching rotation—which consisted of the Niekros, Phil (46) and Joe (42), Guidry (36), Whitson, and 42-year-old Tommy John, whom we'd signed as insurance—engineered a trade with his friend Jerry Reinsdorf, the owner of the White Sox, for Britt Burns, a talented left-hander who'd won 18 games in 1985. I'll never forget the meeting we had at Mr. Steinbrenner's Bay Harbor Hotel in Tampa in December, shortly after I'd been named manager. Clyde, Woody, and all the scouts were there, along with five or six peripheral minor-league

operations people Mr. Steinbrenner always included in the meetings who could be counted on to agree with him on everything. The
discussion was the prospective trade for Burns, which Mr. Steinbrenner assured was going to be a steal for us, even though there
were some medical issues with him. "Young left-handers like this
just don't become available," he declared, "so we have to move on
this quickly before some other team gets to Reinsdorf."

At that point, Dr. John Bonamo, our team physician, stood up.
"George," he said, "I can't emphasize this strongly enough. You cannot trade for this guy. I've seen his medicals and they're awful. He's
got a degenerative hip condition and he's a disaster waiting to happen."

Mr. Steinbrenner looked at Bonamo and frowned.

"Okay, doc, we've heard you. You can go now."

After Bonamo left the room, Mr. Steinbrenner looked around and
said, "He's a doctor, what does he know? We're baseball people here.
You guys all saw Burns pitch last year. Did he look like an accident
waiting to happen?"

Nobody said anything, and a couple of days later we traded Joe
Cowley, who'd won nine games as a rookie for us in '85, and Ron Has-
sey, our hard-hitting backup catcher and a big Yankee Stadium fan
favorite who'd hit .296 with 13 homers, to the White Sox for Burns.

Despite some apprehensions about my starting pitching rotation,
I felt really good about my team—how could you not with a lineup
that included Rickey Henderson, Dave Winfield, Don Mattingly, Willie Randolph, Ken Griffey, and the two kids, Pagliarulo and Meacham, who had performed so well in '85? It was therefore grounds
for much consternation on Mr. Steinbrenner's part that most of them
were absent from the lineup for my debut as the Yankees' manager
on March 8, 1986, against the Orioles at Fort Lauderdale. It didn't
help either that Weaver was back managing the Orioles, having come

out of retirement the year before. For the Yankees' opening game of spring training, Mr. Steinbrenner had invited all his high-powered New York friends, Donald Trump, Chrysler's chairman, Lee Iaccoca, and Bill Fugazy, the limousine mogul, only to have my first lineup stacked with nobodies. Shortly before game time, Mr. Steinbrenner burst into my office.

"What the hell are you doing?" he screamed. "Who the hell are these guys in your lineup? Where's Rickey? Where's Mattingly? Where's Winfield? I've got all my friends from New York here and you're making me look like an idiot. They didn't come all the way down here to see Columbus! And I would think you would want to beat Weaver in your first game."

I tried to explain to him that, in spring training, you want to bring your veterans along slowly while, at the same time, you try to get a good look at your youngsters early on. But he was having none of it, and I wound up telling him to leave me alone and let me run spring training the way I have to. Fortunately, we won the game, but instead of congratulating me afterward, Mr. Steinbrenner came down to the clubhouse holding up a huge sign with a picture of a gorilla and the inscription: "Patience, my ass! I'm gonna kill somebody!" It hung in the locker room the rest of the spring.

A week later we were in Dunedin to play the Blue Jays with Britt Burns making his second start of the spring. In his previous start, he'd demonstrated a 92-plus m.p.h. fastball with good movement, along with a biting curve and changeup, and I'd thought we might really have an ace here. But after covering first base on an infield grounder in the first inning against the Blue Jays, Burns suddenly winced in pain and came limping off the field. He had to be helped to a car, where he was taken back to the Bay Harbor and then flown to Fort Lauderdale. Upon examination by our spring training team physician, Dan Kanell, it was determined Burns was indeed suffering from a degenerative hip disease. That's when Mr. Steinbrenner called me and said, "Don't worry. I've talked to a specialist at the University of Florida who said they can give Burns a hip transplant and he'll be back pitching for us *later in the season.*"

In fact, Burns never pitched again, and I had a gaping hole at the top of my rotation.

Even before Burns broke down, I had determined to get a good, long look at three young starters, the lefty Dennis Rasmussen and the rookie righties Doug Drabek and Bob Tewksbury, with an eye on easing them into the rotation in the likelihood of my older starters breaking down. The six-foot-seven Rasmussen was a hard worker who'd especially impressed that spring, and I was ready to anoint him as my fifth starter when, on a windy day against the Texas Rangers in their bandbox of a stadium in Pompano Beach, he gave up three home runs in front of Mr. Steinbrenner, who was sitting in the stands with Billy. All spring, Billy had been bad-mouthing Rasmussen to Mr. Steinbrenner, saying he was "soft" and didn't throw hard enough, and after that game Mr. Steinbrenner told the writers that Rasmussen had just pitched his way to Columbus. This led to my first major argument with him. I begged him to let me keep Rasmussen, and with Clyde King present, told him how important I thought it was to bring a young pitcher along in our rotation. The next day, he called me and said, "Okay, I've reconsidered. I know this managing job isn't easy and there are times you have to do things you don't want. If you want Rasmussen you can have him, but under one condition."

I was trying to figure out what he was getting at.

"What's that?" I said.

"You've got to release Phil Niekro."

My heart sank. Release Phil Niekro? He was one of the classiest, most decent human beings I had ever known in baseball, a future

Hall of Famer who'd won 16 games in each of the last two seasons for the Yankees. He'd done nothing to deserve this. But apparently Mr. Steinbrenner—and even King, the man who signed him originally—felt that Phil, who would turn forty-seven on April 1, couldn't be counted on to win much more.

This was my introduction to the worst part of being a manager—having to tell a player he's being released. To this day, releasing Phil Niekro was the hardest thing I ever had to do in baseball. I couldn't throw the organization under the bus. I had to tell him this was everybody's decision, but typical of Phil, he made it easy for me.

"I understand, Lou," he said. "I've enjoyed my time here and I wish I could've pitched for you. But I'm not done. I know I can still help some team."

He wasn't done either. He signed on with the Indians a few days later and won 18 more games for them over the next two seasons to finish with 318 for his career. As it turned out, Phil made 34 starts for the Indians in 1986, while the rest of my rotation—with the notable exception of Rasmussen—all fell apart. Guidry and Joe Niekro started out 8–1 up to May 10 before sustaining injuries and went 10–21 the rest of the way. John was also on the disabled list for two months. And then there was Whitson, the high-stress Tennessean who even before his scrap with Billy had a terrible time adjusting to New York after years of pitching in laid-back San Diego and the designated hitter–less National League. The five-year, $4.5 million free-agent contract Whitson signed with the Yankees in 1984 was another example of Mr. Steinbrenner's blind allegiance to the player agent Tom Reich. For that kind of money, the fans expected Whitson to pitch like an ace—and when he didn't, they got on him, in his words, unmercifully, to the point where he claimed they would follow him home from Yankee Stadium and put tacks in his driveway.

I started Whitson against the Royals in the second game of the season and he couldn't get out of the third inning, leaving to a chorus of boos and catcalls from the Yankee Stadium crowd. He pitched much better in his next start against the same Royals, only this time in Kansas City, and at that point, after consultation with Clyde King and my pitching coach, Sammy Ellis, we decided to have Whitson start only on the road. He was actually a pretty good pitcher, but he really struggled in New York, fighting it, and by mid-June, with his ERA nearly 7.00, we decided to trade him. Right before we did, he came to me and said, "I've got to beat this," and asked me to start him in New York. The day he was supposed to start, I was in my office when our team trainer, Gene Monahan, summoned me to the trainer's room. There was poor Whitson, sitting there on the trainer's table, hyperventilating, trying to catch his breath.

"We've got to scratch him," I said, and a couple of days later we traded him back to San Diego.

Meanwhile, I had to find yet another starter, and for the rest of the season I moved Drabek and Tewksbury into the rotation, and they both pitched well. Along with Rasmussen, who justified my confidence in him in the spring by leading the staff with 18 wins, the three young starters were some of the most satisfying aspects of the '86 season. But after being 56–43, only three games out of first place, on July 27, we went 14–17 through August and gradually faded out of the race. We had lost four of the first five games of a road trip when we were playing the Indians in Cleveland on August 2, in the Saturday national TV game.

I was in a bad mood to begin with and looking to take my frustrations out on somebody when I remembered something Mr. Steinbrenner had told me when he hired me as manager: "Remember, baseball is entertainment, and if you get kicked out of a game, put on a nice show!" I knew he'd be watching the game, and when a close call at first base went against us in the sixth inning, I charged out of the dugout, hollering and kicking dirt and quickly earning an ejection, at which point I then flung my hat to the ground and began kicking it as well.

As my tirade continued, our bat boy picked up my cap, which was one of my props, and handed it to me. "Put that cap down!" I screamed at him. "You're ruining my show!"

Terrified, he dropped the cap and scampered back to the dugout.

After the game, which we lost, 6–5, in ten innings, I happened to mention it was Anita's birthday, and when the writers got back upstairs to the press box, they called her to ask if she'd seen my performance on national TV.

"All I can say," she said, sighing, "is that I'm forty-three years old today and I feel like I'm married to a four-year-old."

Considering all the pitching problems, I felt I'd done a pretty decent job to finish the season with 90 wins. Nevertheless, Mr. Steinbrenner was slow to give me a vote of confidence about the next year and was mostly silent after an ominous (or is the word "anonymous"?) column by his pal Howard Cosell appeared in the *Daily News* in early September in which Cosell essentially said I'd done a terrible job and "that at least 10 or more games were lost" because of my managing. When I called Mr. Steinbrenner about the column, he vehemently denied having anything to do with it—even though Cosell was a visible frequent guest alongside him in his private box throughout the season. It probably didn't help either that, across town, the Mets were on their way to winning the world championship. A week after the season, Mr. Steinbrenner finally called and said he was giving me another year.

At the same time, Clyde King was able to convince Mr. Steinbrenner to let him return to being a special adviser, which meant his assistant, Woody Woodward, would be ascending to the general manager's job. I'll say this about Clyde: he was a master at navigating the nomenclature. I actually had worked more closely with Woody during the '86 season, as he made a lot of trips with the team and was usually the person who called me about player personnel decisions the front office was making. Woody and I had a lot in common—he was a native Floridian who went to Florida State and had been a shortstop in the majors with the Braves and Reds in the '60s. He was the same age as I was and he was a very astute baseball man. In one of our first get-togethers after I was officially coming back, we both agreed that, in all our trade and free-agent dealings, we needed to have an eye on getting the team younger. In particular, we needed to make sure we held on to our young starting pitchers, Rasmussen, Drabek, and Tewksbury.

But as Woody quickly found out, Mr. Steinbrenner was not into the future. He wanted to win now, and so, a week before the winter baseball meetings, Woody was ordered to trade Drabek to the Pirates for Rick Rhoden. With 15 wins for a last-place Pirates' team, Rhoden had been one of the best pitchers in the National League in '86, and he went on to lead my staff with 16 wins in '87. But at thirty-three, he was nine years older than Drabek and was out of baseball after the '89 season. Drabek, on the other hand, won 92 games, including a Cy Young Award in 1990, over the next six years. Woody and I begged Mr. Steinbrenner not to trade Drabek, but he saw Rhoden as a sort of trophy, as the best established pitcher on the market that winter, and that was that.

Despite the problematic starting rotation, we reached the '87 All-Star Break in first place, 55–34, three games ahead of the Blue Jays, and we remained atop the AL East until August 8. That was when injuries and age caught up to us and Mr. Steinbrenner caught up to me. The Sunday before the All-Star Break I was in my office at Yankee Stadium when the red phone on my desk rang. (The red phones were private, direct-line phones from Mr. Steinbrenner installed in everyone's office at the stadium. When they rang they kind of glowed like Rudolph's nose.) I picked up the phone, and on the other end, Mr. Steinbrenner declared, "I just won you the pennant, Lou. I just got you Steve Trout!"

There was no question we needed another starting pitcher—Guidry had been bothered by a sore elbow all season, and a month earlier we'd traded Joe Niekro to the Twins for Mark Salas, a catcher with left-handed pop but who was decidedly challenged defensively. Trout was a thirty-year-old left-hander who'd been one of the Cubs' best pitchers, but as I was soon to discover, he was another Ed Whitson when it came to pitching with the pressures of New York.

We opened the second half of the season in Texas, and I decided we would start Trout the third game of that series against the Rangers. Before the game, I told my pitching coach, Mark Connor, to give me a call when Trout was fully loosened up from his bullpen session. But after five minutes, I noticed that Trout had sat down. I called Mark and asked what happened. "I dunno," he said. "He never got loose and just sat down."

This did not bode well, and in his Yankees debut, Trout surrendered nine hits and five runs in five-plus innings. His only saving grace was that our bullpen was even worse. We wound up being slaughtered 20–3, and I finally had to call on Rick Cerone to make his debut as a major-league pitcher to close it out in the ninth. As Cerone recalled for this book, Trout was simply a basket case.

"That first start in Texas, Trout had nothing," Cerone said. "But neither did anyone else Lou brought in—until me. Pat Clements, his fourth pitcher, was trying to get through the ninth with no success. At one point, I went out to the mound to talk to him and I turned and saw Lou coming out of the dugout. He had already visited Clements earlier in the inning and I started waving him off. 'Lou, go back! This is your second trip!' I yelled, but Lou just threw his hands up in exasperation and said, 'Ah, forget about it, Rick. Go to the dugout and take your catching gear off. You're pitching!' I retired the side on almost all knuckleballs. After that first start, Trout just couldn't throw strikes, especially to left-handed batters. It was scary, to the point where I could only call for breaking balls with him."

Trout made eight other starts and five mop-up relief appearances for us in '87, one almost as bad as the next, and after his last start, from which I had to pull him in the third inning after he'd walked four batters, he apologized to me. "I'm sorry, Lou," he said. "I just can't pitch for shit here." Not only did Trout not win me the pennant, he didn't win me a *game*, finishing 0–4, with a 6.60 ERA and 37 walks in 46⅓ innings. (An addendum here: one of the pitchers we gave up to the Cubs for Trout was Bob Tewksbury, who went on to a nice career in the big leagues, winning 110 games.)

Another pitcher Mr. Steinbrenner acquired for me in 1987 who couldn't help was Al Holland. Actually this was the second time in a year we'd signed Holland, another Tom Reich client. We'd signed him as a free agent in 1986 and released him in August after he was mostly ineffective and looked like he was done. I didn't pay much attention when Mr. Steinbrenner, as another favor to Reich, signed him again in April '87 to pitch for our Triple-A team in Columbus. But then, out of the blue, on August 3, I got a call from Mr. Steinbrenner informing me that Holland was being recalled but that I was not to pitch him! I could only assume that this had something to do with Holland needing more major-league service time. The problem was, I had to send out Pat Clements, a lefty reliever who'd been one of my most reliable hands in the bullpen, and it just so happened, the day Holland arrived, Tommy John got knocked out of the game against Cleveland in the third inning. Without Clements, I needed a reliever to give me some innings, and so I called on Holland, who was subsequently rocked for six runs in 1⅔ innings. This was right around the time everything began coming apart—we lost 7 of our first 10 games in August to fall out of first place for the first time since June 24—and when Mr. Steinbrenner called me to scream about me using Holland—"I told you not to use him. You're embarrassing me!" is what he said—I hung up. After that, I stopped taking his phone calls. I just got tired of being beat up and having nothing satisfy him.

Speaking of Tommy John, I'd like to clarify something here about the long-standing myth that Mr. Steinbrenner was constantly making calls to the dugout during games to air his complaints with managers. I don't know about anyone else, but with me that happened only one time: August 24, 1987. We were playing the "Singing Cowboy" Gene Autry's Angels in Anaheim and it was a tight pitching duel between Tommy John and Don Sutton, two wily veterans who allegedly were not averse to occasionally adding a little helpful foreign substance to the ball. In this particular game, the Yankees' WPIX cameras caught Sutton rubbing something on the ball. After the broadcasters noted the Yankees must not have noticed it, Mr. Steinbrenner, watching the game from his horse farm in Ocala, called Anaheim Stadium and had the switchboard operator put him through to our dugout, whereupon he began excoriating me.

"What's wrong with you?" he screamed. "The whole world just saw Sutton doctoring up the baseball and you're just sitting there on your ass and not doing anything about it! Who's paying your salary? Me or the Cowboy?"

"Mr. Steinbrenner," I said calmly, "what's the score of the game?"

"What's the score? We're winning 2–1. What's that got to do with anything?"

"I'll tell you, sir," I said. "It means that our guy is cheating better than their guy."

He hung up in a huff and I never heard another word about it from him—or got another dugout call from him—probably because we wound up winning the game, 3–2, in the ninth inning. I never told Mr. Steinbrenner, but after the game, Mr. Autry, as he frequently did when we visited town, came down to the clubhouse with a bottle of vodka and we sat around talking baseball for a couple of hours before he had his driver take me back to the team hotel. Wonderful man.

It was hard enough trying to hold everything together that season with the starting pitching in such disarray, but I'd also been dealing with Rickey Henderson's ongoing hamstring issue, which had put him on the disabled list most of June and now again in August.

Later that day, "Killer" Kane came to me with a message from Mr. Steinbrenner to be in my hotel room at 2:00 p.m. the next day for a phone call from him. I knew this drill too. Mr. Steinbrenner was famous for telling people to be in their hotel rooms for phone calls from him that never came. One time in '86 he'd done this with me, and I sat in my hotel room, watching TV with three bottles of Heineken, waiting for his call. The next thing I knew it was 4:00 a.m. and I was lying in bed with two empty bottles of beer on the floor and the other one spilled all over me.

Nevertheless, I fully intended to be in my room for his 2:00 p.m. call the next day, except that over lunch with a couple of his Yankees limited partners who lived in Cleveland, I was talked into going shopping. At the same time, I had been lobbying Woody to bring up Joel Skinner, an excellent defensive catcher, to replace Salas, who was leading the league in passed balls. Instead of going back to the hotel, I went right to the ballpark from shopping and called Woody. That's when my general manager informed me he was no longer permitted to talk to me! I couldn't believe it. Rome was burning and the emperor was cutting off his field general.

"I'm sorry, Lou," Woody said. "You're just gonna have to work this out with George. I have to do what he tells me."

The next day in Detroit I called all the writers together and informed them that for weeks I had been trying to get Joel Skinner called up from Columbus but when I called again, my general manager said he was not allowed to talk to me.

Well, that was the match that lit the inferno. After seeing my comments in the papers, Mr. Steinbrenner issued a blistering press release, excoriating me for not being in my room in Cleveland to take his phone call—"I don't know of too many guys—even sportswriters—who if their boss told them to be available for a call at a certain time, wouldn't be there! That type of behavior wouldn't be tolerated at any newspaper and it won't be tolerated by the Yankees either!"

He then followed that up by sending me a letter of insubordination for refusing to take his calls and not being in my room for his call in Cleveland, which he also filed with the commissioner's office. I had no problem with Mr. Steinbrenner's being upset about the missed phone call. I was wrong not to have been there. You should obey your boss, but I was fed up. What I did have a problem with was the rest of the rambling press release, in which he completely undermined me with my players by claiming that in private conversations with him I called Salas "a bum" and accused Rickey of "jaking it."

How do you mend fences with your players after stuff like that comes out? I fired back in the papers, maintaining I never called Salas a bum and had never used that word to describe any player. Same thing with Rickey. I told him the word "jaking" was not even in my vocabulary, but I could understand his bitterness. The whole hamstring thing with him started in a June 4 game in Milwaukee. He'd been complaining about the hammy bothering him, and after he drew a leadoff walk in the eighth inning, I sent him on a 3-2 pitch and he pulled up lame stealing second. He missed three weeks after that and when he came back played cautiously (only three stolen bases) through July before pulling it again, sidelining him the whole month of August. In spring training the following year, Rickey said it probably would have been different if Billy had been managing in '87, which hurt me. Still, I understood because Billy was the one who had brought him to the major leagues with Oakland and, like me with Alex Rodriguez, was almost a second father to him. It took a few years for Rickey and me to mend everything. In 2000, when he was released by the Mets and it looked like his career might be over, I brought him over to the Mariners and he stole 31 bases for me in 92 games. Just an amazing player, and it was an honor to have managed him and been a small part of his career as the greatest leadoff man in baseball history.

It was of little consolation to me that the media all blasted Mr. Steinbrenner for cutting my legs off the way he did. Managing the Yankees—my dream job, for which I was forever grateful to Mr. Steinbrenner—had at that point become a living hell. It took some long talks with my close friends Hawk Harrelson and Bobby Murcer, who were both working as announcers for the Yankees, to convince me to stick it out and just do the best job I could. From August 1 to the end of the season we went 26–33, to finish in fourth place with 89 wins. I knew I was going to be fired, but after all that had transpired in 1987, I almost welcomed it.

CHAPTER 7

Bye-Bye, Boss

As much of a toll the 1987 season took on me, I was not alone. For Woody Woodward, one year of being Mr. Steinbrenner's general manager had been truly hazardous to his health. The first time Anita and I ever went over to Woody's house, we were having dinner in the dining room with Woody and his wife, Pamela, when suddenly I heard this quacking.

"Do you have a pet duck here, Woody?" I asked.

Woody sighed, his eyes rolling upward.

"My Boss phone," he said. "Private line. I had a special ring put on it so I knew it was him and could decide whether I wanted to answer it or not."

By the end of the 1987 season, Woody had absolutely had it. A few days after the '87 season, he told me the Phillies wanted to hire him as their general manager, but that Mr. Steinbrenner was refusing to let him out of his contract. He asked me if I could talk to him and try to reason with him. I told Woody I would, but that I was actually expecting Mr. Steinbrenner to fire me. But when I met with Mr. Steinbrenner at Yankee Stadium, he was like a different person—believe it or not, firing people was always hard for him—and he said nothing about all the acrimony that had transpired between us or the letter of insubordination. Instead, he talked about a grand new plan he had for me.

"I don't know if you know this," he said, "but Woody wants to leave, with two more years on his contract. The Phillies want him, but there's only one way I'm gonna let him go."

"What's that?" I said.

"I'd like you to move upstairs and take over as GM and I'm gonna bring Billy back as manager."

I thought about that for a couple of minutes, a lot of mixed emotions running through my head. *Billy V?* I thought. *This man is absolutely crazy.* At the same time, however, I knew I didn't want to manage for him. I also didn't have any offers from anyone else. Working in the front office, I thought, might actually be a nice reprieve and a way to enhance my baseball résumé. Plus, I would be doing a huge favor for my good friend Woody. The more we talked, the more the idea of being in charge of putting together a ball club began to appeal to me.

As Woody recalls it, "When George called me and said he was letting me out of my contract and that he was promoting Lou to GM my immediate thought was, 'Oh my god! What has he done? Taking Lou out of the dugout is a terrible idea.' It was true, Lou knew talent, but what a waste putting him in the front office. But Lou took the bullet for me, and I was forever grateful."

After agreeing to terms on my new GM contract, Mr. Steinbrenner said, "You're much better off in the front office, Lou. Why would you want to be down on the field, where you were second-guessed by me and everyone else, when you can be up here now and be one of the second-guessers?"

I liked that concept too. Like everything else with Mr. Steinbrenner, however, there were certain requirements about a new job.

"Your first order of business will be to get rid of Trout!" he declared.

"I'll do my best, sir," I said, "but just remember you were the one who said he was going to win me a pennant."

"Never mind!" he shouted, dismissing me. "Just get rid of him!"

It took a while to accommodate Mr. Steinbrenner on Trout, but three days before Christmas I was able to get the Seattle Mariners to give us three pitchers for him—one of them a six-foot-eight left-hander, Lee Guetterman, who went on to have four decent seasons as a workhorse middle reliever for the Yankees. In the meantime, I moved to shore up two of our major weak spots by trading for a catcher, Don Slaught, and acquiring a veteran shortstop, Rafael Santana, from the Mets. The Santana deal especially brought to mind the unintentionally foreboding evidence Woody had left for me. My first day on the job, I sat down at Woody's old desk, opened up one of the drawers, and found it stuffed with bottles of pills— antacids, high-blood-pressure tablets, migraine headache pills—it looked like a minipharmacy! When I got to the winter meetings in Dallas, I soon discovered why. Billy had asked me to try and find a veteran shortstop, preferably with postseason experience, and it so happened the Mets' GM, Joe McIlvaine, had just such a player in Santana who, at thirty, was still in his prime but was being shopped because the Mets wanted to promote their top shortstop prospect, Kevin Elster. Joe and I quickly agreed on a deal—he wasn't looking to hold me up, and he wanted to do right by the popular Santana by trading him someplace he'd like to be. In return, I agreed to give him three borderline prospects: the outfielder Darren Reed, the catcher Phil Lombardi, and the pitcher Steve Frey. All that was needed was Mr. Steinbrenner's approval. But I was not prepared for his reaction.

"Oh, no, no, no," he said. "What's wrong with you? We don't trade with the Mets!"

"But, Mr. Steinbrenner," I countered, "Santana's an established shortstop who's got a World Series ring playing in New York. Those kinds of guys just aren't available."

"Well, then why are the Mets looking to get rid of him?"

I tried to explain how they wanted to break in Elster, but he was having none of it.

"That McIlvaine is taking advantage of you because you're a rookie general manager," he said. "You tell him the deal is off."

I'd been on the job barely two months, and already I wanted to quit. There was no way I was going back to Joe McIlvaine and reneging on the trade. I was this close to getting on a plane and leaving Dallas when I called Mr. Steinbrenner one more time and told him we needed to make this trade and it didn't matter if it was with the Mets.

"All right," he said, "but you tell McIlvaine I have to get one more player back if we're giving up three."

At that point, I rushed up to McIlvaine's room—it was about two o'clock in the morning—pounded on his door, and told him we finally had a deal.

"But I have to have one more player, Joe," I said. "I don't care if it's the third-string catcher in rookie ball. I just have to get my owner off my ass."

McIlvaine agreed to throw in an A-ball pitcher named Victor Garcia who never made it to the majors, but I could have cared less. I could see that being Mr. Steinbrenner's general manager was going to be just as trying as being his manager.

The 1988 season was when Mr. Steinbrenner's war with Dave Winfield over contributions to the Winfield Foundation was just beginning to heat up. The two of them sued each other, each charging the other of failing to make required contributions to the Winfield Foundation as part of the ten-year, $23 million contract Winfield had signed with the Yankees in 1980. Mr. Steinbrenner accused the foundation—and by extension, Winfield—of misusing funds on jun-kets, limousines, and so forth, and the war of words between them in the papers was starting to get really ugly. It was therefore inevitable that Mr. Steinbrenner would come to me—as he did in early May—and order me to trade Winfield.

"Mr. Steinbrenner, you can't trade Winfield," I argued. "In addi-tion to the nearly six million dollars left on his contract, as a player with ten years of service time in the big leagues, the last five with the same club, he can veto any trade."

"You let me worry about that," he said. "Your job is to call around to find what teams are interested and get a list on my desk tomorrow morning."

If there was one thing for which I was very fortunate as a neo-phyte GM, it was the very capable Yankees front office staff that was already in place. My assistant GM, Bob Quinn, had previously been the scouting and player development director with the Indians for twelve years, and our own scouting and player director, Brian Sa-bean, was recognized as one of the brightest young baseball minds in the game. (I should say here that they are probably already pol-ishing up a plaque for Brian in Cooperstown as the architect of three world championships as the general manager of the Giants.) I got together with Brian and Bob, as well as Gene "Stick" Michael (who'd rejoined the Yankees as a scout after managing the Cubs in 1987 and '88), and we began calling around to solicit interest in Winfield. In the end, the only interested team that matched up with us in terms of a player of somewhat equal ability was Houston with Kevin Bass, an outfielder who'd averaged 18 homers and 80 RBI over the past three seasons. The next day I reported this to Mr. Steinbrenner.

"Okay," he said. "Here's what I want you to do. Get Stick, and the two of you go down to Houston and take a look at this Bass and bring me back a report on him. But I don't want anyone knowing about this! This has got to be top secret. That's why I want you to bring raincoats and top hats, and instead of going through the press gate and sitting with the scouts, buy yourselves tickets for the upper deck so nobody will see or notice you."

"Mr. Steinbrenner, I can't do that!" I said.

"Why?" he said.

"Because if I do, I'm liable to be arrested as a flasher or something!"

"What are you talking about?" he snapped.

"Sir, it's a domed stadium in Houston!" I said.

"Ahhhh, get out of here," he grumbled. "Just get me that damn report on Bass."

As I had told Mr. Steinbrenner, it was a wasted exercise. Over the course of the next couple of months, despite his growing hostilities with Mr. Steinbrenner, Winfield reiterated he would not approve any trades. Then, in 1989, he hurt his back and missed the entire season.

It was also no surprise when Mr. Steinbrenner and Billy soon renewed their own hostilities, only this time I was right in the middle of it and I didn't like it. Billy got the team off to a good start—they were in first place as late as June 19—but he wasn't happy with any of the new players I'd brought in, particularly Slaught and Santana, and was constantly critical of them to Mr. Steinbrenner. After a May 6 Friday-night loss in Texas, Billy got involved in a drunken fight with the bouncers in a strip joint called Lace, not far from Arlington Stadium, and was brought back to the team hotel beaten up pretty badly. That weekend I had rented a trailer and driven to Philadelphia with Anita to pick up our son, Lou Jr., from Villanova when Mr. Steinbrenner called to tell me about this latest incident with Billy.

"I don't know what kind of shape he's in," Mr. Steinbrenner said, "but I need you to go down to Texas to manage the team for a couple of days."

"I'm not doing that, sir," I told him, explaining that, logistically it would be impossible and that I was driving my son home from college. I was a little surprised that he didn't give me more of a fight about it, but after finishing loading the trailer up with all my son's stuff, Anita and I began heading home. We were on the New Jersey Turnpike, listening to the Yankees game, when, in the eighth inning, I almost drove off the highway when I heard Phil Rizzuto say, "And pinch-hitting for Santana, here is Chris Chambliss."

"Anita!" I screamed, "did you hear that?"

"Hear what?" she said.

"Rizzuto just said Chambliss is pinch-hitting for Santana!"

"So?" she said.

"Chris is a coach," I exclaimed. "He hasn't played in two years! What's he doing in this game?"

I pulled over to a phone booth and called Mr. Steinbrenner to find out what was going on. He didn't know what Chambliss was doing in the game either, but made it clear this needed to be nipped in the bud. It seemed that Jose Cruz, our primary left-handed hitter off the bench, had come up with a sore knee, and Billy had taken it upon himself to activate Chambliss to replace him.

"I don't care what the reason is," Mr. Steinbrenner said, "get him off the damn roster!"

As it turned out, Chris got only that one last at-bat for his career—but he was paid handsomely for it. Once he was activated, he had to be paid the minimum player salary for the rest of the year, which was about $20,000 more than he was making as a coach. The Chambliss maneuver was just another Billy firestorm with Mr. Steinbrenner that caught me in the middle, and I was fed up with it—fed up with them both complaining about the players I'd brought in, and fed up with their general bickering. So on May 28 I called Mr. Steinbrenner and told him I wanted to relinquish my duties as GM to Bob

Quinn. I told him it had gotten very uncomfortable being the middle-man between him and Billy, and, again, he didn't argue with me. We agreed that I would stay on as a special adviser and scout.

Because we were in first place, Mr. Steinbrenner didn't have much to say publicly about Billy's incident at Lace, even though the papers made a very big deal of it, sending extra reporters down to Arlington to dig up all the lurid details. But anyone who knew Mr. Steinbrenner knew that kind of silence from him was like death, and considering all of Billy's previous drunken tribulations that had led to his firings, he was clearly on borrowed time. It was after a disastrous 2–7 road trip to Boston, Cleveland, and Detroit, from June 13 to 22, which dropped the team to three games behind the then-front-running Tigers, that I got a call from Bob Quinn. I was in Albany looking at our Double-A team, and what Quinn had to say was the last thing I could have expected.

"The Boss is gonna be calling you any minute," he said. "He's firing Billy and he wants you to take over the team again."

I didn't know what to think. My wounds from 1987 had barely healed, and now he was going to reopen them?

I reminded Mr. Steinbrenner how this hadn't worked before and told him that I was very apprehensive about managing for him again, but he kept assuring me it would be different, promising to leave me alone. "I need you to do this, Lou," he said, and I guess the competitive spirit within me, plus encouraging conversations with Hawk Harrelson and Bobby Murcer, convinced me to agree. Still, I tossed and turned all night in my Albany hotel room before driving down to Yankee Stadium, entertaining second thoughts all the way, for the press conference announcing Lou II. If there had been cell phones back then I have no doubt I would have never gone through with it.

I should have known. All I had to do was reread the press clippings from Billy's previous four incarnations as Mr. Steinbrenner's manager: "This time it's going to be different"; "Billy and George understand each other now"; "This time there'll be no interference."

As part of my return as manager, I was able to bring in Stick as my third base coach and Stan "the Steamer" Williams as my pitching coach, and for the first few weeks of my tenure we played pretty well and even climbed back into first place for four days, July 24–27. But I knew it was a fragile, house-of-cards situation, especially the starting pitching; Guidry was bothered by a sore shoulder, and Al Leiter, a rookie lefty who had made the team out of spring training and showed great promise in his first nine starts in April and May, incurred a blister issue that sidelined him most of June, July, and August. Then, on August 24, John Candelaria, who was leading the staff with 13 wins, blew out his knee and was lost for the rest of the season. Once again, August (9–20) was my Waterloo, with our pitching staff compiling a 6.64 ERA for the month. On an off-day in mid-month, I was fishing on Long Island Sound when I got a ship-to-shore radio call from Bob Quinn informing me that Mr. Steinbrenner had fired Stan Williams. Once again, the pattern. As soon as I got back to New York, I called the Steamer and told him how terrible I felt about this and that I was going to get it rescinded.

"No, no, no, please don't do that," Steamer exclaimed.

"Why?" I said.

"Because," Steamer said, "after he fired me he gave me a one-year extension and a $10,000 raise to be a scout!"

Good for him, but not for me! I had no idea who my new pitching coach was until I walked into the clubhouse the next day and there, sitting in my office, was Clyde King.

"I feel bad about Stan," Clyde said, "but I think I can help these pitchers. I'm going to go watch them now and see what I can do."

But later on the home stand, a resigned Clyde came to me and said, "You need to do me a favor, Lou. Call Mr. Steinbrenner and get me out of here. You've got a 'no stuff' staff!"

I had come to realize that Clyde was not my biggest ally. He didn't think I was tough enough on the players, and I'm sure he transmitted that to Mr. Steinbrenner. During the last two months of the season I didn't have a whole lot of communication with Mr. Steinbrenner even as he made periodic comments to the writers about his disappointment with the team's performance. I had no doubt he was once again sharpening his ax, and then I heard he was leaking a story to the writers that I had stolen furniture from him! What had happened was, when I came back as manager the second time, I was told I was required to do a pregame radio show with WABC but that there would be no additional compensation for it. I knew Davey Johnson, across town with the Mets, had a similar pregame radio show arrangement and was paid $75,000 for it. I told Arthur Adler, the Yankees' VP of business, that I would not do the radio show without being compensated, and after arguing that the Yankees would refuse to pay me extra and WABC had no money in its budget for it either, he came up with a compromise in which I would be instead paid in merchandise from the team's radio sponsors. One of those sponsors was a Scandinavian furniture company. Adler sent Anita their catalog to pick out what furniture she wanted, even though it didn't match any of the furniture in our house. Instead, I had it shipped to my restaurant in Woodbridge, New Jersey. Unbeknownst to me, Adler sent the bill to the Yankees. All Mr. Steinbrenner had to do was call me for an explanation, but he never did. The issue festered until the end of the season when, just before we were about to embark on a bus ride from Yankee Stadium to Baltimore for a four-game series against the Orioles, Mr. Steinbrenner summoned me to his office. When I walked in, he was at his desk, shuffling some papers and barely acknowledging me.

"You're in a lot of trouble, Lou," he said.

"What kind of trouble?" I asked, assuming he was talking about the state of the team.

He then proceeded to accuse me directly of stealing from him, charging furniture for my restaurant to the Yankees, while adding that he was probably going to get the Bronx district attorney involved. I couldn't believe what I was hearing. I told him this was all a bunch of bullshit, that the furniture was payment to me for doing the pregame radio show and that Adler should have told him.

"I don't know," he said. "I've got to look into this further."

I think he already knew, but he wanted to have this meeting with me—while the players were all waiting on the bus—to make it look like I was being dressed down by him. On my way out the door, he couldn't resist saying, "You're going down to Baltimore and Weaver's gonna make you look bad again."

I was sorry to disappoint him. We won three out of four from the Orioles, and for the first three games I called all the pitches from the dugout. I was never more exhausted in my life. It takes so much out of you, concentrating on every single pitch for nine innings.

Amazingly, despite all that had gone wrong with our pitching, after the Baltimore series, we were still only 3½ games behind the first-place Red Sox going into a season-ending three-game series in Detroit with the Tigers. The Red Sox lost their final three games but unfortunately so did we. It hardly mattered that we'd set a new home attendance record of 2,633,701 in 1988; both Mr. Steinbrenner and I knew this just wasn't going to work between us.

On Saturday, October 3, after the next-to-last game of the season in Detroit, I told "Killer" Kane to round up all the writers, broadcasters, coaches, and support people for a party at the London Chop House. "Tell them," I said, "this is my last supper!" And what a party it was, the wine and the merriment pouring into the night. The Chop House had a live band on Saturday nights and I vaguely remember getting up on the stage and, in my best Frank Sinatra, starting to croon, *"And now, the end is near, and so I face the final curtain . . ."* before finally giving way to a real singer, Suzyn Waldman, who covered us for WFAN radio at the time and was also an accomplished Broadway performer. Suzyn wowed everyone with a rousing rendition of "New York, New York." It brought tears to my eyes because that was Mr. Steinbrenner's favorite song, which he had played at the conclusion of every game at Yankee Stadium, and I knew I would soon be putting New York in the rearview mirror. At the end of the night, the tab came to a couple thousand dollars, which I told Killer to expense to the Yankees. I figured that was the least Mr. Steinbrenner could do after all he'd put me through in '87 and '88.

Only Anita believed I should stay as manager. The day after the season, when Mr. Steinbrenner called and said he wanted me to fly down to Tampa and come to his Am Ship office at Rocky Point, I told her he was going to fire me again. "Well, then I'm going with you," she said firmly. When we got to the office, Mr. Steinbrenner's longtime secretary, JoAnn Nastal, came out to greet us. Momentarily startled to see Anita there, she rushed back into the office—whereupon Mr. Steinbrenner handed her a fistful of hundred-dollar bills and instructed her to "take Anita shopping for a couple of hours, while Lou and I talk."

I made it easy for Mr. Steinbrenner. Before he could tell me he was going to make a change, I thanked him for the opportunity to manage the Yankees without having had any previous experience, and started to get up to leave.

"Hold on," he said. "Where are you going? Let's talk about the team."

"There's nothing to talk about, sir," I said. "I did the best I could. I've done everything I can here."

"Well, don't you want to know who the new manager is going to be?" he asked.

I really didn't care, but when he told me Dallas Green, I nearly fell off my chair. Big Dallas, who'd managed the Phillies to the world championship in 1983, had a reputation for being a hard-driving, confrontational, old-school guy who was not afraid to rip into his players in public. *This guy's as much of a hardhead as Mr. Steinbrenner*, I thought. *This isn't gonna work out!* I didn't have to guess that it was Clyde King who'd recommended the ultimate tough guy, Big Dallas.

I wished Mr. Steinbrenner well, but again, as I got up to leave, he stopped me.

"Before you go," he said, "I want you to sign an extension."

"An extension to do what?" I asked. "I told you I've done just about everything I can here."

"Well, we'll figure something out," he said.

Then, thrusting a contract in front of me, he said: "Here it is, a three-year extension. Just fill in the figures."

I didn't know what to say. Probably if I hadn't been trying to extricate myself from some serious financial losses with a failed Cadillac dealership in Ossining, New York, and a condominium development venture in Connecticut I'd been partners in, I'd have said no thanks and been on my way. But my oldest son, Lou, was still at Villanova, and my other son, Derek, was in high school and would soon be starting college. Plus, we really liked living in Allendale.

I had been making $300,000 as the Yankees' manager, but as long as Mr. Steinbrenner was suddenly allowing me to have the upper hand, I suggested a raise to $400,000. "You got it," he said. "Just sign the contract and take Anita out to dinner."

This was the mercurial George Steinbrenner. A month earlier he was accusing me of stealing from him and threatening to sic the

Bronx DA after me, and now he was firing me and overwhelming me with generosity at the same time. When I left his office, my head spinning, Anita was waiting for me.

"What happened?" she said.

"Exactly what I told you was gonna happen," I said. "He fired me."

Then, pausing for effect, I added, "But I got a three-year extension and a huge raise out of it!"

Part of my duties in my new contract was to team up with Greg Gumbel on a pregame TV show for the MSG network. The MSG deal paid $80,000, but because of Mr. Steinbrenner's generosity, I didn't feel right about essentially double-dipping and I sent all the checks back to the Yankees. Greg and I had a lot of fun together. He was a real pro and taught me a lot about on-air TV work. It was also nice going to spring training in Fort Lauderdale with no worries or concerns about the ball club, not to mention the daily phone call harangues from Mr. Steinbrenner. In mid-March, I was getting into my car in the parking lot when I saw a familiar face approaching me. It was Syd Thrift, who'd previously been the general manager of the Pirates. Syd, a native Virginian, was a heavyset, convivial sort with big bushy eyebrows and a syrupy southern drawl. In my brief term as the Yankees' GM, I'd had a few drinks with him at the winter meetings in Dallas. He was a great storyteller and not at all hesitant to expound on his knowledge and theories of baseball. I asked him what brought him to the Yankees' camp.

"I'm the new head of baseball operations," Syd announced proudly. "Mr. Steinbrenner thinks I can turn things around here, like I did in Pittsburgh, and that's what I'm going to do! I've got a lot of ideas, particularly in scouting and player evaluation, and I can't wait to get started! I know a lot about psychology and we can put in place some programs here that will help improve our approach to everything."

"Well, good for you, Syd," I said. "But just so you were forewarned—this job here can be very . . . uh . . . challenging."

"That's good," Syd said brightly. "I love challenges."

I didn't see him again until the end of camp, when we crossed paths on the field during batting practice. He seemed a tad more subdued as we discussed the state of the team, and I couldn't help noticing a little twitch in his neck as he talked. Then sometime in late April, after I did my pregame show with Greg, I decided to stop by Syd's office. When I walked in, he was standing by a blender, making himself a diet drink. He looked like he'd lost some weight.

"You better be careful, Syd," I joked. "This is a meat and potatoes job!"

As we talked I noticed that the twitch had gotten more pronounced, and he now had hives on his face. I asked him how everything was going, and he replied that it was hard getting all his plans implemented because of the constant extraneous phone calls and orders from the top.

"I know what you're talking about, Syd," I said. "You've just got to try and roll with the punches around here, because I assure you they're gonna keep on coming."

Then in June, the newspapers reported that Mr. Steinbrenner had ordered all the Yankees' scouts off the road as a cost-cutting measure. Scouting being Syd's bread and butter, I knew this couldn't have gone over well with him. But I didn't see him until about a month later, when he called me into his office in an agitated state. Now, in addition to the twitch and the hives, Syd was sweating profusely, and as he talked, he kept rubbing his head. I noticed his hair was falling out!

"My god, Syd," I said. "Are you all right?"

"No, I'm not, Lou," he said. "This guy is *killing* me! I've got to get out of here!"

Besides my TV work, part of my contract duties with Mr. Steinbrenner was to evaluate the minor-league players and work with the hitters. I was a little reluctant to do the latter since Dallas had his own hitting coach in Frank Howard, but in early May he approached me and asked if I could help Don Mattingly, who was really struggling. I was very appreciative of Dallas reaching out to me like that, and it just showed he was confident in his own skin, as well as in his coaches' loyalty to him, that he would go outside his staff for the sake of helping a player or the team.

About that same time, I got a call from Pat Gillick, the general manager of the Blue Jays, who was about to fire his manager, Jimy Williams. He told me they'd like me to fly to Toronto for an interview, and Mr. Steinbrenner gave me his approval to talk to them.

"What I had always admired about Lou was that he would do whatever it took to win, and I think he got a lot of that from Billy Martin," said Gillick. "Billy and Lou were both innovative in that they'd do things that were unexpected and weren't afraid to make a mistake. That's what I wanted in a manager. When George initially agreed to let us talk to Lou, I was optimistic we could work something out. But then George turned around and said he had to have our top pitching prospect, Todd Stottlemyre, as compensation, and that was it."

I was disappointed Mr. Steinbrenner wouldn't let me go. I'm not sure what would have happened if I'd gone to the commissioner's office about getting released from what was really a special services contract. Pat was in the process of putting together an excellent ball club in Toronto. I told him that as much as I would've loved to have the job, the guy he wound up hiring, Cito Gaston, was the right choice. And he was. Cito went on to win back-to-back world championships with the Blue Jays in 1992 and 1993. I can't count the many times I thought about how that might have been me.

Meanwhile, as I fully expected, Dallas and Mr. Steinbrenner

weren't getting along. After getting over .500 briefly in mid-July, the team lost nine out of ten games to fall into sixth place. That was when Dallas began referring to Mr. Steinbrenner as "Manager George" to the writers, and you knew it was only a matter of time before they would be parting ways. I was home in Allendale when I got a call from Mr. Steinbrenner on the morning of August 19.

"I just want you to know I'm gonna fire Dallas," he said. "I've got a plane coming from Columbus, with Bucky and Stick on it, that'll meet you in Teterboro and from there you'll fly to Detroit to take over as manager."

"Wait a minute, Mr. Steinbrenner," I said. "I'm not doing that. You want to change managers, that's fine. But we both know it won't work with us."

Bucky Dent had been managing our Triple-A team in Columbus and Stick had been out there evaluating the team. I told Mr. Steinbrenner the logical thing would be to make Bucky the manager. He'd been managing for five years in the Yankees' system and had earned a chance, and, grudgingly, Mr. Steinbrenner agreed.

Ten days after the Green firing, it was announced that Syd Thrift had resigned as the head of Yankees baseball operations.

Incredibly, when the team struggled under Bucky in 1989, there were recurring rumors that Mr. Steinbrenner was preparing to bring Billy back for a sixth time! I have no doubt that would've happened, too, had Billy not been killed in a car crash on Christmas Day 1989. I was skiing with my family in Killington, Vermont, when I heard the news. While I was initially shocked, once the details began coming out—that Billy and his friend Bill Reedy, a bar owner from Detroit, had been drinking all day and had driven off an icy road and into a ditch in front of Billy's wife's home in upstate Fenton, New York—I was not surprised, especially when it was revealed that Billy was the driver and, because he wasn't wearing a seat belt, went through the windshield and broke his neck. Billy had a lifelong problem with the booze—when I was his coach I was also his designated driver after games—and he went through life not wearing a seat belt. Still, I felt a sense of deep sadness. I had really grown to like Billy. I didn't respect the fact that he drank so much, but he was mostly a fun guy to be around and he had a great sense of humor. I felt especially bad for his son, Billy Jr., a great kid who went on to become a player agent.

Because of a blizzard in Killington, I was unable to attend Billy's funeral, an elaborate mass at Saint Patrick's Cathedral in New York, arranged by Mr. Steinbrenner's friend Bill Fugazy, who had close ties to the hierarchy of the Catholic Church. Billy was buried in the Gate of Heaven Cemetery in Westchester, where Babe Ruth and the actor Jimmy Cagney are interred. There's no question Mr. Steinbrenner used Billy, and there may well have been a degree of guilt behind the send-off fit for a Yankee icon he gave him. But he also gave him wonderful opportunities that nobody else would have. I only wish he'd made a more concerted effort to get Billy help with his drinking.

As for me, I went to a Catholic church near the ski resort and asked if the pastor would be kind enough to say a special mass for Billy. I gave him a nice donation and even though I think he was a Red Sox fan, he did a wonderful job commemorating Billy. I wasn't one of Billy's buddies, but I can say here that my life was enriched by him.

Billy along with the Boss helped get me started managing, and for that I will always be grateful. It was hard saying no to Mr. Steinbrenner, but at least after turning him down this time, he knew I would never manage for him again—and that the next time another team called for permission to talk to me about being their manager, he would finally let me go.

CHAPTER 8

Red October

As the 1989 season was coming to a close, I began to wonder what the future held for me. As refreshingly therapeutic as it had been, working with Greg Gumbel in the TV booth and content in the knowledge there would never be a "Lou III" with Mr. Steinbrenner, I was getting restless. I needed to sever ties with the Yankees and I very much wanted to manage again, away from Mr. Steinbrenner. I just didn't know where, when, or how that would happen.

And then, twelve days after the season, Bob Quinn, who'd had to endure the humiliation of Mr. Steinbrenner bringing in Syd Thrift over his head back in spring training, resigned as the Yankees' general manager and immediately signed on as GM of the Cincinnati Reds. Whether he knew it or not, in Marge Schott, the chain-smoking, blunt-talking Reds owner (who herself would be repeatedly rebuked by baseball's hierarchy for a series of anti-Semitic and racially charged remarks before eventually being forced to sell the team in 1999), Bob had enlisted for a whole different—but equally frustrating—trip from Mr. Steinbrenner. (For the record, I never heard Marge make any racial or anti-Semitic remarks in my three years there.) Days after Bob took over in Cincinnati, he made a call to me.

The previous August, Pete Rose, "Mr. Red," had been banned from baseball for life for betting on the game during the time he was the Reds' manager, from 1985 to 1989. Rose's longtime Reds teammate Tommy Helms had finished out the '89 season as interim manager, but as Bob explained to me, he wanted to start off with his own manager, someone, who, as he put it, was comfortable enough in his own shoes to step in and handle the intense scrutiny and pressure of replacing a Cincinnati native and the most popular Red of all time. To further emphasize that point, Bob said, "Just so you know, the road you'll be driving in to work at Riverfront Stadium is Pete Rose Way."

None of that mattered to me. I just wanted to get back to the work of managing a ball club, but I still needed Mr. Steinbrenner to let me out of my special services contract.

"Don't worry about that," Bob said, "I'll have Marge call George directly."

After his conversation with Marge, Mr. Steinbrenner gave me the okay to talk to the Reds, but I wondered if this was going to be the same as what happened with Gillick and the Blue Jays—that in the end he was going to want significant compensation for me.

I flew out to Cincinnati and met Marge at Riverfront Stadium, where we subsequently drove out to her house, a big German tudor in the suburb of Indian Hill. That's when I was introduced to her two large Saint Bernards, Schottzie and Schottzie II. We spent a lot of time talking about family, something she made clear was very important to her, and then she asked, "Do you want to come to Cincinnati and manage for me?"

I told her I did but that I was concerned Mr. Steinbrenner was not going to let me out of my contract with the Yankees.

"Oh, honey," she said. "Don't you worry about that. George will do anything I want! I'll call him and work out everything," to which I said, "Good luck!"

Much to my surprise, Marge was right. She did have a way with

Mr. Steinbrenner, and a day later he called me and said if I wanted to go to Cincinnati he wouldn't stand in my way. I figured he realized he was paying me $400,000 a year, for which I wasn't doing very much, and this was a way to save him some money. I think he also saw where the Reds had finished in fifth place, 17 games behind, in 1989, and that, as a small-market team with a tightfisted owner, there was very little chance of my succeeding there.

"I have to say, Marge was very persuasive, Lou," he said. "I hope you realize, though, replacing Pete Rose out there is not gonna be an easy fit for you."

"I understand, sir," I said. "I thank you for letting me go."

Now all I had to do was reach an agreement with Marge, which proved to be somewhat tougher than I anticipated.

"I have one little problem," she said. "Your $400,000 salary with George is more than I want to pay."

"Well how about this, then," I said. "Let's make it $350,000 with an agreement that my salary will be adjusted after the first year."

Once again, I was negotiating without an agent—and in the process agreeing to a $50,000 pay cut. But I was finally getting away from Mr. Steinbrenner and looking forward to a new challenge with a new team. On November 2, the Reds held a news conference at Riverfront Stadium to announce my hiring as manager. I brought Anita and my youngest son, Derek, with me. I had been in the American League my entire life and didn't know the National League, but what most impressed me was how big baseball and the Reds were in Cincinnati. Anita and Marge hit it off right away and I could see that we were going to be happy in Cincinnati. Plus, it was close enough to New Jersey, an hour's plane ride away, so we wouldn't have to sell our house in Allendale.

During the press conference Bob Quinn said that I would have a free hand in naming my coaches, with one exception: the future

Hall of Famer Tony Perez, another Reds icon as the powerful cleanup hitter on the 1975–76 Big Red Machine world championship clubs, would be remaining as first base and batting coach. I certainly had no problem with that. I had the utmost respect for Tony as both a person and a baseball man. In the days to come, I hired my old Yankee colleague Stan "the Steamer" Williams, who'd spent the last year scouting the National League for Mr. Steinbrenner, as my pitching coach, along with Jackie Moore as my bench coach and Sammy Perlozzo as my third base coach. Moore had previously been bench coach with the Expos and before that was Billy Martin's bench coach with the Oakland A's, and Billy had highly recommended him to me. Perlozzo had previously been the third base coach for the Mets. I had also wanted to hire Don Gullett, my former teammate and roomie with the Yankees, to be my bullpen coach and work under Stan to get ready to be pitching coach. I thought it would be a great fit, as Gullett had been the ace of those Big Red Machine pitching staffs. But before I could hire him, Bob Quinn told me the Reds had a very talented pitching coach in their minor-league system, Larry Rothschild, whom they were worried about losing to another organization.

"Would you just talk to Rothschild before you do anything with Gullett?" Quinn asked.

I agreed. I met Rothschild for lunch at Mickey Mantle's restaurant in New York. But what I figured would be a perfunctory two-hour lunch instead turned out to be a four-hour session in which he blew me away with his knowledge of pitching. When I got home to Allendale, I called Bob and said, "This is the guy!" To this day, Larry, who later worked for me with the Cubs, remains one of the most respected pitching coaches in baseball, with the Yankees.

I remember vividly that one of the first Reds people I talked to was Johnny Bench, who told me, "You've come into a great situation, Lou. I don't know what happened here last year, but this is a very good team you're taking over. They're ready to win. They just need to be shown how."

That was very reassuring, but as Quinn said, there were still a few pieces we needed to add. As such, Bob and I and our three main scouts, Jimmy Stewart, Chief Bender, and Gene Bennett, got to the winter meetings in Nashville a couple of days before they were officially scheduled to begin, and went to work. We had a situation with our All-Star closer, Johnny Franco, who'd saved 32 games for the Reds in '89. He'd just gotten almost a million-dollar raise in arbitration and was coming into free agency, and Quinn said we needed to trade him because we weren't going to be able to afford him after the '90 season. At the same time, we couldn't trade him without having a replacement for him. Jimmy Stewart said the Mets had interest in Franco, who was a Brooklyn native, and thought they might be willing to swap Randy Myers, a twenty-seven-year-old lefty who appeared to be coming into his own as a potentially dominant backend reliever. (As I would later find out, Myers was also a bit of a wild man in terms of his habits and demeanor. He liked to wear army battle fatigues under his uniform jersey and kept a couple of deactivated hand grenades in his locker.) Quinn was able to move quickly on that deal, only to have Marge nearly kill it.

"I'd shaken hands with Joe McIlvaine, the Mets' GM, and now I just had to call Marge for her approval," Quinn recalled. "I couldn't imagine any problem. But when I told her what the deal was, she screamed, 'No, no, no! You can't trade Johnny Franco! He's my favorite player! Tell them the trade is off!' That's when, coward that I was, I turned the phone over to Lou, who managed to sweet-talk Marge into giving her okay."

As the winter meetings were coming to a close, it looked as if the only things we were going to be able to accomplish were the Myers trade and the taking of Tim Layana, a young right-handed reliever, from the Yankees in the Rule 5 draft. But then I got to talking with the Stick, Gene Michael, who was now the Yankees' GM. Stick was looking for a starting pitcher and asked me about Tim Leary, a workhorse right-hander who'd been 8–14 with a 3.52 ERA and in 207 innings for the Dodgers and Reds in '89.

During that summer of '89 I'd taken some time off from broadcasting to tour the Yankees' minor-league system—that's where I saw Layana—and I'd been particularly impressed with a twenty-four-year-old left-handed-hitting outfielder, Hal Morris. Morris was a big kid—6' 3", 200 pounds—who had a very unorthodox hitting style but made really good contact. He was also really a first baseman, but with Don Mattingly entrenched at first with the Yankees, they were trying to force him into an outfielder. One of the "pieces" Bob Quinn and I had talked about adding was a left-handed hitting first baseman to platoon with our incumbent, Todd Benzinger. So when Stick asked me if we'd be willing to trade Leary, I said to him that I liked Morris while pointing out to him that his path was pretty much blocked with the Yankees. Stick agreed and we had a deal. Later that summer, when Morris was on his way to hitting .340 and Layana was doing a really nice job as a middle reliever for us, Mr. Steinbrenner sent word to me to "leave my players alone!" and then accused me of being a fox in the henhouse with the Yankees in 1989. I got a kick out of that.

Having added a left-handed power closer, a left-handed bat at first base, and a right-handed middle reliever, I couldn't wait to get to spring training, even if it was in Plant City, a small town nineteen miles east of Tampa with little or no nightlife or fine dining places. And then, just before the start of camp, negotiations between the owners and players over a new collective bargaining agreement broke down and the owners imposed a lockout of spring training. As the lockout dragged on for nearly a month, I became more and more agitated—I needed to get to know these kids!—and when camp finally did open I admit I probably acted like a man possessed. At least that's what Barry Larkin recalls:

> Before the first full-squad spring training workout, Lou had a meeting with us which was brief and to the point. He told us he didn't like losing, didn't accept losing, and that we were not going to lose. We kind of looked at each other and said, "Okay? Is that it?" During that spring, he really jumped all over on a couple of players—which he later explained to me were "teaching moments"—and we'd think, "Oh my god, this guy is *scary*!" I remember one time in particular when he got all over Paul O'Neill for throwing to the wrong base from right field. We quickly came to see that Lou wasn't going to accept the mental mistakes we'd had in the past.

At the same time, I like to think the players were learning some things too. Sammy Perlozzo remembers how "we'd be standing there in the dugout and our pitcher would get two strikes on the batter and Lou would turn to us and say, 'This guy can't hit a curveball,' and then he would get on the top step of the dugout and shout to our catcher, 'Call a curveball!' The batter would look back at him and smile as if to say, 'Are you kiddin'?' and Lou would smile right back and call again for the curveball and the batter would strike out. He must have done that a dozen or more times during that 1990 season—'Guy can't hit the inside fastball!'—and damn if it didn't work every time! We'd just stand there and laugh and laugh."

I will say this: I wanted to prove Mr. Steinbrenner wrong in the worst way, and I kept remembering what Bench had said to me about this Reds team being extremely talented, all coming into their prime, and just needing to be shown how to win. Early on in spring training Tony Perez said essentially the same thing. I'd asked Tony, "What was wrong here last year?" He replied, "You've gotta push 'em, Lou. At times they give up on themselves." I just knew I'd come from an organization where the pinstripes were all about winning, and so throughout the spring we pushed them. I told them over and over, "You guys have talent. It's time you knocked that door down."

In the lefty Tom Browning and the righty Jose Rijo, we had two legitimate top-of-the-rotation starters, while Myers joined the holdovers Rob Dibble and Norm Charlton to give me a trio of power-arm relievers, any one of whom could close. I thought we had the makings of a really nice pitching staff, and Joe Oliver, though only in his second year in the big leagues, was an excellent catcher who called a good game and could catch and throw well. With Larkin at short, Chris Sabo at third, and Mariano Duncan at second, I had both power and speed in my infield. Ironically, Larkin, Sabo, and Hal Morris had all played together at the University of Michigan—they were my "scholars," although Sabo was also a little goofy. In the outfield, O'Neill in right and Eric Davis in center were ages twenty-seven and twenty-eight respectively and had combined for 49 homers and 175 RBI in 1989. Davis was one of the most cordial and intelligent players I ever managed and had a world of talent, but after the 1990 season he just couldn't stay healthy, and had it not been for the many injuries he incurred I have no doubt he'd have been a Hall of Famer. He was that good. O'Neill, on the other hand, reminded me a lot of myself. He and Sabo were my two redasses. They hated making an out and took a beating out on many a bat. I particularly enjoyed watching O'Neill get mad.

"Lou was always getting on O'Neill, who he always called 'Big O'Neill'," said Larkin. "One time he was giving O'Neill batting tips in the cage and said to him, 'Can you dance?' O'Neill looked at him, quizzically, and Lou goes on, 'You know, dance? You need to establish a little rhythm up there, get a little music in your head!' With that, he gets into the cage and starts dancing right there in the batter's box! Eric Davis and I were standing behind the cage watching this, laughing our asses off, shaking our heads and thinking, 'This guy is certifiably nuts.' But in retrospect I don't know anyone who knew more about hitting than Lou."

Despite the aborted spring, I was able to get all the things I needed accomplished with the kids, and because we were a young team we were able to get in shape faster. About all we were lacking was a bona fide leadoff hitter, and at the end of spring training, Bob took care of that by acquiring Billy Hatcher, who'd averaged over 35 stolen bases the previous four seasons, from the Pirates.

Above all, we needed to get off to a good start, which is what we did.

We started off on a six-game road trip to Houston and Atlanta and won all six, and continued that streak with three more wins at home. After the 9–0 start we kept on winning through the rest of April and May, and by June 3 our 33–12 record was the best getaway by any team in Reds' history. Most of that was accomplished without the services of Davis, who was on the disabled list with a strained knee ligament from April 24 to May 19.

The big key to our success was the late-inning bullpen trio of Myers, Dibble, and Charlton, who came to calling themselves the "Nasty Boys." And they were nasty—Dibble with his 100 m.p.h. unhittable fastball, Charlton with a 97–98 m.p.h. splitter, and Randy with that 96 m.p.h. slider that he used to pound the outside corner. They revolutionized baseball. Dibble did not allow an earned run in his first 15 outings, and Myers had a win and two saves the first week. By season's end, they'd combined as relievers for a 1.89 ERA, 44 saves, and 234 strikeouts in 184⅔ innings. Charlton was almost as dominant as my principal seventh- and eighth-inning setup man, but in mid-July when Rijo went down with an injury, I had to move him into the starting rotation. Charlton was the ultimate competitor who, when I called him into my office and told him I needed him in the rotation, answered, "I'm ready."

Another big factor in our flying start was the breakthrough (or at least we thought it was a breakthrough) by the right-handed starter Jack Armstrong, who, after spending most of the previous two seasons in the minor leagues, won a spot in the rotation out of spring training and won eight of his first nine starts. By midseason, Armstrong was 11–3 with a 2.28 ERA and was named the National League's starting pitcher for the All-Star Game at Wrigley Field in Chicago. And that was about the last Armstrong ever did in the major leagues. He lost six of his next nine starts after the All-Star Break and at the end of August I had to take him out of the rotation. He pitched three more full seasons in the big leagues, never approaching that first-half brilliance in 1990, and was out of organized baseball before he was thirty. I was always mystified at what happened to Armstrong (whom I even left off the roster for the first round of the playoffs in 1990) but Stan Williams offered this theory:

> I think after getting the All-Star start, that satisfied him. I remember complimenting him at the All-Star Break at what a nice season he was having. I couldn't believe it when he told me he'd had enough work on his mechanics and he was ready to go home. To him, he had proven other people wrong.

My only regret of the 1990 season was that after that hellacious start, we played .500 ball the rest of the way and the fact that we were in first place from start to finish was never fully appreciated by the fans and media. We received a lot of criticism for what was perceived to be lackluster play in the second half, even though the smallest our lead ever got was 3½ games. Despite how it may have looked, I knew I was getting the effort and didn't feel a need to air the team out. More often than not, after a tough loss, I would vent my frustrations with my coaches. According to Larry Rothschild, one such venting session early in the 1990 season left the coaches speechless and in disbelief.

"I hadn't yet seen Lou's volcanic temper," he said, "but after this particularly bad loss he came into the coaches' office ripping mad. Just before, I had come into the room with a Styrofoam cup of beer which I set on this small, low refrigerator. Lou starts pacing back and forth, grousing about the team's play, and suddenly kicks the container of beer. What happened next was nothing short of amazing. The top rim of the cup was severed cleanly, as if with a razor or something, and it landed on the floor in front of us while the cup itself remained upright on the refrigerator with not a single drop of beer spilled! We were just astounded. But Lou didn't even notice. He just kept pacing and venting while all of us were sitting there, staring dumbfounded at that lip of the cup lying on the floor. To this day I am in total disbelief at that incident."

I honestly don't remember losing my temper much during that 1990 season, except for perhaps the August 21 game against the Cubs, which earned me a lifetime dubious achievement award since it's still aired on TV almost as much as George Brett's pine tar explosion. We had lost five games in a row and maybe I was having visions of those three disastrous Augusts with the Yankees from 1986 to 1988. I just felt I needed to do something to get my team out of the August doldrums, and I used a close play at first base early in the game— which Dutch Rennert called against us—to do it. Didn't matter that Dutch was one of the better umpires. I wanted to let off some steam. I charged out there and after getting in his face and screaming the magic words to earn myself an ejection, I looked down and saw this beautiful shiny white base. So I reached down, pulled it out of its moorings, heaved it thirty feet toward second base, then picked it up and threw it again into right field. I'm told that was the first time in anyone's memory a manager had pulled up a base and thrown it in anger. I'm not proud of having that distinction—I did it once again years later with Seattle—but it did serve its purpose. In my absence we went on to win that game, 8–1, to break the losing streak.

About the only other time I got really mad that 1990 season had nothing to do with a bad call in a game or a mental mistake or lack of effort by any of my players. Rather, it was an unwelcome intrusion back into my life by Mr. Steinbrenner. In the aftermath of his being suspended from baseball for giving $40,000 to an admitted gambler named Howie Spira in exchange for supplying damaging information on Dave Winfield's foundation, the transcript of Mr. Steinbrenner's testimony to Commissioner Fay Vincent was released in mid-July— with me smeared all over it. In attempting to explain away why he gave the money to Spira, Mr. Steinbrenner said he did it to protect me because Spira supposedly had information that I had a gambling problem. I was completely blindsided by this outrageous claim on Mr. Steinbrenner's part and now, in the middle of the pennant race, was forced to call a press conference to defend myself.

You have to remember, I was in a very difficult position as the man- ager of the Reds who replaced Pete Rose after he was banned for life for betting on baseball, and now Mr. Steinbrenner was claiming that I, too, had a gambling problem. The only gambling I did was on the horses and dogs. I went to the track a lot to get my mind off baseball, especially on the road, rather than be bored hanging around the hotel.

That spring, I'd gotten a call from Vincent, who then sent his secu- rity director, Kevin Hallinan, to meet with me for a couple of hours in Plant City. I wasn't sure what any of this was about other than baseball doing its due diligence regarding gambling after the Rose investigation. I told Hallinan that I enjoyed betting on horses and the dogs but that I absolutely never gambled on sports and didn't know any bookmakers. Shortly thereafter Vincent called me back to tell me everything was okay. He never once mentioned Spira, whom I never met, and I thought that was the end of it. Now, at my press conference, I told the writers emphatically that if I'd had any skeletons in my closet I'd have never come to Cincinnati, and then I added, "George is always saying how much he likes me and my family. And this is how he repays me."

Looking back, I'm thinking it was rather ironic Mr. Steinbrenner would be connecting me to gambling and horse racing since, a few years earlier, we had actually gone into the racehorse business together. After a Yankees spring training workout in Fort Lauderdale, Bobby Murcer and I went down to Hialeah for the yearling sale. I'd already done my homework and had a list of five or six horses with good bloodlines I thought would be worth buying if the bidding didn't get too out of hand. But when we got there, who do we run into but Mr. Steinbrenner, who immediately wanted to see my list.

"Who gave you this? This is garbage!" he declared. "These horses are no good. You come with me. I've got my own list. I've done my studying and you'll invest with me."

With that, he showed me the name of this filly who was supposed to also have great bloodlines, and instructed me to sit across from him in the bidding area and raise my hand when he gave me a signal.

"If I do the bidding myself, it'll run the price up," he said.

We wound up getting the horse for $55,000, and shortly thereafter Mr. Steinbrenner ran her at Monmouth Park in New Jersey. In three races there, she never passed a horse. Meanwhile, I couldn't help noticing how small she was compared with the other fillies and how fragile she looked.

"I don't know, Mr. Steinbrenner," I said, "this horse is really small. I'm even taller than her!"

"That's okay," he said. "She's a young two-year-old. She'll fill out. We may have started her out in too strong competition up here at Monmouth. I'm going to send her down to Tampa Bay Downs where I can keep an eye on her progress. I'm also going to get a new trainer."

The end of the story is she never passed a horse at Tampa Bay Downs either.

After Mr. Steinbrenner's testimony about me with Vincent became public, it was a long while before we ever spoke to each other. Our mutual friend Malio Iavarone was the peace broker when one day we both happened to be in his restaurant and he sent me over to Mr. Steinbrenner's table. It was like nothing had ever happened. He never mentioned anything about it and never apologized to me, and by then, I had just let it go. (An aside here: Malio had a special private room off the main dining room that he named the "Piniella-Steinbrenner Room." But one day I came in and noticed the placard over the door had been changed to the "Steinbrenner-Piniella Room." As Malio explained weakly, "What can I say? He wants everyone to know who's the boss here.")

Still, while Mr. Steinbrenner's comments were a distraction, I tried to keep my head down and manage a team that I knew had what it took. There were a lot of people who had doubts about us going very far in the postseason, but I wasn't one of them, because I had seen how every time we were tested, we answered—most notably when we lost three in a row in mid-September to see our lead shrink to 3½ games over the Dodgers and proceeded to win six of our next seven to put the NL West division away. As it was, no Reds pitcher won more than 15 games in 1990—Browning was 15–9 and Rijo 14–8—and no Reds batter hit more than 25 homers. Davis, with 86, led the team in RBI. It was truly a team effort. I also have to give a lot of credit to Pete Rose and the scouting director, Julian Mock. They had put this team together.

Our biggest challenge of the 1990 season was Jim Leyland's Pittsburgh Pirates team, which we met in the National League Championship Series. They had won 95 games in the regular season, had the best all-around outfield—Barry Bonds, Andy Van Slyke, and Bobby

Bonilla—in baseball, and in my old Yankee protégé Doug Drabek, they had the National League Cy Young winner at the top of their rotation. To beat them we were going to have to play our complete game.

When the Pirates won game 1, overcoming a 3–0 deficit against Rijo at Riverfront Stadium, it was a jolt. It was the first time all season we were behind in games to anyone. But as I said, every time that '90 team was tested, they answered. In game 2, Browning gave up singles to Gary Redus and Jay Bell to open the game, setting the table for Van Slyke, Bonilla, and Bonds. This was the mettle of Browning: he retired all three, the latter, Bonds, by strikeout, to end the inning unscathed. Leyland later said that was the turning point of the whole series. The three of them, Van Slyke, Bonilla, and Bonds, had driven in 311 runs that season, but our pitchers held them to a collective .190 average and 5 RBI in the six-game series. O'Neill was the game 2 hero for us, singling home one run in the bottom of the first against Drabek and doubling home the winning run in the fifth. He also made the defensive play of the game, throwing out Van Slyke at third base after catching Bonds's fly to right for a 9-5 double play in the sixth. In game 4 we demonstrated more of that complete-game finesse when Billy Hatcher gunned down Sid Bream trying to score from second on a single to center by José Lind, and Davis threw out Bonilla at third trying to stretch a double into a triple. For the series, our outfielders had four assists and no errors.

We were a complete team in every way. That was no better illustrated than in the final game 6. I used six different lineups in the series, including three different batters in the number three spot. My game 6 number three hitter was O'Neill, who had a .471 average for the series when, much to his dismay I'm sure, I sent a pinch hitter, Luis Quinones, up for him with runners at first and third and one out in the seventh inning against the Pirates' tough lefty Zane Smith. After we scratched out a run against Smith in the first inning, he'd held us scoreless into the seventh, and in this situation I was looking for someone just to make contact. Paul had not had a whole lot of success against Smith, so I figured with Quinones being a switch hitter, I'd let Leyland make the choice as to whether to stick with Smith. He left him in and Quinones, who'd hit .241 with just 17 RBI in 83 games during the regular season, made me look brilliant when he singled to right for what proved to be the winning run and series-clinching hit. It was a further tribute to our bench that Glenn Braggs, a reserve outfielder who'd replaced O'Neill, recorded the next-to-last out of the game with an excellent running catch of a Carmelo Martinez drive to deep right field.

Beating the Pirates reinforced my feeling we had a really good team. I was able to rest my pitching the last month of the season and I didn't have to apply the whip. But now, in the World Series, we were faced with an even bigger challenge in the Oakland A's, managed by my old Tampa pal and Pony League teammate Tony La Russa. The A's had won the most games (103) of any team in baseball, and with the "Bash Brothers," Jose Canseco and Mark McGwire (combined 76 homers), plus Rickey Henderson (65 stolen bases, 1.016 OPS) at the top of the order, they had the most formidable lineup we had faced all year. Very few people gave us a chance, but they overlooked three things: (1) our kids were confident now; (2) we had a power-pitching staff and the A's hitters had not seen that kind of velocity in the American League; and (3) they had a fastball staff and our hitters hit fastballs better than any other team in the National League.

I first saw Jose Rijo in 1984 when he was a nineteen-year-old rookie with the Yankees, and you could tell right away this kid had the makings to be a dominant starting pitcher in the majors. All he needed was confidence. That confidence fully manifested itself in 1990, when he finished fifth in the National League in ERA (2.70) and second in hits per nine innings (6.899). He was the hardest thrower of our starters and I figured the A's were not going to be too comfortable facing him. They weren't. Rijo tossed seven shutout innings in our 7–0 game 1 win, in which the Bash Brothers were held to a collective 0-for-5.

I had hoped to pitch Browning in game 2, but his wife was having a baby and we didn't know when he'd be able to get back from the hospital. So I went with our other lefty, Danny Jackson, who wasn't able to get through the third inning, and after four we were trailing 4–3. That's when I got scared. We needed innings, but from whom was I going to get them? Enter Jack Armstrong, whom I'd left off the roster for the Pittsburgh series. Jack had certainly had plenty of rest, and he gave us a much-belated encore to his All-Star-worthy first half by shutting down the A's on one hit through the fourth, fifth, and sixth. A triple by Hatcher and an RBI infield groundout by Braggs enabled us to tie the game in the eighth and knock out Tony's 27-game winner, Bob Welch, and Joe Oliver won it in the tenth with an RBI single off Tony's future Hall of Fame closer Dennis Eckersley. It was only the fourth time all season Welch hadn't made it through eight innings and only the third time in 53 chances Eckersley had blown a save. But we were on a roll and undeterred by the stats or pedigree of Tony's stars. In the top of the tenth inning, I looked down at the end of the dugout and there was Browning. I couldn't believe he'd left the hospital and his newborn baby and rushed back to the stadium. "I'm here if you need me, Skip," he said.

Thanks to Oliver, I didn't need Browning until two days later, when the series resumed in Oakland for game 3. He didn't have his best stuff, but he didn't need it as we rocked the A's Mike Moore for eight hits and six runs in 2⅔ innings, including two homers by Sabo, a leadoff shot in the second and a two-run blast in the third. Browning gave up three runs in six innings and then I turned it over to the Nasty Boys, Dibble and Myers, who shut the A's down in the last three innings.

We completed the sweep, which some people have called one of the biggest upsets in World Series history, with Rijo pitching another gem—8⅓ innings, two hits, one run, and nine strikeouts—in game 4. Rijo's dominating performance was fortunate, as we lost both Eric Davis, who suffered a gruesome injury (lacerated kidney) diving for a ball in left field, and Billy Hatcher, who was hit by a pitch in the hand, in the first inning. Neither one of them would have been able to play in any more games had the series continued.

To this day, all these years later, I still cannot fully describe the elation—and redemption—I felt sitting in the visiting manager's office at the Oakland Coliseum in the aftermath of winning the World Series. That same night, Mr. Steinbrenner, who was on suspension from baseball, was the host of *Saturday Night Live* in New York, and in his opening monologue he joked that at 11:15 p.m., he bought the Cincinnati Reds. He then later made a quick reference to "Lou winning game 4." No public congratulations. After most of the reporters had left, I was sitting there with Suzyn Waldman and a couple of New York writers when somebody mentioned that Mr. Steinbrenner had been playing the buffoon on *Saturday Night Live* while I was winning the World Series, and asked me if there was anything I wanted to say to him.

I thought about it for a few seconds and then replied, "Yes there is. George . . . I can manage!"

It was the wrong response. I reacted out of pride. What I should have said was, "I just want to thank Mr. Steinbrenner for the opportunity to manage and instilling in me the will to win."

A couple of days later, I did get a congratulatory telegram of sorts from Mr. Steinbrenner that said simply, "I taught you well."

Never once did he tell me "job well done" when I worked for him. I tried to please him but I always fell short. I've been told he said the same thing about his relationship with his own father.

CHAPTER 9

Nasty Doings and Doggie Poop

Only in the insensitive, oblivious, penurious world of Marge Schott could the joy of winning the world championship all but be extinguished in just a couple of hours. I'd like to say we partied into the San Francisco night—as we deserved to do—and woke up Sunday morning, with a beautiful hangover, basking as the champions we were. Unfortunately, the only person in the baseball universe on whom the supreme accomplishment of sweeping the winningest team in baseball in the World Series was lost was our owner. At our supposed victory party back at our hotel in San Francisco, Marge neglected to buy any food. It seemed she wasn't happy that we won the World Series in Oakland and didn't bring it back to Cincinnati where she could have gotten another gate. We were starving by the time we got back to the hotel and I remember winding up celebrating in a little hamburger joint around the corner with eight or nine players and wives at 3:00 a.m.

Meanwhile, Eric Davis was lying in a hospital room in serious condition as doctors worked to repair his kidney, and we had to leave him behind. I called him in the hospital as soon as we got back to Cincinnati, and he was distraught about having to miss the parade. He had to remain in the hospital for six days. Making matters worse was Marge's refusal to pay for either his plane fare home or the approximate $6,000 hotel bill for his family while he was hospitalized. It left a sour taste in all our mouths and left me wondering just how long I was going to be able to put up with Marge's mercurial and crude behavior.

After her husband, Charles, died of a heart attack in 1968 and left her his auto dealership and stakes in some other local industries, she lived by herself with her Saint Bernards in that big house in Indian Hill. She'd bring the dogs to the stadium every day, and before the games she'd come out on the field with a cigarette in her hand and one of the dogs would invariably get away from her and run out to right field and take a dump. Then he'd come running back to the infield, circle around second base and take a leak on the pitcher's mound. That's when two guys in tuxedoes would come running out with pooper-scoopers to clean up the messes and the grounds crew would have to repair the mound—all of this holding up the start of the game.

Of course, my Yankee teammates might say I'm a fine one to talk when it comes to on-field shenanigans delaying the start of games.

"Everybody knows Lou was obsessed with hitting, to the point where he couldn't walk past a mirror without stopping to practice his batting swing," related Ron Guidry. "Everywhere he went, he'd be practicing his swing—just walking down the street in visiting cities, getting up in the middle of restaurants. But I remember this one time in particular, early in 1977 at Yankee Stadium. I was on the mound, preparing to throw my first pitch, waiting for the sign from Thurman, when suddenly, Thurman lifts up his mask and starts walking toward me.

"'What's going on?' I said to him.

"Thurman points out to right field where Lou, his back to the field, is practicing his swing, totally oblivious to the fact that the game is beginning.

"'We have to wait for him to get done out there,' Thurman said.

"We both stood there, laughing, until Thurman yelled over to Willie Randolph at second: 'Ask Lou when it will be all right with him start this damn game!'"

Then there were Marge's superstitions, in which she would rub dog hair over everybody and everything for good luck. One time she was sitting behind our dugout and pulled out a clump of dog hair and gave it to the bat boy and told him to sprinkle it all over the bat rack to wake up our hitters. The problem was it was 100 degrees that day and the dog hair all stuck to the pine tar on the bats and we had to painstakingly scrape it all off. On the road, Marge would send me these "doggie grams" saying things like, "Doggone shame you lost" or "Doggone good game," which she would follow up with a phone call, saying, "Did you get your doggie gram today, honey?"

Marge left me alone when it came to managing the team and she wasn't demanding and tough like Mr. Steinbrenner. But where Mr. Steinbrenner greatly differed from her was that he'd spend money to win, while Marge was frugal and wouldn't spend money on anything, even a World Series victory party. Once a month she'd call me up to her suite to talk about the team with her lady friends and she'd ask, "What would you like to drink?" I'd answer vodka and she'd pull out this big jug of vodka that was absolutely vile. Finally, the next time she called me up, I brought my own bottle of Absolut vodka.

"Oh," she said, "we'll save this for a special occasion."

"No, Marge," I said. "*This* is the special occasion."

Marge was a big patron of the Cincinnati Zoo and the Children's Hospital in Cincinnati and she frequently had parties at the house with some of the zoo animals. At one of them she had this elephant and encouraged everyone to take a ride on him. People didn't want to say no to Marge and one of the people she convinced to do it was Steamer, who subsequently fell off the elephant and jammed his shoulder. I was never quite sure why, but Marge never liked the Steamer and after the 1991 season she ordered Bob Quinn to fire him over my strong objections.

"I'm pretty sure I know why," said Steamer. "One time before the game, I was standing on the field next to the gate where Marge always went through to get out onto the field. She came down with one of the Saint Bernards and I said to the guard, 'Open the gate to let the two dogs on the field.' I'm sure Marge heard me."

One time at a fundraiser she held for the zoo at Riverfront Stadium, Marge wanted to arrange a race between a cheetah and Randy Myers.

"A race?" I said. "Randy's my closer. What if he pulls a muscle? I can't take that chance."

"You never mind," Marge said, "the cheetah's going to start four hundred feet away at the outfield wall and Randy will start behind second base."

All of a sudden the cheetah came flying over the mound and almost knocked Randy over.

Another time in spring training Marge rented out a restaurant on Dale Mabry Boulevard in Tampa for a twenty-fifth anniversary party for Anita and me. All the coaches and our friends from Tampa were there, and at one point Marge thought it would be cute if she handcuffed Anita and me together. It was funny for a while as Anita and I strolled the restaurant "inseparably" handcuffed. But then Marge confessed that she'd somehow lost the key to the handcuffs and we had to call a cop to saw them off. That was truly funny. Marge did have a great sense of humor and I did like her, as did my wife and my kids.

Marge's quirkiness notwithstanding, I had a lot of fun in Cincinnati, especially that first year. Sammy Perlozzo loves telling the story about how I tried to help the *Magnum, PI* and *Blue Bloods* TV star Tom Selleck get a hit off a major-league pitcher but finally lost patience:

> Selleck was a big Tigers fan and was in spring training as a celebrity guest with them in Lakeland when we came over there for one of our first games of the spring. In the ninth inning, the Tigers asked our permission to allow Selleck to pinch-hit, and much to my surprise, Lou agreed. Tim Layana, who had this great knuckle curve, was on the mound for us, and Lou decided he was gonna let Selleck get a hit. So he yells out to Layana, "Let him hit it!" Layana laid one in and Selleck fouled it off. This happened three straight times, Layana laying it in and Selleck fouling them off. Finally, Lou throws up his arms and screams at Layana, "Okay, that's *enough*! I'm tired of this. Throw him the damn knuckle curve!"—which Layana did and Selleck struck out. We were all standing there in the dugout, doubling over with laughter.

One of my pals, Bill Parcells, spent a lot of time around the team, in spring training and periodically on the road, and he'd kid me about how much easier it was to manage a baseball game than it was to coach football. So at one point, I told him I was appointing him as my "runs" coach, meaning he would sit up in the press box and relay signs down to me on what to do in certain situations. This one game, in Philadelphia, we went into the seventh inning trailing 2–1 when Hal Morris led off with a triple and twenty-five minutes later we'd batted around for seven runs. At the end of the inning, I looked up to the press box and there's Bill, grinning from ear to ear, shouting down to me, "Is that enough? This game is easy!"

Bill was a real baseball fan and he knew the game and spent a lot of time picking the brains of my coaches, in particular Perlozzo, with whom he loved talking about signs. Sammy always used to tell people that I didn't really have any signs and instead lip-synched them to him, which is only partially true. I always felt the other team could steal signs, which is why a lot of the time I had my bench coach give the actual signs.

"When it came to signs, we used to call it 'holler ball,'" said Perlozzo. "Lou got impatient giving signs and more often than not he'd just lip-synch them. The other coaches told me that my most important job was to not ever get sick because I was the only one who could read Lou's lips. I'll always remember this one game we played against the Astros in the Astrodome where the dugouts were very close to the field and you could see and hear the manager in the other dugout real easy. We had a runner on first and Lou wanted to call for a hit-and-run. He's on the top step of the dugout lip-synching 'hit-and-run' to me. I look over at the other dugout and Art Howe, the Astros' manager, is laughing because he could read Lou's lips too. Now I have to decide: Do I put the hit-and-run on anyway? I gotta do what Lou says, so I put it on and, of course, Howe calls a pitchout and the runner's thrown out at second. When I got back to the dugout, Lou says to me, 'I think they got your signs!'"

The 1990 Reds were only the fourth team in major-league history—the 1927 Yankees, the 1955 Brooklyn Dodgers, and the 1984 Tigers were the others—to go wire-to-wire and win the World Series (in 2005, the White Sox later joined that list), and I was eager to see what Marge had in mind about that salary adjustment we'd agreed to after I took that initial $50,000 pay cut when I signed on as manager.

After all, we couldn't have done much better, and I was looking for an adjustment from $350,000 to $500,000. But all through November, December, and January I had no communication from her, so in early February I called Bob Quinn and asked him to check into it. But when he called Marge, she told him to stay out of it, so I called her myself.

"Don't worry, honey," she said. "I'll get back to you."

Right. Now I called David Fishof, my marketing agent in New York, and asked him to see if he could get this resolved. A day later, he called and said he'd worked out a deal that would pay me $650,000. All those years I never had an agent negotiate my contracts, and all I could think of was all that money I'd cost myself. It was not until I hired Alan Nero a few years later when I'd gone to Seattle—where I was still underpaid—that my contracts really went up. Alan was having breakfast with Randy Johnson, who was one of his clients, in a hotel on the road when I met him, and during the course of our conversation he asked me what I was making. I had a flashback to Gabe Paul all those years ago with the Yankees telling me, "Don't tell anyone what you're making." That's how they kept salaries down. When I told Alan, he was aghast.

Even though we were defending world champions, Bob and I knew we needed to add pitching, and we went to the winter meetings in Miami Beach with the scouts determined to fill that need. But when Marge showed up, she all but shut us down. "Oh, no, no!" she shrieked. "You all won last year. You can't trade any of these players. I love these players! You all can do it again."

Marge's problem was she got attached to her players, and there was nothing wrong with that except we were very thin pitchingwise and we all knew standing pat was a recipe for losing. I only wish she'd had an equal loyalty and affection for our scouts. Instead, Marge was constantly complaining about the scouts, one time moaning publicly,

"All they do is sit around and watch baseball games. Why should I have to pay them for that?" It was that attitude that prompted Jimmy Stewart, my right-hand scout, to jump ship after the 1990 season and sign on with the Phillies. The Reds had one of the smallest scouting staffs in the majors, but, lucky for Marge, they were all top notch. The proof was in all those homegrown players on the 1990 team.

We started the '91 season with essentially the same team and we held our own, finishing April in first place, and later winning 9 of 11 games from June 23 to July 5 to pull within three games of the first-place Dodgers. That was as good as it got for us. In late June, Rijo, Charlton, and Scott Scudder, my fifth starter, all went on the disabled list, and the thin pitching that had been so much a concern to me back in the winter manifested itself the rest of the season. Rijo, after missing five weeks with a broken ankle, did come back to make a strong run at the Cy Young Award (15–6, 2.51 ERA), but after Browning, with 14 wins, none of our other starters won more than seven games, and Randy Myers (3.55 ERA after 2.08 in '90) had a major regression in the bullpen. Myers's struggles disarmed the Nasty Boys, and at one point I had to take him out of the closer's role, a decision he found difficult to accept. Randy was an extremely competitive guy, sometimes a little volatile. He was a big, strong guy and before games, dressed up in that bivouac outfit and army helmet, he liked to roughhouse with my son Derek. One day, however, he body-slammed him! Derek came into my office and said, "That Myers is really rough!" and I had to have a talk with Randy.

In early August Randy began grousing every day about wanting to be traded. His locker was right outside my office, and I had finally heard enough of this when Hal McCoy of the *Dayton Daily News* asked me about the Myers trade talk. The door to my office was open, so I knew Myers could hear me when I responded rather emphatically to Hal: "Myers is paid to wear the uniform he's wearing. He takes the checks, doesn't he? Does it ever occur to him that nobody wants him? He needs to shut up and pitch when he's asked to pitch. If not, he should just take the uniform off and go home! How's that!"

Remembering Dick Howser, I guess that was my way of telling Randy he could "brick it."

The '91 season was frustrating for all of us. Besides the pitching, Eric Davis was plagued with leg problems all year, missing most of August, and had only four RBI in September and October when we were in the process of finishing up 10–23. My frustration hit the breaking point on August 3 when, in the bottom of the eighth inning, Billy Doran hit a solo home run for us just inside the foul pole to cut our deficit to the Giants to 7–4. Dutch Rennert, the first base umpire, had run all the way down the line to make the call, only to have the home plate umpire, Gary Darling, overrule him. I went a little berserk, screaming and kicking dirt at Darling, and after being ejected, I threw my hat at his feet and scooped up more dirt and buried it. I was already upset with Darling from the day before when he ruled a foul dribbler by the Giants' Willie McGee—which McGee didn't even run out—a fair ball that knocked in a run in a 5–4 loss for us. But it was what I said about Darling the next day to the writers, when I was still steaming, that really got me in trouble:

> If I had a shovel, I would have dug up home plate and thrown it at him. He has a bias against the Reds. All year we've never gotten a call from him and I don't think we'll get a call from him. He should be professional enough, if he doesn't like us for whatever reason, to at least call a good game.

Well, that sure did it. A couple of days later I got a registered letter from Richie Phillips, the head of the umpires' union, informing me that I was going to be sued for $5 million by Darling, who contended that my remarks had severely damaged his reputation. I went to Marge and showed her the letter and asked if she could help. I pointed out that I had done this in defense of the team, and her response was, "Honey, this is your problem. You got to protect yourself. Have fun in New York." I never forgot that. This was the reward I got? It wound up costing me $120,000 in legal fees and fines. That winter, I was sitting at home in Allendale when Bill White, the National League's president, called me and said, "Let's get this resolved."

Needless to say, it had been weighing heavily on me. In a meeting with White and Phillips, without any lawyers, we reached a settlement in Fay Vincent's office in which I agreed to make a contribution to a fund for indigent umpires, perform some charity work for the umpires, and issue a public apology to Darling. I went to Marge again to see if she would help me, and again she said, "No, this is your problem." She was right. I was the one who had created the problem, but the club should have backed me. When I told this to Bill White, he said, "Let me handle this," and a couple of weeks later I got a check for half the amount.

I'll always be grateful to Bill, a real baseball man, for the way he handled that situation.

At the end of the '91 season Myers came to me and asked me what my plans were for him.

"My plans are to trade you for a leadoff hitter," I said honestly, which we did. On December 8, we traded Randy to the Padres for Bip Roberts, the 5' 7", 165-pound "speed flea" who went on to hit .323 with 44 stolen bases for the Reds in '92.

There wasn't much of a big deal made of my verbal clash with Randy, other than it was a typical situation in which a struggling, prideful player is unhappy about being demoted or benched and the manager has to do what's best for the team. That was not the case, however, the following year when I got into a truly ugly and regrettable violent confrontation with my other Nasty Boy Rob Dibble. On September 17, we were in an increasingly difficult pursuit of Bobby Cox's first-place Braves when I used four relievers—none of them Dibble, who was now my closer—to preserve a 3–2 win over them. After the game, the reporters asked me why I hadn't used Dibble and I explained to them that he had been complaining of a stiff shoulder and I didn't want to take a chance with him. During the course of the game I'd had Larry Rothschild check three times with Dibble to see if he was available and he'd repeatedly said no. But after the reporters left my office and asked Dibble if his shoulder was in fact the reason he wasn't called into the game, he responded, "The manager is a liar."

When Hal McCoy reported that to me, I lost my head. I raced out of my office and confronted Dibble and the next thing I knew the two of us were grappling on the clubhouse floor, punching and screaming, right in front of the TV cameras and all the media. Fortunately, Tim Belcher, one of my other pitchers, broke it up before either one of us was seriously hurt. It's something I regret to this day. As a manager, I should've had more control over my emotions, but I didn't appreciate being called a liar.

The next day, Rob and I talked it out, and today we are the best of friends. I'd like to say right here that those Nasty Boys—Rob, Randy, and Charlton—were three of the greatest competitors I ever managed. I loved those three guys. I loved guys who put it on the line every time out, and they did.

I will say this about Belcher, too: I'm forever grateful to him for saving me from getting my ass kicked by Dibble! We had acquired him (not as a bodyguard) the previous November in one of the most difficult trades I ever had a part in—for Eric Davis. God knows, I hated to trade Eric, who was one of my favorite players of all time—a five-tool guy who always had a smile on his face. Every once in a while I enjoyed having a brandy with him. But Eric's body was breaking down from all those games on Riverfront Stadium's artificial turf and we desperately needed another proven frontline starting pitcher behind Rijo and Browning. So we sent Eric to the Dodgers for Belcher (who was 10–9 with a 2.62 ERA in 209⅓ innings in '91) and a minor-league right-hander named John Wetteland, on whom we had great reports from Jimmy Stewart.

A week later, at the winter meetings in Miami Beach, we felt most of our off-season business was done, but Dan Duquette, the general manager of the Expos, kept showing up at our suite every morning—unannounced—asking us about Wetteland. Finally, on the last day, Bob Quinn noted that, in Davey Martinez, a .275 hitter with a little power and speed, Duquette had a center fielder who could help replace Davis for us. At the same time, our assistant GM, Jim Bowden, said he loved this third base prospect in the Expos' system, Willie Greene. So after much discussion we finally gave in to Duquette and traded him Wetteland for Martinez, Greene, and another righty reliever, Scott Ruskin. For us, Greene was the key to the deal off Bowden's high recommendation.

I remember that within a one-week period in late August and early September, Wetteland made four appearances against us and absolutely threw the hell out of the ball, and I said to Quinn, "That Willie Greene better be a helluva player for us or else Dan Duquette really fleeced us!" Wetteland wound up closing for the Expos in his first year with them, saving 37 games, and he later went on to be one of the preeminent closers in baseball with the Yankees. As for Greene, he had a couple of good years for the Reds in '97 and '98, long after I was gone, but was plagued by injuries most of his career.

We made a good run at Bobby Cox's Braves in '92 and were in first place as late as August 1, but we suffered two devastating injuries.

Sabo, who'd hit 51 homers the two previous seasons, sprained his ankle in the second game of the season and wasn't the same all year, and on July 1, Browning blew out his knee, and we were never able to adequately replace him. We were a half game behind the Braves coming into Atlanta, August 1, for a three-game series and had a 5–2 lead in the eighth inning when they scored five runs off Charlton. The Braves went on to sweep the series and, unlike 1990, we were never able to recover. Still, I was proud of the way we played at the end, winning 9 of 11 from September 17 to 27, but the Braves, who were up by 10½ games on September 13, were just too far ahead to be caught.

On a stifling hot day at the end of September, we were posing for the team picture in the outfield at Riverfront Stadium. It was 100 degrees on the field, with no ventilation, and I noticed this air-conditioned truck, with a closed back, pulling out onto the field. Browning was standing there on crutches and I said to myself, "How nice of Marge to bring a truck to take Browning out to the photo shoot"—which was 425 feet away in deep center field. Except that wasn't what the truck was for. Inside the truck was Schottzie, nice and cool, and poor Browning had to hobble by himself all the way to where we were taking the picture. Then Marge decided it would be cute if Schottzie sat on my lap for the picture, and all of a sudden this enormous Saint Bernard was slobbering all over my face in the 100-degree heat. That was enough.

Even though Marge and I had agreed we would not talk about a new contract until after the season, I had pretty much made up my mind I was not coming back. I was tired of the "doggie grams" and still harboring resentment over her complete lack of support in the Darling situation. But I still loved Cincinnati and its great fans, and a part of me still wanted to stay. So when Marge called and asked me to meet her at Riverfront Stadium to discuss a new contract I agreed. But soon after I got there, she said disparagingly, "I don't want to discuss this here around all these staff people" and said we'd have our meeting at the Cincinnati Club downtown.

That really rubbed me the wrong way. I hated the dismissive way Marge treated her employees and was aware of the fact that she was about to fire Quinn, whom she never appreciated or respected. When we got to the Cincinnati Club, she had her attorney there and we started talking about a two- to three-year extension at $800,000 a year, which I thought was very fair. But then I kept thinking about all that had upset me with her and the fact that Quinn wasn't going to be there, and I just blurted out, "Thank you for the opportunity here, Marge, but it's time for me to go home. I don't want the extension."

Marge just looked at me, flabbergasted, but said nothing. I got up, gave her a hug, walked out, and that was the last time I ever had any communication with her.

When I got back to the apartment, Anita had the car totally packed, and I said to myself, "What did I just do?" Anita was very upset and so were the kids. We'd all loved Cincinnati, and on the drive home to New Jersey, through the beautiful foliage of Ohio, West Virginia, and Pennsylvania, I could not stop myself from periodically welling up with tears.

CHAPTER 10

Saving in Seattle

I had no intention of working in baseball for the 1993 season.

When I got home to Allendale from Cincinnati I knew I was going to need time to resolve all my financial issues. I needed to sell my restaurants and divest myself from a condominium project in Connecticut I'd invested in. I also had decided to take the year to personally manage the automobile dealership in Ossining to try and get it profitable again.

I'd been home for only a couple of weeks after the World Series, when, out of the clear blue sky, I got a call from Woody Woodward, who had gone west to become GM of the Seattle Mariners in July of '88 after barely a year and a half with the Phillies.

"When I took over the Mariners in '88, I told ownership there was only one man I wanted as my manager and that was Lou, who had just signed that personal-services contract with George Steinbrenner," Woody recalled in 2016. "Lou flew out and we had this really nice meeting with George Argyros, the Mariners' owner at the time, but after talking it over with Anita, he turned us down, saying it was just too far from Tampa. It was very disappointing. But now, in '93, the circumstances were a little different. Lou needed to work, and even though the media on the East Coast and a lot of his friends told him baseball could never work in the Northwest, I realized this also represented a real challenge for him."

When Woody called and asked me to come out and meet the new Mariners owners, I told him I'd be happy to but it would still be a waste of time. Seattle was so far away and I had so much stuff to deal with. Plus, I was planning to move back to Tampa, even farther away. But Woody was persistent. He said, "Just do me a favor and come out and meet with these people." In 1992 Hiroshi Yamauchi, the president of Nintendo, had bought a 49 percent share of the Mariners, a move that had saved the team from being moved to Tampa. And in John Ellis, the managing general partner, and Chuck Armstrong, the team president, whom I already knew, Woody felt he had two very personable and convincing people who might be able to change my mind.

So even though it was Woody who owed me a favor when I agreed to be the Yankees' GM so he could escape to the Phillies back in '87, I said okay to going out to Seattle, where he'd arranged a dinner meeting at the Snoqualmie Falls Lodge, overlooking this spectacular waterfall about thirty miles from downtown. I have to say that was the first time I'd ever been taken to dinner by a baseball owner. Ellis, Armstrong, Howard Lincoln (the former chairman of Nintendo), and three or four of the minority partners were there, and we had a great time, with a lot of laughs, until the minority owners started peppering me with questions about how I managed. That's when Ellis cut them off. I found it rather amusing, but he was afraid they'd start to aggravate me with all their ideas of how to run the team. I already knew Armstrong was a great guy and now I'd gotten to know that Ellis was likewise, and while no offers were made, I flew home feeling a little less firm in my convictions about not managing in 1993.

The next day, Woody called to thank me for coming out and asked me what I thought of the meeting. I told him I really liked all the people there, especially his bosses, but that, frankly, all of my friends, both in and out of baseball, had said Seattle was a dead-end place. In their sixteen years of existence since 1977, the Mariners had had only one winning season, and they were stuck with a horrible stadium situation. The Kingdome was a dreary, deteriorating facility with particularly hard artificial turf and a lot of overhead wires and structures that periodically obstructed fly balls. The Mariners had sustained over $50 million in losses the previous two years because of the lack of revenue from skyboxes and luxury suites. For years, the Mariners had attempted to get funding for a new baseball-only stadium, only to have the state legislature and taxpayers continually vote it down. "Baseball is slowly dying there," my friends all told me. "Why would you ever consider going there?"

Woody listened patiently as I recited all the reasons why I'd be better off just sitting out the '93 season than going to Seattle, and then said, "Okay, Lou, I hear you, but this is precisely why I want you as my manager here." He told me to think about it and we hung up. One thing I had noticed, however, in our conversations: Woody had learned a lot from Mr. Steinbrenner in the time he worked for the Yankees. When Mr. Steinbrenner wanted something, he could really turn on the charm and Woody, I saw, had adopted a lot of that smoothness. A day later, he called me again and this time he had Ellis and Armstrong on the phone with him.

"I'm gonna be honest with you, Lou," he said. "You are our first and only choice for our manager."

"I'm flattered," I said, "but I still just don't think it's possible."

At that point, Ellis jumped in.

"I don't understand, Lou," he said, "are you scared of this situation?"

"Well," I said, "they did have the second-most losses of any team in baseball last year."

"This is a great challenge for you, Lou," Ellis countered, "and I know you love challenges."

John was very convincing. "Let me think about this," I said again.

But when I talked it over with Anita, she almost freaked out. "No, no, no!" she said. "You can't do this! It's all the way across the country. All your friends have told you that you can't succeed there!"

"That's the lure of the job for me," I said. "This is a real challenge. But it's a young team, with a superstar player in Ken Griffey Jr. I really believe the situation can be turned around."

Probably if I didn't need the money and had an actual income to help me turn around my financial situation, Anita would have prevailed. But we both knew it was going to be tough sledding if I didn't have a regular income in '93. I called Woody back and told him I'd take the job. We'd never discussed money or a length of contract but we quickly agreed on a three-year deal for $800,000 a year, along with an attendance clause of $50,000 if we drew more than 1.2 million, and a fourth-year team option for another $800,000. Once again, I didn't have an agent and I should have said I wanted $800, $900, and $1 million. Still, I was now one of the highest-paid managers in the game, and even though I didn't do a very good job of negotiating, what made it easy was my relationship with Woody. I loved working with Woody. He had a great way with people, he knew baseball, and I was confident we could turn the Seattle situation around.

I was able to bring in four of my coaches from the Reds—Sammy Perlozzo for third base, John McLaren for the bullpen, Lee Elia for my bench coach, and Sammy Ellis as my pitching coach. We also hired Sammy Mejias, a Dominican-born former outfielder with the Reds, Cubs, and Expos, for first base, and he turned out to be about the best outfield coach I ever had. As I told the writers at the press conference announcing the coaching staff, "I brought everyone over from Cincinnati with me except Schottzie!"

At the same time, Woody asked me how I felt about bringing in as batting coach Ken Griffey Sr., who was working as a roving instructor in the Mariners' minor-league system after retiring as a player with them in 1991. If I hadn't played with and managed Kenny with the Yankees, I might have been a little concerned about having him on the staff with Junior there as my best player. But I knew Kenny to be a hard worker who'd been a really good player and hitter, and who'd commanded a great deal of respect in the clubhouse. I told Woody I thought this was a great idea, and Kenny did an excellent job with our hitters if only for two years, after which he resigned to take care of some personal business back home in Cincinnati. I remember a conversation I had with Kenny at the tail end of spring training in which I conceded it wasn't going to be easy for him coaching his son.

"Oh, shit, he don't need any coaching from me," Kenny said. "All Junior needs is a batting cage, a batting practice pitcher, and a bat!" He was right.

The team I inherited in Seattle already had a pretty good nucleus despite having lost 98 games in 1992. Junior, though only twenty-three, was already an established superstar in center field. At third base, we had Edgar Martinez, who led the American League in batting (.343) and doubles (52) in '92. Jay Buhner, my "gift" to the Mariners from the Yankees in 1988, was becoming a force in right field with 52 homers over the previous two seasons. Tino Martinez, a first-round draft pick in 1988, was just coming into his own as a powerful lefty bat at first base. (I'd grown up with Tino's dad, Rene, on West Conrad Street in Tampa and played stickball with him on a neighborhood lot.) Omar Vizquel was a Gold Glove shortstop, and Randy Johnson was on the verge of becoming the most dominant left-handed starting pitcher in baseball. It was Woody's and my opinion that we didn't have to improve all that dramatically on the talent at hand.

Our top priority was a right-handed starting pitcher to slot in number two behind Randy at the top of the rotation, and we were able to accomplish that by signing Chris Bosio, who'd been 16–6 and logged 231⅓ innings for the Brewers in '92. We also needed a closer, and, to that end, we were able to acquire my former Nasty Boy Norm Charlton from the Reds for outfielder Kevin Mitchell, who was still a fearsome hitter but had been sidelined with injuries for large stretches of the previous two seasons.

In the spring of 1993, the Mariners opened their brand-new complex in Peoria, Arizona, which they shared with the Padres. It was also my first spring in Arizona, and I was especially eager to get a firsthand look at Junior. I'd heard wonderful things about him, all of which were confirmed in those first few weeks of camp. I watched how graceful he was shagging fly balls, how he ran with those long, smooth strides, and how, when he swung the bat, it just flowed. He'd hit these towering fly balls over the fence and I'd say to myself, "Damn, the ball really carries in Arizona," except I soon found out it carried just the same everywhere for him. "There's thunder in this young man's bat," I said.

Buhner's power was just as tremendous. He was strong as an ox. Back in '88, he inadvertently created a lot of problems for me when I traded him from the Yankees to the Mariners for Ken Phelps. The reason for the deal was that both Billy Martin and I felt we needed another left-handed bat, and Phelps had averaged 25 homers over the previous three years with the Mariners. But bringing in Phelps (who had 10 homers and 22 RBI in 45 games down the stretch for the Yankees in '88) also meant taking at-bats away from Jack Clark, the Yankees' other designated hitter, who complained bitterly about me. Meanwhile, Buhner was considered a top prospect and Yankees fans were none too happy about the trade. But now, at least, I was finally the recipient of the deal.

Despite the promise of all this young talent, we got off to a terrible start (0–10) in my first Cactus League exhibition season and I started questioning what I'd gotten myself into. A big part of the reason was that our new stadium in Peoria wasn't completed and we had to play every game on the road that spring. I remember one day on the bus ride back to Peoria after we'd been blown out, 10–6, by the Cubs in Mesa, we passed a baseball field where there was a pickup game going on. I hollered out: "Stop the bus! Maybe we can beat these guys!"

I said it for effect, but right after that, we started turning things around and won our last eight spring training games to finish up 16–14. I was feeling much better about my new team.

Opening Day at the Kingdome bore that out for me. "The Big Unit," Randy Johnson, struck out 14 batters in eight innings, and in Junior's first at-bat of the season, he hit a monster three-run homer in the first inning off Jack Morris, and we handily beat the defending world champion Blue Jays, 8–1. What a great start to my first season as the Mariners' manager.

Still, I didn't have to be told Seattle wasn't a baseball town. Only once in their first sixteen years had the Mariners drawn over two million fans, taking a backseat to pro football and pro basketball (where George Karl was in the process of turning the SuperSonics into an NBA power). It was common for me to pick up the morning papers in Seattle and see our game stories kind of buried in the back pages of the sports sections, with the Sonics and Seahawks on page one. My coaches and I regularly had breakfast in this little diner where the owner had no idea who we were until very late in the season.

After that most satisfying Opening Day win, we kind of sputtered out of the gate in '93, losing five out of six on our first road trip to Toronto and Detroit, including an embarrassing 20–3 shellacking in Detroit. But after that, we won six of nine at home and played a little under .500 ball up to July 1. It wasn't great, but it was also clear that this team wasn't going to lose 98 games again. The high point of the season was a six-game winning streak from July 6 to 15 that put us within two games of first place in the American League West. That same month, Junior tied a major-league record by hitting homers in eight consecutive games, and he would finish the season with 45. (I should note here that I was equally proud to be the manager when Don Mattingly also tied the record for eight consecutive games hitting a homer, with the Yankees in 1987.)

I had gotten to know Junior years before when his daddy, Ken Sr., was a teammate with me on the Yankees. Senior would bring him to the ballpark and he'd shag flies in the outfield with us during batting practice. Now, four or five years later, he was a man. He'd filled out some and you could see that natural ability in everything he did. More than that, though, you could see the natural joy he had just playing the game. He laughed a lot and was a clubhouse prankster. And he was by far the most talented player I'd ever managed, and that really excited me. I was a fan, like everybody else. It didn't take long for him to establish himself as the best player in the game.

We finished the season 82–80, only the second time the Mariners had a winning record, and I have no doubt it could've been much better had we not lost Edgar for over 100 games and Tino for 50 games with injuries. We also lost Bosio for the whole month of May with a broken collarbone and again for another 3½ weeks when he reinjured it on June 6, in one of the worst baseball brawls I've ever seen. In the seventh inning of our game against the Orioles in Baltimore, Mike Mussina hit my catcher, Bill Haselman, with a pitch in the shoulder. Haselman, who had homered earlier, charged the mound, and quickly both benches and bullpens emptied out onto the field. There were punches and bodies flying everywhere, and only after twenty minutes were the Baltimore city police finally able to restore order. At 6' 3" and 220 pounds, Bosio was a bull and a real competitor who, the inning before, had thrown a few close pitches to the Orioles' Harold Reynolds, and I always assumed Mussina's hit on Haselman was a retaliation pitch. In all, seven players were ejected in the brawl along with one manager—me.

By improving from seventh to fourth with 18 more wins in '93, we drew just over two million fans and I was able to get my $50,000 attendance bonus. I was never one to take credit for attendance, however. It's always an entire organization's effort, and instead of pocketing it, I donated it to the United Way. When I told Chuck Armstrong what I wanted to do, Bill Gates, the big man in Seattle as the founder of Microsoft, said he would match the contribution. I called Bill to thank him for his generosity, and he said to me, "Don't worry, Lou. I've got a lot more money than you."

On rare occasions, Bill would come into my office just to talk baseball, but he always had these lineups with him that were all based on analytic formulas he'd drawn up. He'd explain these formulas and I would listen and nod my head until one time he implored, "C'mon, Lou. Why don't you try this lineup today?" I said, "Okay, Bill. Today we'll go with yours," and damn if we didn't win, 7–4! Bill Gates had all the formulas and analytics before "moneyball."

One of the most pleasant surprises of that first season was the emergence of Mike Blowers at third base. Blowers, who'd played college baseball at the U. of Washington, had been acquired in a trade from the Yankees in 1991 and spent most of '92 at Triple-A Calgary. He was not even on my radar in spring training, as a nonroster invitee. But when Edgar tore a hamstring in an exhibition game in Vancouver, Blowers took over at third. He was an excellent fielder with a gun for a throwing arm, but I told him if he was going to keep the job I was going to need more power from him. That's what I got. He had an outstanding season, hitting .280 with 15 homers, including grand slams on consecutive days, May 16–17.

It was because of Blowers's play at third, and the fact that Edgar was having recurring leg problems playing on the Kingdome's hard artificial turf, that I made the decision in 1994 to move Edgar off third base to become my primary designated hitter. I have no doubt that decision enabled Edgar to play in the majors until he was forty-one and accumulate the stats—.312, 2,247 hits, 309 homers, .933 OPS, and a 21st all-time .417 on-base percentage—that made him most worthy of the Hall of Fame. He did all that in spite of an eye abnormality called strabismus that prevents the eyes from moving in tandem. The doctors said he was basically one-eyed at times, when the right eye refused to go straight. When the right eye would go out, he lost depth perception and the ability to see a change in the pitch velocity. The strabismus would occur at any time, sometimes in the middle of a game—Edgar never knew when—although a major factor for it was fatigue. Few people knew this, but Edgar had to do special exercises every day for his eye. He had a special machine in the batting cage that would spit out little rubber balls, coming at great speed at him, all around the strike zone, so he could focus.

Despite this, he was one of the most lethal hitters I ever saw. He was a machine. He reminded me of Jim Rice, with that good, compact right-handed swing that produced so much velocity. One of the most amazing things about Edgar's swing was that every so often, he'd hit a ball that was three or four feet foul when it left the bat, only to have it curve around the left field foul pole fair. He had that great ability to stay inside the ball and get that spin. He was a skinny kid when I first got him—he stole 14 bases the year before—but as he started to fill out he began having hamstring issues, which curtailed his running, and that's why I felt making him a DH was the right thing to do. At the same time, I am concerned the stigma of being a DH is what has kept him from getting close to the 75 percent needed from the Baseball Writers Association for election to the Hall of Fame. I don't understand that thinking. Hopefully, what David Ortiz has accomplished as a likely first-ballot Hall of Fame inductee has put the DH in a new light with the voters, and Edgar will get his due.

A week after the '93 World Series, Woody and I went to the general managers' meetings in Naples, Florida, where, ordinarily, there aren't any trades consummated. But we had a bit of urgency in that Dave Valle, our catcher in '93, was a free agent, and Woody said we couldn't afford to re-sign him. I told Woody that in spring training in Plant City with the Reds in '92, all the pitchers kept asking me if this young catcher, Dan Wilson, could catch them. I told Woody his bat was iffy, which was why he was still in the minors, but that I knew he could handle the pitching staff. Woody agreed to explore it. He wound up working out a deal with the Reds' GM, Jim Bowden, to send Bret Boone, our starting second baseman in '93, and Erik Hanson, a former second-round Mariners' draft pick who'd won 11 games, with a 3.47 ERA in 215 innings, to Cincinnati for Wilson and a right-handed reliever, Bobby Ayala. It was a really gutsy trade on Woody's part, but it turned out to be one of the best he ever made. Wilson was the Mariners' number one catcher for the next eleven seasons, becoming a pretty good hitter to match his defensive prowess, and Ayala was a solid workhorse reliever and part-time closer for me the next four seasons.

In addition to Valle, Woody had another pending free-agent issue with our shortstop, Omar Vizquel, who, in '92, had gotten an arbitration bump from $360,000 to $1.1 million and was now looking to double that. So very reluctantly, we traded Vizquel to Cleveland for Felix Fermin, a decent shortstop who made just $975,000 in '93. I regret I had Vizquel for only one year. Vizquel, who won the first of his eleven Gold Gloves in '93, is the greatest fielding shortstop I ever saw and another of my players I will be proud to see go into the Hall of Fame.

We got off to a 0–5 start in 1994—which turned out to be the strike year that was never completed—and we were 40–62, in fourth place and 8½ games behind, as late as August 1. But I still felt we were the best team in the division, and from that point on, we won 9 of our last 10 games, and I have no doubt that if the season hadn't been canceled on August 11, we'd have won the division.

I went home for the winter in '94 brimming with confidence about the next season, especially after the way we'd finished up before the strike hit. Part of that confidence was due to the fact that, with an eye on the stadium referendum vote in the state legislature due in September '95, the Mariners' ownership had let Woody know they would allow the payroll to increase. So unlike previous years, we weren't going to have to trade any players because of salary constraints. Instead, on May 15, Woody was able to trade for my old "bodyguard" in Cincinnati, Tim Belcher, who was making nearly $3.5 million with the Reds.

We did make a few coaching changes in '95. I moved Lee Elia from bench coach to hitting coach and John McLaren from bullpen coach to bench coach. "Uncle Elia" proved to be one of the best batting coaches I've known in the game, and "Mac" was my bench coach and right-hand man for the next eleven years, right through my tenure in Tampa. We also brought in Bobby Cuellar as our new pitching coach and replaced McLaren as bullpen coach with Matt Sinatro, who'd been my advance scout the previous two years. Matty, I have to say, is one of the funniest guys I've ever been around. He was the one I could always count on to relieve the tension and make me laugh.

Unbeknownst to me, my optimism about 1995 was soon to be blunted by two dire events. The first was when I arrived in Peoria in early February and was confronted by a group of strangers—imposters, if you will—in Mariners uniforms. With the players' strike still on and no resolution in sight, the owners had elected to start the season with replacement players, an absolutely horrible and game-damaging decision on their part. When I walked out onto the field at Peoria, Woody had put a table in the outfield and the "players" from all walks of life were lined up to fill out forms. It reminded me of my days in the National Guard reserves. Fortunately, the replacement players experiment was terminated (appropriately on April Fools' Day). Right before the spring training games were set to begin, a federal judge, Sonia Sotomayor (who later went on to be appointed to the Supreme Court), agreed to hear arguments on the National Labor Relations Board's request for an injunction—which ultimately led to a settlement of the strike. Two days after her decision, the real players returned to work, but the damage was done. Spring training was reduced to a three-week cram session and the start of the regular season was pushed back from April 2 to April 26.

The second dire event, which proved personally catastrophic for the Mariners, occurred May 26 in Seattle when Junior made one of his typical sensational catches in center field, racing 100 or so feet and crashing into the fence to pull down a rising liner that robbed the Orioles' Kevin Bass of an extra-base hit. I had talked to Junior many times about the reckless abandon with which he played center. The angles in the Kingdome's outfield walls were severe, and the big wall was not padded. Watching him race into that right-center-field wall, fully extended, and then hit the wall so hard, I feared the worst. When I ran out there and saw what had happened—his wrist was shattered—I was sickened. Here was the best player in all of baseball, and, in an instant, his career was in jeopardy. For a hitter, the most important thing is the wrists. Later, after taking X-rays, our team doctor was very concerned. All I could think was what the impact of losing a player like Junior was going to have on Major League Baseball, not to mention for us. The problem was, he thought he could catch anything. (Three years later, on August 9, 1998, in

Detroit, he made an even better catch, chasing a long drive by the Tigers' Luis Gonzalez all the way to the fence in right-center field, then leaping three feet off the ground to snare the ball before it went over the wall.)

I always said Junior played center field like one of God's angels.

Fortunately, the doctors were able to repair Junior's wrist and he never had any ill effects from the complicated surgery. But he was lost to us from May 27 to August 15, during which time we were 36–37. By the time Junior came back we were in third place, 11½ games behind the first-place Angels. And even though Woody had done a great job of continually patching the starting rotation behind the Big Unit, Chris Bosio, and Belcher, by acquiring Andy Benes from the Padres at the July 31 trading deadline and Salomon Torres from the Giants, I told my players frankly that we were playing for the wild card. I never thought winning the division was possible, because the Angels were a very formidable team.

I should've known better than to lower expectations for my team. Just as Junior came back and gave us a huge boost, the Angels went into a stunning free fall, with two nine-game losing streaks between August 25 and September 26. At the same time, nine days after he returned to action, Junior hit a game-winning two-run homer in the ninth inning, on August 24, against the Yankees' closer, John Wetteland, and we went 24–11 the rest of the season. The one unsettling part of our great comeback was the vote, on September 19, in which King County's residents rejected a subsidy tax amendment to fund a new stadium. Immediately after the vote was announced, our owners threatened to sell the team.

The 1995 AL West division race came down to the last series of the season—the Angels playing three games against Tony La Russa's A's, who had just swept them in Oakland the week before, and us playing four games against Texas. We, in turn, had swept Oakland the week before, enabling us to go into first place for the first time all season. With a two-game lead and four to go, I got a call from Tony telling me, "If you just split with Texas, you're in, because we've played well against the Angels all year."

That may have been true, except Tony got swept by the Angels, and after winning the first two games against the Rangers, we lost our last two and suddenly it was back to 1978 for me—tied for first place and faced with a one-game sudden-death playoff for the division title. *Here we go again*, I thought. After all this, win or go home. At least unlike 1978, when Al Rosen lost the coin flip for the Yankees and we had to go to Boston, this time the Mariners got the home field on account that we'd had a better regular-season record against the Angels. Even though it all happened on such short notice, there were 52,356 people in the Kingdome, and I don't think there was ever a louder place in baseball.

The pitching matchup—Randy versus Mark Langston—was ironic because six years earlier they had been traded for each other. In the fifth inning, Vince Coleman, the six-time National League stolen base leader, whom Woody had acquired in a trade with the Royals on August 15, broke up a 0–0 game with an RBI single through the hole at shortstop. Two innings later, we really broke it open with four runs against Langston, the big blow being a bases-loaded double by Luis Sojo. The game ended up a 9–1 blowout, with Randy dominant throughout with 12 strikeouts. As Junior said afterward, "There was something about the Unit when he stepped on the field today. It was as if he said, 'Just give me the one run and I'll take care of the rest.'"

What a feeling. The Seattle Mariners were division champions for the first time in their nineteen-year history and now we were going to play the Yankees in the first round of the playoffs. I couldn't help thinking of the similarities—the '78 Yankees overcoming a 14-game deficit, the '95 Mariners being 13 behind as late as August 2, and both teams winning sudden-death elimination games. And just like Bob Lemon had had to use our ace, Ron Guidry, to win the playoff game in '78, I'd had to use Randy in this one.

We played the Yankees tough the first two games of the best-of-five division series in New York, which was encouraging to me, even though we flew back to Seattle 0–2. In game 1 in New York, after the Yankees knocked out Chris Bosio in the sixth inning, Junior hit his second homer of the game to tie it 4–4 in the seventh. But then the Yankees scored four runs off my bullpen in the bottom of the inning to put it away. Game 2 became a baseball classic, a five-hour, thirteen-minute marathon in which we outhit the Yankees 16–12, but blew four separate leads. It all came down to the bottom of the 15th inning when, with one out, Jim Leyritz homered over the right field wall off Belcher. Almost as soon as Leyritz's ball landed in the seats, the heavens over Yankee Stadium opened and it began pouring. It was still raining hard as we got into our bus to the airport, and the Yankees fans hovering around the parking lot were really heckling us unmercifully. That was when I decided to show some bravado, letting my team know I had confidence in them. As I started to get on the bus, I turned to the fans and shouted, "Enjoy this while you can. This is the last game you'll be watching this year!"

I truly felt, down 0–2, we had them right where we wanted them. I certainly felt good about having Randy rested and ready for game 3, and he shut the Yankees down on two runs over seven innings, outpitching Jack McDowell, the 1993 Cy Young Award winner who'd won 15 games for the Yankees during the regular season in '95. After Tino Martinez took McDowell deep for a two-run homer in the fifth, we knocked him out of the game by loading the bases with one out in the sixth. That's when we broke it open against Buck Showalter's bullpen, Tino delivering an RBI single off Steve Howe to put us up 3–1, followed by three more runs against Bob Wickman.

To be honest, I thought Buck may have made a tactical mistake pitching McDowell against Randy, who was unbeatable at the King-dome. While it was true McDowell was probably rusty after not hav-ing pitched since September 21 due to a back injury, it wouldn't have made any difference if he sat out one more day. Buck could have skipped him and made Scott Kamieniecki or someone else the sac-rificial lamb against Randy. If he had saved McDowell for game 4, there's a good chance the outcome might have been different. In-stead, Kamieniecki pitched the fourth game and we jumped all over him for nine hits, four walks, and five runs in the first five innings. Nevertheless, it turned out to be a kind of slugfest as my guy, Bosio, didn't have much either, getting knocked out of the game in the third inning when my old pal, Big Paul O'Neill, hit a two-run homer to put the Yankees up 5–0. That was about the only time in the series I was really worried. We needed to hold the Yankees right there, and Jeff Nelson did just that, pitching four innings of shutout relief. That enabled us to come back and win the game against the Yankees' bullpen, the big blow being Edgar's grand slam off Wetteland in the eighth. Edgar's seven RBI in the game set a postseason record.

For the deciding game 5, I was really short, pitchingwise. I needed to get a good start—and some length—from Andy Benes against Da-vid Cone. I was really up against it. Before the game, Randy came up to me and volunteered to pitch in relief. "If you need me," he said, "I'll give you what I got." That was Randy. I told him, "I want you to stay in the dugout and if the game is close in the seventh inning, I want you to walk out to the bullpen. The place will go crazy. They'll tear the roof off the Kingdome." And that's exactly what happened.

Benes wasn't great, but he hung in there and got us to the seventh inning trailing only 4–2. The events from there made this one of the two greatest games I've ever been part of (the '78 playoff game being the other). One thing that was very clear: Buck didn't have a whole lot of confidence in his bullpen, especially Wetteland. For the first seven innings, Cone had been a real warrior, shutting us down on two runs, striking out nine, and stranding five base runners, but also using up 118 pitches. He began to tire in the eighth after giving up a solo homer to Junior that cut the Yankees' lead to 4–3.

After a groundout by Edgar, Tino worked Cone for a walk and Buhner singled to center. At that point, I sent Alex Diaz, a switch-hitting reserve outfielder, up to hit for my shortstop, Felix Fermin, and he, too, drew a walk. Cone was really laboring now, his pitch count over 130. Still, Buck did not make a move. He was hoping, I'm sure, his gallant right-handed ace could get him just one more out.

Once again, I gave Buck a choice by sending up another switch-hitter, Doug Strange, for Danny Wilson. Strange was my super utility guy, a good professional bat off the bench who had gotten some big hits for us down the stretch, most notably a huge, ninth-inning, game-tying two-run homer off Texas' right-hander Jeff Russell two weeks earlier. Cone was exceedingly tough on right-handed hitters and Strange was my last left-handed option on the bench. Again, though, Buck didn't budge, and Strange worked Cone to a 3-2 count before drawing a game-tying walk when Cone bounced a splitter in front of the plate. It was his 147th pitch of the game.

That was all we got in the inning. Buck replaced Cone with a skinny rookie right-hander named Mariano Rivera, whom we didn't know a whole lot about, since he'd spent very little time with the Yankees in '95. We'd gotten our formal introduction to him in the 15-inning game 2 when he'd come out of the bullpen and completely dominated, no-hitting us over the final 3⅓ innings, striking out five. I remember saying to Uncle Elia, "Where has this guy been?"

Rivera struck out Mike Blowers to end the eighth and leave the bases loaded. He was back out there for the ninth, but was replaced by McDowell, who pitched out of a first-and-second, one-out jam.

Once again, we were in extra innings, and I took the occasion to bring in my big weapon, the Big Unit, who struck out the side in the tenth, but gave up an RBI single to Randy Velarde in the eleventh. For the fourth time in seven days, we were facing the end of our season. But we were home and the Kingdome was a din with 57,411 screaming fans imploring us for one more comeback.

Little Joey Cora started us off in our half of the eleventh against McDowell, beating out a bunt down the first base line, barely eluding Don Mattingly's tag, and Junior followed with a single up the middle. Now to the plate came Edgar, who, to that point, had been a one-man wrecking crew against the Yankees in the series—11-for-20 with 2 homers, 2 doubles, 8 RBI, and 19 total bases. Red-hot Edgar versus a spent McDowell. I felt very good about where we were now. On an 0-1 pitch, Edgar launched a laser shot to left field, and as Cora crossed the plate with the tying run my eyes focused on Junior, running full tilt with those long, loping strides. I looked briefly over to the third base coaching box where Perlozzo was preparing to put on the stop sign, but Junior was having none of that. I was astonished to see him keep on running, steaming past Perlozzo, all the way to the plate where he slid safely just ahead of the throw. We had done it. Mariners 6, Yankees 5. I thought getting the Mariners to their first postseason was about the best feeling I'd ever had, but this was better. I will savor that game to my dying day.

I would be remiss if I didn't also mention the subplot of the series—the hitting exhibition that played out between Edgar and Mattingly. Though he hadn't said anything official, everyone assumed that Donnie, who had really struggled with his bad back the previous few seasons, was going to retire after the 1995 season. But what a finish! In his final five games against us, Donnie was somehow able to reach back with a hitting display reminiscent of the mid-'80s, when he was the best player in the game. He seemed to match Edgar hit for hit, with a .417 average, 4 doubles, a homer, and 6 RBI. Donnie was always one of my favorites (and one of my earliest pupils)—a humble kid with no ego, a blue-collar player who became a star. It had hurt watching him those last few seasons, when balls off his bat that he used to drive out of the park became routine flies. That's why it was so heartwarming for me to see him go out a star as well.

I haven't ever discussed that series with Donnie. I know how painful it was for him. But his performance spoke for itself. After the last game, Showalter came over to our clubhouse and congratulated us. I thought that was very classy and I never forgot it. As for the Boss? Radio silence.

I wish I could say the thrilling game 5 against the Yankees was not our last hurrah in 1995, but the Cleveland Indians team we ran into in the American League Championship Series was quite formidable, with speed (Kenny Lofton and Omar Vizquel) at the top of the lineup and heavy thunder (Carlos Baerga, Albert Belle, Manny Ramirez, Jim Thome, Eddie Murray, and Paul Sorrento) throughout the rest of it. They also had superior starting pitching in Orel Hershiser, Charles Nagy, and Dennis Martinez, and a top-notch closer in Jose Mesa.

For game 1, I was totally out of pitching, and after a long debate as to who to start, our assistant general manager, Lee Pelekoudas, cited this obscure rule that stated any player who had been on the major-league roster before September 1 was eligible for the postseason. So I decided to go with Bob Wolcott, a twenty-two-year-old rookie right-hander from Medford, Oregon, whom we'd left off the division series roster. Wolcott had pitched fairly well for us after being brought up from the minors in mid-August. However, when he walked the first three Indians batters of the game, I had to go have a talk with him.

"Do you like to hunt?" I asked him.

Wolcott looked at me curiously. "Well, uh, yeah," he said.

"Why don't you think about being out in the woods back home in Oregon and having fun," I said, before walking off the mound.

Darned if the kid didn't pitch out of it by retiring the next three batters, and from there he did a heck of a job in getting us off to a 1–0 lead in the series, holding the powerful Indians lineup to two runs over seven innings. In game 2, Belcher did not fare as well, getting knocked around for nine hits and four runs in 5⅔ innings. At the same time, we couldn't get anything going against Hershiser, who held Junior, Edgar, Tino, and Buhner to a collective 3-for-15 in the Indians' 5–2 win. In game 3, Randy gave us a strong eight innings (four hits, two runs) in out-pitching Nagy, and my closer, Norm Charlton, followed up with three no-hit innings to set the stage for Buhner's game-winning three-run homer in the eleventh.

And that was it. We didn't win another game.

On the flight from Seattle to Cleveland, Andy Benes told me he couldn't wait to start game 4 because it figured to be cold in Cleveland and he pitched well in cold weather. I'm sure he felt that way, but the Indians knocked him out of the game in the third inning, and Ken Hill and four Indian relievers shut us out, 7–0. Our hitters just shut down those final three games. We hit .184 for the series. Hershiser held us to just two runs in six innings in game 5, and Dennis Martinez and two relievers shut us out again, 4–0, in game 6.

I remember after game 5 letting my braggadocio get the best of me by telling the writers that we would win the series back in Seattle. It was meant to show my confidence in my team, but it was also stupidity because it probably put extra pressure on them. I learned that later on in my career from Joe Torre, who always made his team the underdogs.

As much of a letdown it was to lose the ALCS, 1995 remains one of the most satisfying seasons of my career. I'd gone to Seattle, where the Mariners had never won anything, where everyone had told me taking a job was a dead-end proposition, and I'd proved them wrong. Not only did we win games, we won fans.

As if the 1995 season itself weren't proof enough of what we'd accomplished, on October 23, the Metropolitan King County Council reversed the earlier vote and approved a financing plan for a new $320 million baseball stadium in Seattle, eight days before the Mariners' deadline to put the franchise up for sale.

That was the biggest win of all. We had saved baseball in Seattle.

CHAPTER 11

Don't Like Good-Byes

There has probably never been more eager anticipation of the baseball season in Seattle than in the spring of 1996. The first appearance by the Mariners in the postseason—which proved to be the impetus for the Metropolitan King County Council to approve the funding for a new stadium—sounded the alarm that baseball in Seattle was here to stay, and now the people wanted more. They had come to embrace the superstar talent—Junior, Edgar, the Big Unit—on this Mariners team, which had previously been mostly ignored, and they were not unaware that, in 1996, a fourth supreme talent would be joining that trio.

Alex Rodriguez had gotten his first exposure to the big leagues in July 1994, when he was just nineteen years old. The Mariners had signed him on August 30, 1993, after making him the overall number one pick in the June amateur draft out of Westminster Christian High School in Miami. I didn't have a whole lot to do with the pick other than being asked by Woody Woodward to look at films and offer my opinion of both Alex and Darren Dreifort, a right-handed pitcher from Wichita State whom the Mariners were also considering as the number one pick. I looked at Alex playing in his high school games and what I saw was a man among boys, a tall, rangy shortstop with a fluid batting swing and a strong arm, a kid who you could see just from the films knew how to the play the game. A complete player. For me, it was a no-brainer. Because he signed late, he did not start his professional career until 1994, but we knew it would not take long for him to make his major-league debut.

Alex immediately impressed me in spring training with his speed and athleticism, and I made a mental note to monitor his progress in the minors. We started him out at Class A Appleton of the Midwest League, and after he hit .319 with 6 homers in 65 games there, we moved him up to AA Jacksonville, where he continued to excel. Even though we had projected him to be our starting shortstop beginning in 1996, I wanted to see more of him firsthand, and in early July of '94, I asked Woody if we could bring him up. Felix Fermin was doing fine for us at shortstop, hitting over .300, and Woody was very hesitant to rush Alex. He finally agreed, but with one condition: "Only if you play him every day," he said. "I don't want him coming up here and sitting on the bench."

I agreed, and Alex was our regular shortstop for most of the month of July in '94, but he struggled with the bat (.204, 2 RBI in 54 at-bats) before we sent him to Triple-A Calgary at the end of the month. In retrospect, Woody was right. Alex wasn't near ready. We did the same thing with him in '95, calling him up for three separate stints when injuries hit our infield. But despite his early struggles in '94 and '95, I thought being around a big-league clubhouse and seeing how major leaguers conduct themselves was an invaluable experience for him. I can understand if Alex didn't quite see it that way.

"In '94, I was just a baby," Alex recalled in an interview for this book, "and they already had a good shortstop in Felix Fermin and a second baseman in Joey Cora, so getting sent back didn't hurt, because I knew it was a long shot that I'd be staying. Woody drafted me and I was a big fan of Woody and Lou, so I knew I was gonna be part of the big club soon. But in '95, I was brought up and down three times. On the third time, Lou brought me into his office. He was smoking a cigar and had a beer on his desk, and he said, 'I'm gonna have to send you down to the minors again,' and I just remember being heartbroken. That almost broke me. I remember driving home and calling my mom in Miami and telling her I was going back to the minor leagues again and asking her if my eligibility to play quarterback at the University of Miami was up. She said, 'Son, you're gonna stop this nonsense right now! You need to go down there and bear down.'

"When he sent me down that last time, Lou said, 'You need to be strict with the fundamentals—making routine plays, bunting guys, being a better base runner—to play up here.' He told me I had to be more consistent with my hitting, making better contact, and I vowed to myself, 'Lou will never have a reason to send me down again.'"

When we brought Alex back the last time in '95 and kept him on the roster for the postseason, I said to him, "Don't put too much pressure on yourself. You're gonna have a wonderful major-league career. Just don't try to make it all happen now." That was my message. As I said, we knew Alex was going to be our regular shortstop in 1996, but it's so much easier if you first let him get his feet wet. In those stints when he was up, in '94 and '95, he learned a lot from Luis Sojo and Edgar. We just wanted to make sure that, in 1996, he was really ready. The only thing he didn't have was the knowledge of the strike zone. I said to him, "You're getting yourself out when you're not swinging at strikes. Go talk to Edgar." His bat speed, his athleticism, his defense, were all off the charts. He was smart, he knew the history of the game, and he had a passion for the game. You could see he wanted to be great.

Early on in spring training '96, I told Alex to just relax, that he was our shortstop, and starting off I batted him second, in front of

Junior, so he'd get his share of good pitches to hit. Did we expect him to win the batting title that first year? No. But at the same time we knew it wouldn't take long for him to have serious impact. Edgar and Uncle Lee Elia took him under their wings and he just took off, an instant superstar, winning the 1996 batting title with a .358 average, along with a league-leading 141 runs and 54 doubles, plus 36 homers and 123 RBI. What a first season! At the same time, Junior established personal highs in homers (49) and RBI (140) despite missing 20 games with a broken hamate bone in his right wrist after fouling off a pitch on June 19.

Although it had been preordained for two years, Alex's ascension as our everyday shortstop in 1996 became even more imperative after Woody was forced to make yet another payroll-driven trade that previous December. Tino Martinez, a number one Mariners draft pick in 1988, was coming into his free-agent walk year, and after a career season in 1995 (31 homers, 111 RBI), Woody was certain the ownership would not be willing to shell out for the kind of multi-year, big-bucks contract it would take to retain him. Right after the '95 World Series, I told Tino's uncle, Tony Gonzalez, who's one of my best friends in Tampa, that we were going to have to trade him. When Tony told Tino this, Tino asked him to talk to me about trying to trade him to the Yankees, who were his favorite team growing up and had just moved their spring training from Fort Lauderdale to Tampa. I knew the Yankees were looking for a first baseman to replace Mattingly, so Woody called Gene Michael to tell him we were looking to trade Tino but were going to need to get back some good, young, inexpensive players who were ready for the big leagues. A few days after that conversation, I was sitting at home in Tampa when I got a call from Mr. Steinbrenner.

"Are you trying to fleece us again?" he said.

"No way," I said, explaining that we needed to trade Tino and I was looking to put him in the best place for him, if I could.

"Well, it's going to be hard replacing Mattingly," he said. "Can this kid do it?"

"Just look at his numbers from last year," I said. "He's just now coming into his own."

"Okay," Mr. Steinbrenner said. "Why don't you come over to Malio's and we'll talk about this over lunch."

Between Mr. Steinbrenner, Stick, myself, and Woody, we were able to agree on a deal to send Tino and Jeff Nelson, one of my best relievers, to the Yankees in exchange for Sterling Hitchcock, a promising twenty-four-year-old left-hander who'd won 11 games for the Yankees in '95, and Russ Davis, a power-hitting third base prospect.

We were able to replace Tino at first by signing free agent Paul Sorrento, who had a nice year (.289, 23 HR, 93 RBI) for us in '96. Hitchcock, meanwhile, wound up leading my staff in victories with 13. But while I never like to use injuries as an excuse, it's fair to say our inability to follow up the breakthrough '95 season with a return trip to the postseason can be directly traced to the loss of our two top starting pitchers, Randy Johnson and Chris Bosio. Randy, the defending American League Cy Young Award winner, was bothered by a bulging disk in his back, missing all of June and July, and he didn't start a game for us after August 24. Bosio was plagued by a recurring knee issue and was out June, July, and September. In all, I used fifteen different starting pitchers in '96. (In addition, Davis broke his leg on June 7 and never returned.)

The one saving grace in all that starting pitching scrambling was Woody's July 30 trade-deadline deal with the Red Sox for Jamie Moyer. To get Jamie, Woody had to give up my "bobo," Darren Bragg, the gritty, blue-collar outfielder I loved having around me. Although initially criticized by the Seattle media, the deal turned out to be a huge win for Woody.

Jamie was a soft-throwing lefty with a tremendous knowledge of pitching who was probably ill-suited for Fenway Park and, before that, when he was with the Orioles in their own small ballpark, Camden Yards. He was thirty-three at the time of the trade, and most scouts probably thought he was about done. But from 1996 to 2006, Jamie won 145 games for the Mariners, including 20-win seasons in 2001 and 2003, and in 2012, at age forty-nine with the Phillies, he became the oldest pitcher in baseball history to win a game in the big leagues. Unlike most pitchers today, who want to throw harder and harder, Jamie wanted to throw softer, much like Tommy John. He would baffle hitters with 84 m.p.h. stuff, a big, sweeping curveball, and his "out" pitch changeup. It was the most amazing thing I ever saw. Jamie also became an instant leader in our clubhouse, as the pitchers, especially, all gravitated to him to pick his brain.

Despite the injuries, we finished the '96 season 85–76, missing the wild card by two games. From September 12 to 21, we ran off 10 straight wins to close within 1½ games of front-running Texas in the AL West, only to lose six of our last eight. It was disappointing, but the season attendance, 2,723,850, was by far the highest in Mariners' history, and I looked forward to getting back on track in '97 with all my big guns and a healthy Unit.

Over the winter, Woody made one significant trade, sending Chris Widger, our very capable backup catcher, to Montreal for Jeff Fassero, a thirty-four-year-old left-hander who'd won 15 games for the Expos in '96. Bosio's bum knee had forced him to retire, and Fassero stepped right in, winning 16 games for us in '97 with a team-leading 234⅓ innings. But after a winter of rest for his back, it was the revitalized Unit who played a leading role in our second AL West title in three years, going 20–4 with a 2.28 ERA, including two 19-strikeout games. Between May 1994 and October 1997, Randy was 53–9, including a 16-game winning streak.

After the truly rewarding '97 regular season—in which Junior won the AL MVP, leading the majors with 56 homers and 147 RBI and we won the AL West by six games over the Angels while setting a major-league record (that still stands) with 264 homers—I felt good about our chances of taking it all the way to a first World Series for Seattle. Junior was in a tremendous zone that entire season. He was just so focused. He didn't take any bad swings. He didn't chase any bad pitches. His timing was impeccable, and we all thought he might very well beat Roger Maris's American League home run record of 61. The amazing thing is, if you look at his swings, from his first at-bat in the big leagues to his last, they're all the same. But his 1997 season was by far the best season I ever had from any of my players. He never felt any pressure and his performance never varied the whole year.

Our only weakness had been a particularly porous bullpen—which came to a head for me on July 30, when we were up 7–2 in the eighth inning against the Red Sox and wound up losing 8–7. With that loss, our bullpen achieved the highest ERA in the majors (6.20) and had given up the second-most homers (16). Right after that, Woody moved boldly—too boldly, I suppose, in retrospect—to shore up the problem, first trading our promising young left fielder and 1995 number one draft pick, Jose Cruz Jr., to the Blue Jays for righty setup reliever Mike Timlin. A few minutes later he sent two top prospects, catcher Jason Varitek, our 1994 number one draft pick, and right-hander Derek Lowe, to the Red Sox for Heathcliff Slocumb, a right-handed closer who'd saved 63 games over the previous two seasons. While Timlin and Slocumb did help stop the bullpen bleeding in '97, Varitek and Lowe in particular went on to have long and productive careers, both playing major roles in the

Red Sox's "curse-breaking" 2004 world championship team. Still, if Woody hadn't made those deals I don't know if we could have survived August and September.

"We desperately needed relief," said Woody. "The Slocumb deal was one you wish you could have back, especially because Varitek and Lowe were my draft choices. But that's the nature of the beast. There isn't a GM in baseball who hasn't made a bad deal. I'm sure Dave Dombrowski, one of the best GMs in the game, would like to have back the deal we made with him in which we got Randy Johnson in the first place—for Mark Langston. At the time, Langston was one of the best lefties in the game and one of the faces of the Mariners, and Dave looked at him as being the key to getting the Expos to the postseason."

As it turned out, my optimism about an extended 1997 postseason was quickly dampened when Davey Johnson's Orioles knocked out Randy after only five innings in game 1 at the Kingdome—and did likewise to Jamie, after just 4⅓ innings, in game 2. Thanks to a superb effort by Fassero (8 innings, 3 hits, 1 run), we were able to win game 3, but the Orioles clinched the series by beating Randy, 3–1, the next day. Looking back, I maybe underestimated the Orioles. I *know* I underestimated Davey when I saw his game 4 lineup, which had a .237 hitter, Jeff Reboulet, at second base and hitting second, instead of Roberto Alomar, a future Hall of Famer who'd hit .333 during the season. Reboulet proved there was, in fact, a method to Davey's madness by shocking us with a homer off Randy in the first inning, and the Orioles, who scored a second run in the inning on a double by Geronimo Berroa and a single by Cal Ripken, never trailed in the game.

It wasn't long after that the seeds were sown for Randy's departure from Seattle. With free agency looming for him after the 1998 season, he engaged our ownership about a contract extension only to be rebuffed. Even with the new ballpark coming in 1999, nothing apparently had changed insofar as the Mariners' being able or willing to retain their top stars when they neared or became free agents. The reasoning given in this case was that Junior would be coming up on free agency in 2000 and the priority was to have a war chest full of money to sign him.

From the get-go in '98, it was clear to everyone that Randy was in a funk and allowing his contract situation to affect his pitching. On Opening Day against the Indians at the Kingdome, we staked him to a 9–3 lead after five innings and I had to remove him in the sixth when the Indians scored three runs on a pair of doubles and a pair of singles. We wound up losing 10–9.

On July 5, after giving up eight runs in eight innings, including a pair of homers to Juan Gonzalez, against the Rangers, Randy's record stood at 7–8, with a very un-Unit-like 5.07 ERA. His sulking and all the trade rumors swirling around him were bringing down the whole team, and I finally had to have a talk with him. He didn't want to leave Seattle, but he also wanted to be paid.

"Look," I said to him, "the better you pitch, the better the chances to stay here."

He didn't believe that. I should say here that Randy was never a problem in the clubhouse as much as he was to himself. The whole time he was with me in Seattle, we had very few conversations. Randy kept to himself—he'd be sitting there in his locker with his headphones on, or sifting through his photography. He used to say to me, "Damn, you don't ever talk to me," and I'd say, "That's because I don't want to talk to the back of your head!" But when I called him to congratulate him in 2014 on being elected to the Hall of Fame, we talked longer than the whole time he was with me in Seattle. I couldn't get him off the phone!

Randy was basically an introvert. I'd see him often on the road, walking around the city by himself, with just his camera. I think he was also maybe a little self-conscious about his height. When you're 6' 10", there's a lot of moving parts there, and he worked exceedingly hard on his repetition and in becoming more compact. He always wanted to be great and would not accept mediocrity. He had this reputation for being sullen, but his teammates all liked him. And unlike guys like Nolan Ryan, Bob Gibson, and Don Drysdale, who were absolutely mean out there, more than willing to grind a fastball into a batter's ribs, Randy was conscious of his overpowering stuff and was always concerned about hurting someone. His mere size was intimidating enough to batters. But as evidenced in the 1993 All-Star Game, when he threw his first pitch to John Kruk over Kruk's head, he had a sense of humor about it as well.

As we approached the trading deadline in 1998, 10 games under .500, two things had become apparent: we weren't going anywhere, and we needed to bite the bullet and trade Randy. Considering the fact that Randy was, in fact, a two-month "rental" player pending his free agency, I again give credit to Woody for getting a tremendous return from the Astros for him—a power-hitting infield prospect in Carlos Guillen and two young starting pitchers, Freddy Garcia and the lefty John Halama. Garcia stepped right in at the top of our rotation with 17 wins in '99 and won 59 games for me from 2001 to 2004. Halama won 35 games from 1999 to 2001 as my number four starter, and in 2001 Guillen did a nice job for us upon replacing Alex as our shortstop. As for Randy, he left the Astros at the end of the season after they failed to make the playoffs and signed a four-year, $52 million contract with the Arizona Diamondbacks.

We had expected at least 18 wins from Randy in '98 and wound up getting nine. Leading up to his trade, we were 8–20 in June. Once the deal was done, it was up to me to restore morale. But this was a team of professional veterans—Junior, Edgar, Jamie, Buhner, Danny

Wilson—and our 39–34 record after the All-Star Break—without Randy—was the best in the AL West, just not good enough to make up for the underperformance of the first half.

The encouraging second-half comeback in 1998 could not mask the fact that we went into the 1999 season with a very uncertain starting rotation, as well as with the general perception that we were gradually tearing down the team to get ready for the new ballpark. And then, with the season having barely gotten started, I lost Alex for a month and a half with knee surgery, as well as his replacement, Guillen, for the entire season after he, too, was felled by a knee injury. In addition, the regression by Fassero (4–14), whom we traded to Texas in August after he'd won 16 and 13 games his first two seasons with us, put a major crimp in my already thin starting rotation.

The fact that, in midseason, we had to make the transition to a totally new ballpark and a totally different brand of baseball, with natural grass and wider expanses in the outfield, made it particularly tough on Woody in his efforts to make trades. Despite a second-straight losing season, we drew over three million fans for the first time in Mariners history, including 56,530 for the last game in the Kingdome, June 27 (in which Junior, fittingly, hit a game-winning three-run homer), and 44,607 for the opening of Safeco Field, July 15.

Behind the scenes in 1999, I could see that the frustration of two straight losing seasons, the inability to keep our best players, and the increased involvement of Howard Lincoln in the baseball operations had tempered Woody's excitement over the new stadium. There were strained relations between him and Lincoln, who felt Woody was too obliging with me on player personnel moves. On September 18, one of the saddest days in my managing term with the Mariners, Woody announced his retirement. Woody was always very composed, but the press conference—in which he insisted he wasn't forced out—was one of the few times I ever saw him get emotional. He'd done a great job of leading the organization to where it was, and now he wasn't going to be there to fully enjoy the new ballpark. As Woody walked off the podium, I started to think about my own situation. I'd been in Seattle nine years and there was always the possibility a new GM would want his own manager. John Ellis had relinquished his position as CEO, Lincoln was getting more and more involved, and I thought, *How much longer do I have here?*

That's why I was so delighted when, a month later, the Mariners announced the hiring of Pat Gillick, who had just quit as GM in Baltimore, as Woody's successor. When John Ellis, who still had tremendous influence in the organization, had asked me about Gillick a few weeks before, I encouraged him, saying that Pat was the only guy to bring in. I knew Pat to be an outstanding baseball executive, the architect of two world championship teams in Toronto who'd then built winning teams in Baltimore. I had missed the opportunity of working for him in Toronto when Mr. Steinbrenner wouldn't let me out of my contract in 1988, and now I was getting a second chance.

Unfortunately for Pat, he was coming into the job under the worst possible circumstances, as his first order of business was going to be dealing with Junior's contract and whether we could afford to keep him. I had a very special relationship with Junior. Not just because he was a great player, but because he was a great person. I had played with and managed his daddy, and I admired what a devoted husband and father he was. On the other hand, Junior was also a great needler, who made me laugh, and I think he understood everything I was doing.

"For a guy who seemed disorganized, Lou was the most organized manager I ever knew," Junior said. "We respected him because of his knowledge and understanding of the game of baseball and his insistence that it be played the way it's supposed to be played. The small details, he preached them day in and day out. I was twenty-three when he got there. We were all kids and we just needed guidance from a guy who genuinely cared about us and our families and who'd been there before.

"At the same time, we stirred it up with him. I'd walk by his office and say, 'Anything wrong, Skip? You ain't been ejected in a while.' We had many laughs with him, like the time he kicked the water-cooler in the dugout and really hurt his toe. They had to remove his toenail and the toe was all purple and bleeding. Then they had to cut the top of his shoe off so it could breathe. Every day, I'd say, 'How's that air-conditioned shoe, Skip?' But the funniest one was after a game in Oakland. We were playing lousy and Lou starts reading the riot act. He says, 'In times like this you have to man up to adversity and stay united. But you guys are like soft shit in the rain. You know what that is?' And then he like makes the 'safe' sign, blows in his hands to make this loud *ploof* noise, and says, 'All squishy like that!' I looked at Buhner and the both of us just burst out laughing, which really pissed him off. The next day I said to him, 'Soft shit in the rain! That was a good one, Skip.'"

For all the talk of Junior coming up on free agency in 2001 and the enormous amount of money it was going to take to retain him, after we traded Randy I never thought the Mariners would trade him too. I always believed they would sign him long term and he'd be a Mariner for life. But in early November, when he rejected the Mariners' initial offer of eight years, $138 million, and expressed a desire to play closer to his home and family in Orlando, I knew I would soon be saying good-bye to another one of my star players. It wasn't a matter of the Mariners coming up with the money to sign him. Junior wanted to go.

"When I got there, one of the first things I did was to go down to Orlando, with Lincoln and Chuck Armstrong, to talk to Kenny," said Gillick. "I told him we didn't want to trade him, that we were building the team back up and aiming to go to the World Series, and didn't he want to be part of that? But he said, 'Nope, I want to move on.'

"I firmly believe the reason he wanted to move on was A-Rod. He didn't want to share the spotlight with him, even though he was the more popular player in Seattle, who'd won an MVP award in '97 and had led the American League in homers the previous three years."

I'm not sure if that was the main factor. If you ask me, I believe Junior's overriding reason for wanting to leave was geography. His family was growing up and he wanted to get closer to Florida. I do know he didn't want to leave his teammates, like Buhner and Edgar. The problem Pat had was that there were only a limited number of teams with the resources to sign Junior once they traded for him. And then Junior made it even harder by rejecting a deal Pat had with the Mets—which would have netted us a base-stealing center fielder, Roger Cedeno, and two hard-throwing relievers, Armando Benitez and Octavio Dotel. Instead, he now declared the only team to which he would approve a trade was the Reds.

I had grown very close to Junior in the eight years I'd been with him. He was a great young player who became a superstar talent. He was also hardheaded and wanted to do things his own way, and from time to time I would have to have a conversation about that. I had a way of handling those talks. I would call him into my office and tell him to sit behind my desk, as if he were me, and I would sit in the chair facing the desk and play the role of him. I would then say to him, "Okay, Junior, you're the manager and you'd like to have Junior conform to what all the other players on the team are being asked to do. How would you answer that question?" He would answer right away and then we'd switch chairs and we wouldn't have a problem. I did that a few times with him and we'd have a chuckle over it. It's how we became very close.

"Being that I was playing both him and me, it went well," Junior later said.

Junior also had a great sense of humor and was the clubhouse prankster. One time we had a bet in spring training on March Madness for a steak dinner, which I won. After a couple of days had gone by, I asked, "Where's my steak?"

Junior replied, "Don't worry, it's coming."

An hour later, I came back off the field in Peoria and there in my office was this big old cow! Everyone got a big laugh out of that, except when I looked around the office I saw where the cow, like Schottzie in Cincinnati, had dumped all over the floor.

They still talk about the time, in 1994, when Alex was a nineteen-year-old rookie and Junior talked him into auctioning off his sperm to the highest bidder. At the time, I was totally unaware of this caper and learned about it only years later. As the story was reported, Junior told Alex that Randy and Buhner were going to auction their sperm off, and that he should, too, because he had great genes. The more Junior went on about it, the more Alex started believing him, finally asking, "How much do you think we could make?"

Junior. What a prankster.

There's no question there was a clubhouse rivalry between Junior and Alex—they were never particularly close—but it was never anything that had any undercurrents in the clubhouse. They both had egos and, in effect, competed against each other. And even though Junior had also made no secret of his disappointment at the ownership's trading of Randy and Tino, I truly believe that the overriding factor in his desire to leave was that his kids were growing up, he'd bought the house in Orlando, and Seattle was just too far away. I could certainly relate to that. I do know this: nobody was more affected by Junior's departure than Buhner. They were the closest of friends, center fielder and right fielder, and almost inseparable. Shortly after the trade, Jay said he wanted to retire. Fortunately I was able to talk him out of that, and he rewarded me by rebounding from two previous subpar seasons with 26 homers and 82 RBI in a part-time role in 2000.

What was truly amazing was Gillick's ability to get a very decent package back from Cincinnati, the only team Junior would let him talk to. In return for the best player in baseball, Gillick got center fielder Mike Cameron, a serviceable right-handed reliever in Brett Tomko, and a highly regarded Dominican third base prospect, Antonio Perez. I'd remembered seeing Cameron when he broke in with the White Sox in the mid '90s. He was very athletic, played the right way, and had average power and good speed. His only negative was he struck out too much. One day in Chicago, I was talking to my good friend Hawk Harrelson, who was now the White Sox's broadcaster, and telling him that I really liked Cameron and that I thought I could help him with his hitting. Hawk had Cameron call me, and that winter Cameron even flew down to Tampa to work with me. While Cameron would never be confused with Junior, he was an excellent defensive center fielder who became a real force for the Mariners over the next four years, averaging 22 homers and 86 RBI.

Once he had Griffey traded, Gillick set about doing what he did best—putting together a championship-caliber team. The 40-plus homers, 120-plus RBI? That was almost impossible to replace. Instead, he filled in all around the places where we were lacking in 1999. From the free-agent market, he signed John Olerud, a professional hitter and superb defensive first baseman whom he'd originally drafted and signed in Toronto; Mark McLemore, a speedy handyman who could play almost any position; and Arthur Rhodes, one of the most proficient left-handed relievers in the game.

We still needed a closer, however. Jose Mesa, my closer in '99, had done a creditable job, saving 33 games, but too many of them had been high-wire acts. In talking to our scouts in Japan and our Pacific Rim operations director, Jim Colborn, Pat got some interesting reports on a thirty-two-year-old right-hander, Kazuhiro Sasaki, who'd had an ERA of around 1.00 the previous three years in Japan and was said to have a deadly split-finger pitch. We signed Sasaki and brought him into spring training to compete with Mesa for the job. It reminded me a little of 1978 when the Yankees signed Goose and had him compete with Sparky, who'd only won the Cy Young Award as our closer the year before. Mesa was just as jealous as Sparky was.

"I don't like this," Mesa told me one day early in the spring. "Dammit, I did a good job for you last year!"

I could understand his bitterness, but once he saw Sasaki, he realized Colborn and our Japan scouts were not wrong. Sasaki wound up saving 37 games in 2000 and after the season broke my record as the oldest player to win Rookie of the Year honors.

Sasaki, Rhodes, Mesa, Tomko, and Jose Paniagua, a hard-throwing Dominican right-hander we'd acquired off waivers from Tampa a couple of years earlier, gave me the deepest, most effective bullpen I'd had in Seattle. You could say, however, that the entire staff showed great improvement in 2000, and for that I have to give credit to Bryan Price, whom we promoted to pitching coach after he'd spent ten seasons working in our minor-league system. Before Bryan, I had been criticized by some people in the Seattle media for being too hard on young pitchers and pitching coaches. But I had nothing to do with the dismissal of the four previous pitching coaches, and if you look at my history, I gave more opportunities to young pitchers than anyone else did. But it's always been my contention that if you want to win in the majors, your pitchers have to be tough and throw strikes. When a starting pitcher starts nibbling and not pitching in the strike zone, that's a formula for losing. You can either coddle young pitchers or react. I reacted. I loved giving young pitchers chances, but you still want to see performance. I got paid to win. If I just tolerated mediocrity, I wasn't doing my job.

Nevertheless, after sitting down with Bryan and listening to his philosophy on pitching and realizing it was the same as mine, I told him in spring training, "You know the system. The pitching staff is yours. Do with it what you want." The result was an improvement in team ERA from 5.24 in '99 to 4.49, second in the league in 2000, and in 2001 an American League best of 3.54.

Despite our greatly improved pitching, our numbers one and two, Jamie Moyer and Freddy Garcia, missed significant time with injuries in 2000. As a result, after leading the division from June 29 to September 28, we were unable to hold off a scorching Oakland team that won 18 of their last 22 games, and we had to settle for the wild card. I was still greatly buoyed about our chances of going to the World Series when we swept the White Sox in the AL Division Series. I was especially pleased at how we won the final game—on a ninth-inning squeeze bunt.

The score was 1–1, with one out and Rickey Henderson (whom Gillick had signed in May as outfield insurance) on third base, and Carlos Guillen, pinch-hitting for my catcher, Joe Oliver, at bat. I told Guillen in the dugout, "I'm going to pinch-hit you here, but all I want you to do is lay one down to Frank Thomas at first base." I knew Thomas couldn't throw, and with Rickey's speed, he could score easily on a good bunt. So what happens? Guillen swings away at the first pitch! Fortunately on the next pitch he got the bunt down and it eluded Thomas as Rickey crossed the plate. After the game, I asked Guillen what the hell happened on that first pitch.

"I'm sorry, Skip," he said. "I just got caught up in the moment."

Because the Yankees were extended to five games before they were able to win their division series with the A's, we had three days of rest in Seattle, which should have been a good thing—except the day before he was supposed to fly to New York to be our game 1 starter in the ALCS, Moyer was hit by a line drive in the knee on his final pitch of a simulated game. Just before, Jamie had asked to pitch to a couple more batters without the protective screen. I wasn't comfortable about that, but I take full responsibility. It was a devastating loss. Jamie, the master of illusion, had pitched well against the Yankees with all their big left-handed bats. My lineup was as good as Joe Torre's, but without Jamie, we were one ace short against the Yankees' formidable trio of Roger Clemens, Andy Pettitte, and Orlando "El Duque" Hernandez in the ALCS.

I suppose the one thing that will be forever remembered about our 9–7 loss in the final game of the ALCS in New York was the monster three-run homer David Justice hit off my lefty setup man Arthur Rhodes in the seventh inning. The homer, which caromed off the upper-deck facade in right field, touched off a six-run Yankees rally and broke our backs. On the pitch before, it looked to me (along with a whole lot of other people) that Justice had swung, which would have made the count 2-2, but John Hirschbeck, the home plate umpire, ruled he checked his swing. As I said at the time, it was a huge call, in that Rhodes now had to throw a 3-1 fastball instead of a 2-2 slider. Such are the breaks of the game. It was just too bad, because afterward I would have much preferred to be talking more about the great night Alex had. Starting with doubling home our first run in the first, Alex went 4-for-5 with a homer, 2 doubles, 2 RBI, and 2 runs scored.

It wasn't until a couple of weeks later that I came to realize this had been his good-bye to me.

CHAPTER 12

Rising Sun, Setting Sun

Only a couple of days after the loss to the Yankees in the 2000 ALCS, the Mariners' high command of Howard Lincoln, John Ellis, Chuck Armstrong, and Pat Gillick had redirected their attention to a matter of pressing importance to the future of the franchise: Alex Rodriguez's pending free agency. Despite the constant speculation in the press, it was something I hadn't given a whole lot of thought about during the 2000 season, primarily because I couldn't conceive of the Mariners ever letting Alex leave, especially after having had to trade both Randy Johnson and Junior.

Alex was now the face of the franchise. I'd had him for seven seasons, "raised" him, if you will, from when he was a nineteen-year-old summoned to the big leagues in 1994, barely eleven months after being the number one overall pick in the amateur draft out of high school, and I'd watched him quickly grow into a superstar of unlimited greatness. I never imagined that greatness being achieved anywhere else but in Seattle. I still felt that way when Pat, Howard, John, Chuck, and I went to the December winter meetings in Dallas and prepared to make our pitch to Alex and his agent, Scott Boras. I especially hoped to talk personally to Alex.

Pat and the others had informed me that they were prepared to offer Alex a six-year deal worth $120 million. I felt very comfortable with that. It was a helluva commitment. But when Boras arrived at our suite, without Alex, I immediately felt uneasy. There was very little small talk. Boras got right to the point and wanted to know what our offer was. When Pat presented it to him, Boras said simply, "Okay, thanks. You're not even close," and walked out the door. That was it. Not even a counteroffer. We were astounded. We didn't know if he was bluffing or if he really meant it.

The next day we found out he wasn't at all bluffing. We knew the Texas Rangers were heavy in the bidding for Alex, but like everyone else in baseball, we were stupefied when their owner, Tom Hicks, announced he had signed Alex to a ten-year contract worth $252 million—more than double our offer. Until then, the richest contract in baseball history had been the eight-year, $121 million deal the left-hander Mike Hampton had gotten from the Colorado Rockies in 2001. When word of Alex's contract spread around the winter meetings there was mostly outrage. Sandy Alderson, who was Major League Baseball's head of operations, called the numbers "beyond alarming." My friend Brian Sabean, the GM of the Giants, put it in even more perspective as far as Alex was concerned when he said, "All I know is, he better be pretty good for a long time. Just figure out the percentage that contract is going to be against their payroll now and in the future. It's a lot to live up to."

As for us, I was shocked, while Pat was just disgusted.

"When we lost Griffey and then A-Rod there was absolutely no pushback from Lou," Gillick later said. "Griffey wanted to go, and with A-Rod, it wasn't as if we didn't do everything we could to keep him. We were willing to go to six years for one hundred and twenty million until Boras spit in my face. I knew we had no chance. Hicks was a new owner and the winter meetings were in Dallas and he wanted to walk away with the big trophy."

I wished I could have gotten the chance to talk to Alex personally. I couldn't blame him for taking that offer. It was a business decision and Boras didn't open the door any further for us, not that it would have mattered with an offer in hand more than double ours. I was almost as disappointed that Alex was staying in our division. The bottom line is, when you hire an agent, you're telling him, "I'm gonna play and you're gonna handle the business," and Boras was as good as any doing that.

I did feel that if we'd gotten Alex in that room we could have convinced him to stay, but Boras came in alone, and once he took over, all the emotions went out of it. It became all business. I had grown much attached to Alex, and he had grown very close to me and Anita—to the point where he used to call her "Mom." This was much more than just a player-manager relationship. Rather, it was more like father and son. I'd watched him grow. I was responsible for bringing him up the right way in baseball, teaching him the ropes. But there was no way he could've turned down that kind of money—twice as much as anyone else offered him. So now I had to watch him go. It was not unlike a parent sending his kid off to college, knowing he was on his own now. When Alex called me to say good-bye, it was a very painful conversation for both of us.

"I called Lou right after I made my decision," Alex said in an interview for this book. "I told him, 'I'm gonna sign with Texas but I wanted to tell you first so you wouldn't have to read it in the news.' Obviously, it was a very sad day for me because playing for Lou, I was spoiled. I had great protection and he was a great mentor for me. There were tears on both sides. He was the only manager I'd ever had for six and a half years in the big leagues. In many ways I wish I'd had another five years under Lou's tutelage and protection. But I don't look at it in 'what might have been' terms anymore. Everything that's happened in my life and career, good or bad, I look at myself in a much different light now. I've tried to learn from it and make the best of it. But Lou made me a better person and a better player."

So for the second time in a year, Pat Gillick was faced with the task of replacing a superstar and keeping intact as best as possible a championship-contending team. We had already decided that Carlos Guillen, one of the key players we got in the Randy Johnson deal from Houston, would replace Alex at shortstop. The original plan, before Alex's signing with Texas, was to have Guillen take over at second base and David Bell, who'd done a nice job at second for us the previous two seasons, move over to third. With second base now a need, Pat signed Bret Boone, who'd broken into the majors with the Mariners in '92 and whom we'd very reluctantly traded to the Reds two years later for Dan Wilson. Ironically, both Boone and Bell were third-generation major leaguers in that their fathers and grandfathers had also played in the majors. In the history of baseball, there have been only four three-generation families to all play in the majors, and we had two of them on the same team. Not surprisingly, Boone and Bell were two of the smartest baseball players I ever managed, as well as being class acts.

About the only good thing in not being able to re-sign Alex was that Pat had some $20 million extra in the kitty to spend on free agents for 2001. He spent $3 million on a one-year deal for Booney and another $14.5 million on Aaron Sele, a right-hander who'd won 37 games the previous two season for the Rangers, to fill in the starting rotation behind Jamie Moyer and Freddy Garcia. Even before Alex departed, however, Gillick used $27.1 million to sign a spindly (5' 11", 175 pounds) twenty-seven-year-old singles-hitting right fielder who'd never played a single day in the major leagues.

For nearly four years, Jim Colborn, the Mariners' Pacific Rim scouting director who'd signed Kazuhiro Sasaki in 2000, had been following Ichiro Suzuki, waiting and hoping for when he became a free agent in Japan and would aspire to play in the majors. That day came in mid-October 2000 when Ichiro's team, the Orix Blue Wave, for whom he'd won seven Japanese Pacific League batting titles, agreed to "post" him (the blind bid system, in which any of the thirty major-league teams could make an offer to Japanese teams for their free-agent players). Whenever Colborn had mentioned Ichiro to the Mariners' owner Hiroshi Yamauchi, the Nintendo chief expressed skepticism.

"You can't get him," Yamauchi said. "They'll never let him leave Japan."

But Colborn knew different. He'd gotten very close to Ichiro, to the point where Ichiro told him he was looking forward to becoming a free agent and taking his talents to the United States. And the team he'd love to play for was the Mariners. Once Yamauchi realized that, he ordered our top executives to do whatever they had to do to make him a Mariner.

Actually, the seeds to the Mariners' signing Ichiro were sown the previous spring, when Colborn arranged to have him come to our training camp in Peoria in an exchange program. He trained with us for a couple of weeks but was not permitted to play in any of the exhibition games. Still, we'd been able to get a firsthand look at his abilities, which were considerable: an extremely disciplined contact hitter, with a keen batting eye, great speed, and a plus throwing arm in right field. You could see he was a polished, well-coached player. Once we won the posting, with a bid for $13.1 million, everyone was comfortable with the three-year $14 million contract it took to sign him, especially since, with Jay Buhner now reduced to a part-time player, we had an opening in right field. It didn't hurt either that the heavy Asian population in Seattle figured to make his transition to the United States all the more comfortable.

Nevertheless, when Ichiro arrived in camp at Peoria in February

2001, I was one who still had some concerns about him. I remembered from my days with the Yankees that Billy Martin always wanted to see bat speed from the rookies and new players on the team. For the first few days of camp Ichiro was hitting almost everything to left field and down the third base line. I liked most everything else about him, but I was getting a little nervous about whether he was going to be able to hit major-league fastballs on a consistent basis. Finally, during a spring training game, I went to his interpreter and said, "Tell him I want to see bat speed. I need to see him pull the ball." I watched as the interpreter went down to the end of the dugout, said something to Ichiro, and Ichiro nodded and smiled. The next inning, he hit a high fastball onto the hill behind the right field fence. When he got back to the dugout he came up to me and said, "You happy now?" I replied, "Yes, yes. I'm very happy. From here on out you can do whatever you want!"

The most homers Ichiro ever hit in the majors was 15 for the Mariners in 2005, but I have absolutely no doubt that if he'd wanted to, he could have easily hit 15 to 20 a year on a regular basis. You couldn't teach American kids to do what he did—pull the inside pitches, steer the away pitches, on a line, to the opposite field. There was no way to defend him. He'd be already in motion toward first base, with his upper body still stationary, when he swung the bat. I always said if they'd put him in the home run contest at the All-Star Game he'd have won it. In batting practice he consistently hit the ball three to four hundred feet to the pull field. Instead, he settled for two batting titles, the all-time record for hits in a season (262 in 2004), and the only man in history with ten consecutive 200-hit seasons and 3,000 hits in both the United States and Japan. He's another one of my players I'm looking forward to seeing accept his Hall of Fame plaque in Cooperstown, but first he's gotta stop playing or it may not happen in my lifetime!

Ichiro later said he was very nervous throughout that first season, desperate to make good as the first Japanese everyday position player in the majors. But if he was, he sure didn't show it. At the end of April, he was hitting .336, and he never stopped. He wound up compiling one of the most phenomenal first-year seasons of any player in history, leading the league in batting (.350), stolen bases (56), and hits (242). Naturally, with Alex gone, we all wondered what Ichiro could bring to the table in his place. All he did was join Fred Lynn as the only players in baseball history to win the Rookie of the Year and Most Valuable Player awards in the same season. And for the second straight year, I had been supplanted by one of my own players as the oldest Rookie of the Year. When it came to the MVP, I have to admit I was torn between Ichiro and Bret Boone. Booney, in 2001, became our Alex, hitting .331 with 37 homers and a league-leading 141 RBI. He was a cocky kid when I first had him, but now he was a seasoned pro and an equally great defensive player who could turn the double play better than any second baseman in the game. At one point, Gillick asked me, "How in the hell could you trade this guy?" I explained to him we had to get rid of the salary of Erik Hanson, the pitcher we included in the Wilson deal, who was coming up on free agency. Like I said, it was a coin flip between the two for the MVP. Booney, who also got off to a torrid start in April, hitting .344 with 22 RBI, wound up finishing third.

Taking Ichiro's and Booney's lead, we finished April 20–5, in first place by nine games—the only team in history to win 20 games in April. From there, it merely steamrolled to one of the greatest seasons baseball has ever known. Our 116 wins tied the 1906 Cubs for the most ever in a season. We led the AL West from start to finish— another wire-to-wire for me—and won it by 14 games. We won more games on the road (59) than at home (57), and from May 23 to June 8, we won 15 in a row. Edgar, at thirty-eight, had his typical season:

.306, 23 HR, 116 RBI. Mike Cameron had 25 homers and 110 RBI and won a Gold Glove in center field. John Olerud hit .302 with 21 homers and 95 RBI as an All-Star at first base. My top four starters, Jamie, Garcia, Sele, and Paul Abbott, were a combined 70–21, and Sasaki had 45 saves. I should also add that Buhner tore the arch in his left foot in spring training and was on the disabled list almost the entire season. But he was in that clubhouse every single day, lending support and leadership. He was my enforcer to the end, a true professional.

"The 2001 team was special, and epitomized Lou teams in that it was one of the best fundamental teams I ever had," said Gillick. "There was, however, one night in August when it didn't look that way. We were playing in Cleveland on the ESPN Sunday-night game. I was home in Seattle watching the game on TV and after three innings we were losing 12–0. We wound up losing the game, 15–14, in eleven innings, and about a half hour after the game I got a phone call from Lou, screaming, 'I need a pitcher!' I said to him, 'Okay, Lou, okay. It's all right. Look at the standings! We're almost fifty games over .500 and leading the division by nineteen games!'"

It was by far the best—and the easiest—team I ever managed. We began September winning 10 of our first 11 games, crossing the 100-win mark. On the morning of September 11, I was asleep in my hotel room in Anaheim when I got a phone call from Anita, who was extremely distraught.

"Did you see what's happened in New York?" she said. "Turn on the television!"

I quickly flipped on the TV and for the next three hours watched in horror, frozen in my bed, at the sight of the twin towers in flames, then crumbling to the ground into rubble. The city of New York, my second home, was under attack. Thousands of people killed. It was just unfathomable. For the next three days we were grounded in Anaheim, with no-fly restrictions in effect and I spent much of the time in my hotel room glued to the TV, watching the horrifying events in New York. The season didn't resume until September 18, when Freddy Garcia shut out the Angels, 4–0, at Safeco. The next night, Jamie and four relievers shut the Angels out again in what turned out to be the division clincher, as Oakland lost to Texas to fall 18 games behind.

Before the game, Pat and I talked about what we should do when we clinched. We both agreed this was no time for any kind of celebration or partying. Instead, after we learned Oakland had lost, our players got out an American flag and paraded it all around the infield, then kneeled on the mound, said a prayer, and raised the flag again. That was my all-time favorite moment in my ten years in Seattle. I was so proud of my players. Hanging on the wall in my den at home is a picture of them holding up that flag, dated September 19, 2001. As this was going on, the sellout crowd at Safeco, 45,459, got eerily quiet and then emptied silently when the ceremony was over.

With the division clinched so early, Pat and I had a bit of a quandary: Do we go for the major-league record of 116 wins in a season, or do we rest our team? I talked it over with my players and they all wanted to go for the record. So we decided we could still watch our pitching and rest our lineup and at the same time keep playing hard with the idea of accomplishing something no other team had ever done.

From September 24 to October 6, we won 10 of 11 games to reach 116 wins, tying the record, with one game to go. We were playing the Rangers—who were in last place—that final series, at home, and I wondered what Alex was thinking and feeling across the way when we tied the record. Unfortunately we had to be satisfied with just a share of the record—which had stood for 95 years—when the Rangers beat us, 4–3, on the last day on a ninth-inning run against Jeff Nelson.

After the game, I made an impromptu address to the team in which I congratulated them on doing something only one other team had ever done, and for also setting the American League record for most wins in a season. Pat and Chuck Armstrong came down to the clubhouse and essentially said the same thing on behalf of the ownership. We were all extremely proud of them. But now, I said, we had to put this loss behind us and get ready to play a tough Cleveland team in the first round of the playoffs.

In the years when there was only one wild card, the team with the best overall record in the league usually got to play the wild card team in the first round. But because the A's were in our own division, we had to play the Indians, who'd won the AL Central, while the A's played the AL East champion Yankees. Cleveland was a proven, professional team with very few weaknesses. After splitting the first two games in Seattle, they clobbered us, 17–2, in game 3 and suddenly, after winning 116 games during the season, we were on the brink of elimination in the first round of the playoffs. Thanks to a homer and 2 RBI by Edgar and the combined five-hit pitching from Garcia and three relievers, we were able to tie the series with a 6–2 win in game 4, and in game 5 our pitching—this time Jamie and three relievers—prevailed again to win the series. But it had been hard fought and had taken its toll.

Before the series, Carlos Guillen contracted tuberculosis, and we were concerned the rest of the team might have been infected. In addition, Edgar pulled a groin muscle and was hobbling badly in the series. He played the rest of the postseason essentially on one leg. Our strength was our bullpen and because we were extended the full five games, I was unable to start Jamie until game 3 of the ALCS.

Even though the A's were the wild card and a team with whom we were most familiar, my preference was for us to play the Yankees in the ALCS. It's always special to beat the defending world champions to get to the World Series. I should've known to be careful for what I wished for. Unlike the A's, or any other team for that matter, the Yankees had four proven aces—Mike Mussina having now joined Roger Clemens, Andy Pettitte, and El Duque—to our two, Garcia and Jamie. In game 1, Pettitte shut us down on three hits in eight innings, and the next night Mussina gave up only four hits and two runs in six innings, with the Yankees' bullpen shutting us out the rest of the way. Down 0–2, I caused quite a commotion in my postgame media conference when I vowed, "We are coming back here to play game six. Don't ask any questions. Just print it!" The New York newspapers had a field day with that, and even though I believed firmly in what I said, it would have been best to keep it to myself. You can let your team know it but not the entire country.

New York was buzzing like I'd never seen it before, but there was no escaping the grief and unspeakable horror still enveloping the city from the attack of 9/11. Before game 3, Major League Baseball officials asked us if we would visit Ground Zero and a couple of firehouses. We spent the entire day visiting with the workers at Ground Zero, the firefighters, and the police wards. It tore your heart out to see the devastation at Ground Zero and to realize all the lives that had been lost. Our hearts poured out for the people there.

When I was with the Yankees, I'd go down to the financial district from time to time, and seeing it now, in ruins, was just unreal. The devastation and then the stories the fans and people there were telling us, it was overwhelming. Watching the bravery of the cops, firemen, and first responders all working feverishly there at Ground Zero made us feel proud, and I remember thinking, *If we can just bring one little piece of joy and hope by being here . . .* As it turned out, the resilience of the city was exemplified by the Yankees.

When we got to Yankee Stadium, however, it was time to refocus on baseball. I knew I had to talk to them, so before the game I called my players together in the clubhouse and held up a copy of the *Daily News*.

"Do you see this newspaper?" I said. "This is not the *Daily Planet*. Those guys in the other dugout aren't supermen and we're not just any other baseball team. We can beat these guys!"

With Jamie on the mound, we pounded El Duque and three other Yankees relievers for 15 hits, including homers by Olerud, Boone, and Buhner, in a 14–3 rout. I thought we were on our way, and that if Paul Abbott, my fourth-game starter who had a really good changeup, could keep the Yankees at bay for six or seven innings, we could get the series back to Seattle—as promised—where I'd have Garcia and Moyer ready and rested for games 6 and 7.

I was right about Abbott, who pitched five innings of no-hit ball, but walked eight and used up 97 pitches doing so, and I had to go to my bullpen two innings earlier than I'd hoped. Norm Charlton and Jeff Nelson kept the game scoreless through seven, and then in the eighth, Boone homered off Ramiro Mendoza to give us a short-lived 1–0 lead. In the bottom of the inning Bernie Williams homered off Arthur Rhodes to tie it. Now Joe Torre and I were both down to our closers. But after Mariano Rivera retired us in order in the ninth, Sasaki gave up a two-run walk-off homer to Alfonso Soriano in the bottom of the inning, and Yankee Stadium exploded in delirium.

It was a truly tough loss, and now I had to decide whether to bring back my right-handed horse, Garcia, on three days' rest, or go with twenty-three-year-old Joel Pineiro, who was the future of the organization but had not started since September 22, when he'd lasted just two innings against the A's. The third option was Sele, my game 1 starter, who was 0–5 in six previous postseason starts. Gillick, my pitching coach, Bryan Price, and I went over and over the possibilities before finally settling on Sele, who, unfortunately, was not able to contain the Yankees' bats. We were down 9–0 after six innings and lost, 12–3.

It was a terrible letdown after winning 116 games in the regular season, and I'd wanted badly to beat the Yankees. Throughout the three games in New York, the Yankees fans had chided me pretty good, shouting stuff like, "No game six! No game six!" and that hurt me because I'm a sensitive person. These were, after all, the same fans who cheered and supported me unconditionally all those years ago when I was playing hard for them and later doing battle with Mr. Steinbrenner.

On the other hand, the city of New York and these fans had gone through so much devastation that winning this series was in a way therapeutic for them. They needed healing and I felt good for them. I even said so publicly before game 5, but adding, "That's a strange thought coming from a manager who's getting his ass kicked." When you'd played and managed in New York and formed as many lifelong friendships there as I did, you couldn't help feeling good about the Yankees going back to the World Series, bringing a little joy back to the Bronx and taking everyone's minds off the death and destruction still being sorted out at the lower end of Manhattan.

The next day we flew back to Seattle, but as if we hadn't gone through enough calamity already, soon after we were airborne there was a fire in the back of the plane! All the air masks came down, and we had to make an emergency landing back in Newark. After touching down, I looked out the window and saw all these fire trucks and ambulances furiously motoring toward the plane. Having a little private gallows humor, I thought, *Where the hell were all these people last night when I needed them?*

We ended up sitting in Newark Airport for hours, waiting for a new charter plane to take us home, but at least that gave me time to reflect. It had been a highly emotional week in New York, and I wondered why in the world I had wanted to play the Yankees in the ALCS, with the coast-to-coast travel, and then getting caught up in all the aftermath of 9/11, when Oakland would have been so much simpler. But then I looked around at my players and coaches, and there was no complaining, no head-hanging, and I realized just how good this team was and how great this season had been. Also in my den at home I have my original signed lineup card from the 116th win, October 6, 2001, as well as a signed team ball. It's time to give them to the Hall of Fame. I know it doesn't have the 116-win lineup card from the 1906 Cubs.

In 2001, the Mariners led the majors in attendance—3,507,326— the first time they'd ever drawn over three million. The franchise couldn't have been more thriving, and I was still happy about how well the transition had gone from Woody to Pat, who kept making sure I had good teams to manage. Coming off a 116-win season, Pat didn't feel a need for any major changes, and instead signed James Baldwin, a right-hander who'd won in double figures the previous six years for the White Sox, to supplement the back end of the starting rotation. He also did some fine-tuning with the bench, signing thirty-six-year-old switch-hitter Ruben Sierra, who'd hit 23 homers as a fourth outfielder and DH for Texas the year before, and trading David Bell to the Giants for another switch-hitter, the utility man Desi Relaford. To replace Bell at third base, Pat traded Jose Paniagua, who'd done an excellent job as a workhorse middle reliever for me the previous four seasons, and a couple of other minor-league relief pitchers to Colorado for Jeff Cirillo, a career .300 hitter with modest power.

During this time, however, my father's health had started deteriorating, and I began thinking more about how far it was from Tampa to Seattle and how hard it was, with no direct flights, to get back home in the case of an emergency. Much as I loved everything about Seattle, especially the sockeye salmon fishing, for the first time I started thinking about managing closer to home when my contract expired in two years.

If repeating as division champions isn't hard enough, trying to live up to expectations after a season for the ages was impossible. It wasn't until late July 2002 that this became a reality for us. Despite a recurring, disabling hamstring issue with Edgar, significant drop-offs in production from Cameron and Boone, and disappointing performances from Baldwin and Cirillo, we climbed into first place on April 10 and hung on for four and a half months. All the while, though, I knew we were going to need help at the trading deadline. Surprisingly, when I expressed my feelings to Pat and John Ellis, they told me Howard Lincoln's position was that the team was good enough and that he was unwilling to sacrifice any more prospects or raise the payroll. We would be sitting out the trading deadline. In a meeting in early June, Lincoln made it clear to all of us this was a business and his main interest was making money. Howard was a lawyer for Nintendo, not a baseball man, and he liked the idea of that Brinks truck arriving at the stadium twice a day. He ended the meeting by saying, "That's it. There'll be no more conversation about this. If the World Series happens, it happens. I don't want to read anything about trades or improvements in the papers. Is that clear?"

It was deflating for everyone in the room. A couple of weeks later, we were in Houston for an interleague series against the Astros, and one of the Houston writers asked me about all the players—Carlos Guillen, Freddie Garcia, and John Halama—we'd gotten in the Randy Johnson trade back in 1998. The writer noted how they were all still doing well for us four years later, while Randy had left the Astros after just two and a half months in '98 and signed as a free agent with Arizona. Rather than gloat about how well the deal had worked out for us, I complimented Houston's general manager, Gerry Hunsicker, for his boldness. "They were trying to win the World Series and they thought Randy could be a big factor in that," I said. "I think if you have a team that's one piece short, you owe it to your fans and your players to go for it." I then qualified that just a bit, saying, "You have to make darn sure that's the right piece. You can decimate your farm system pretty quick."

It was an innocent comment and I didn't think anything more about it until I got back to Seattle and Gillick came into my office and informed me that Lincoln was very upset with me. With that, he showed me a memo Lincoln had sent out in which he said he was disappointed to read my remarks in the paper because they weren't consistent with the understanding he had with the baseball staff about the public discussion of potential moves. As I read the memo, my blood began boiling.

"He wants your response," Gillick said.

"Yeah, well, I'll give him my response!" I said. "Tell him I'll meet him here tomorrow morning. I can't believe this. This is embarrassing to me. If he's upset about something I said, why didn't he just pick up the phone instead of putting out this damn memo?"

Howard obviously thought I was showing him up, even though when I said what I did to the Houston writer, I hadn't given a thought about that meeting he'd had with us. The fact still was, I came from the school of Mr. Steinbrenner, who always went for it, just as I'd learned from Marge in Cincinnati what happens when you don't go for it . . . We were never able to catch Atlanta in 1992.

I was still steaming about the memo the next day when I entered the conference room at Safeco for my meeting with Howard. As usual, Anita gave me the advice she always gave me: "Be kind and gentle." But I was in no mood for that. I was expecting a private audience, but instead there were a half dozen other people there including Pat, John

Ellis, Chuck Armstrong, and our assistant GM, Lee Pelekoudas. It reminded me of meetings Mr. Steinbrenner always used to have, in which he stacked the room with all his subordinates whom he could count on to vote the way he wanted them to.

Howard started off by demanding to know what I meant by my comments in Houston, and I explained to him they were simply an innocent compliment to the Astros. I told him I meant no harm and that I hadn't even been thinking of our situation. But then I told him, as good as our team was, we weren't at all assured of getting to the postseason, adding that I didn't agree at all with his philosophy. I knew behind the scenes he felt I'd been given too much power by Woody, which was not true, and that he thought, as a manager, I shouldn't have that much influence in player personnel matters. From there, we got into it pretty good, to the point where I finally said to him, "If you don't like the job I'm doing, Howard, feel free to fire me and send me the hell home!"

To his credit, Howard didn't lose his cool. He was very pragmatic. He said he wouldn't fire me, but that if I wanted to quit, to go ahead. "You're a paid employee here and you'll do what your bosses say."

I didn't want to quit. I still had a year and a half on my contract, which, thanks to Alan Nero, had crept up to $2.1 million a year, and I wasn't going to forfeit all that money. At the same time, I couldn't help thinking of all we'd done in my ten years there, saving baseball in Seattle and turning the franchise around into one of the most successful and prosperous in the game, with record attendances and revenues, and now here we were, acting like it was 1979 again. There was only one wild card, and nobody was better at making deals than Pat Gillick, but his hands were tied. At my induction into the Mariners Hall of Fame in 2014, John Ellis came up to me and said, "My biggest regret in all my years in Seattle was not going for it in 2002."

It would have been nice if we could have left our disagreements at that, but after the trading deadline came and went without us doing anything, I was shocked when Lincoln, in defending our inaction, told a *Seattle Times* columnist, Larry Stone, "The goal of the Mariners is not to win a World Series. It is to field a competitive team, year after year, to put itself in position to win a World Series, and hope at some point it happens."

One thing was sure: I knew I wasn't working for Mr. Steinbrenner anymore. And I also suddenly had a huge morale problem in my clubhouse. How do you explain that kind of thinking to your players? I held a meeting and I told them, "We're good enough to win with what we have, and I don't want to have any distractions from here on out."

We didn't have any more problems the rest of the year. But also, as I had warned Lincoln, we didn't have enough—especially on our bench—to hold off Oakland and Anaheim, which won 103 and 99 games respectively to our 93.

My frustrations boiled over on September 18, when, with two out and the score tied 2–2 in the bottom of the ninth inning against the Rangers, C. B. Bucknor called my backup catcher, Ben Davis, out on a bang-bang play at first base. There had been runners at second and third, and Davis had hit a line shot back at the pitcher, which the Rangers' second baseman, Michael Young, had picked up and fired over to first. I was sure Davis had beaten the throw, which would've given us the ball game (and later, the replays showed the first baseman's foot was off the bag as well). I raced out to first and confronted Bucknor, who quickly gave me the thumb. But I wasn't finished— not by a long shot. When I saw the smirk on Bucknor's face, I completely lost it, throwing my cap and kicking dirt on him. Then when I started heading back to the dugout, John Moses, my first base coach, handed me back my cap. Or should I say my prop, which I proceeded to throw at Bucknor. That provided the momentum to continue this tirade. Next, I went over to first base, and like the stunt I had patented years ago in Cincinnati, pulled it from its moorings and tossed it into right field. I then ran the base down and tossed it again, before finally making my unceremonious exit.

Happily, we won the game the next inning on a pinch-hit RBI single by Sierra, so as I said to the writers afterward, "I ran a minimarathon out there, but we got the job done."

I later heard that Lincoln had gotten tired of my tantrums, telling a reporter, "You can't have prima donnas out there." For what it's worth, I'm not proud of the way I acted either. I hate seeing the replays of my histrionics on TV today. It's frankly embarrassing now. But the truth was, I was tired of Howard too. I didn't like the fact that he pushed Woody out, or the way he was increasingly imposing his will on Pat in the baseball operations. So at the end of the season, with my dad's situation weighing heavily on me, I told Pat, "I don't think I'm coming back here next year."

Pat begged me to reconsider. "Play it out one more year here," he said, "and we'll win another championship and then both leave together." I believed we could, and I would've loved to have worked with Pat for as long as I was managing. There were so many other people I was also going to miss sorely in Seattle; in particular, Dave Niehaus, the Mariners' legendary Hall of Fame broadcaster and his radio partners, Ron Fairly and Rick Rizzs. I really enjoyed having dinner on the road with those guys and we all became very close. Dave was a walking encyclopedia of the Mariners, and Ronny and I loved talking hitting. My all-time favorite memory with them was a trip we took to the wine country on an off-day in Oakland one year. I had it all planned out and rented a Thunderbird convertible, and we were going to drive through Napa all the way up to Calistoga, then head back south through Sonoma. There was just one small problem. After stopping at three wineries, we were all loaded, and I had to hire a driver to get us back to Oakland. When I got home to Tampa, Anita wanted to know why the FedEx guy had brought us twelve cases of wine!

Ten years in Seattle, countless friends and memories. But my mind was made up.

"Lou and I had three really good seasons together in Seattle," said Gillick. "He's a lovable character, with a big heart and a real softy down deep. We never had one disagreement, which I know is rare for a manager and a general manager. I did everything I could to keep him from leaving, but I knew why. Lincoln wanted to win on the bottom line, but not on the field. I tried to hold it together, but Lou likes winning and success more than money."

A few days later, Pat, Howard, and Chuck flew to Tampa to meet with me. I had my good friend and consigliere Mondy Flores with me. By this time, there weren't any lingering hard feelings on my part. I told them I just wanted out. We talked about the one year left on my contract and that, if possible, I wanted to manage somewhere closer to home in 2003. They went back to Seattle and made the announcement that I would not be coming back, leaving unsaid the status of my contract. In the meantime, Alan Nero got on the case for me.

Through intermediaries, the Mets' owner, Fred Wilpon, was put in touch with Alan. Wilpon had just fired Bobby Valentine and was looking for an established, successful manager who was popular in New York. I guess I fit that profile. I let Alan know that I would love to manage for Wilpon, whom I knew to be a real gentleman. I knew also, in New York, I wouldn't have to worry about payroll issues. Lastly, the thought of managing right across the Triborough Bridge, in Mr. Steinbrenner's backyard, was especially intriguing. (When word began to spread in New York about me possibly coming to the Mets, Mr. Steinbrenner called my pal Malio to have him try and dissuade me. I was having lunch with Malio at his restaurant and he kept saying things like "You don't want to go to the Mets" and "You know as well as anyone that the Mets are second-class citizens in New York to the Yankees." I knew exactly where all this was coming from.)

What I did not realize was there was no way Howard Lincoln was going to let me manage in New York. Lincoln let Nero know that he would let me out of my contract but he was going to have to be compensated from whatever team I went to. Howard played hardball with Wilpon. He told him if he wanted me he was going to have to fork over the Mets' number one prospect, Jose Reyes. Wilpon, rightly, refused, while hoping he could wait Howard out.

In the meantime, however, Howard had gotten himself another bidder for my services—my hometown Tampa Bay Devil Rays, the worst team in baseball, which had finished in last place all five years of its existence and had averaged nearly 100 losses a season in the process. Once it became known that my services were available, the Devil Rays' owner, Vince Naimoli, who I knew only casually in Tampa, aggressively pursued a deal with Alan and the Mariners. For me, he offered a four-year contract for $13 million, which was over $1 million a year more than my Mariners salary, and to the Mariners he offered as compensation the left fielder Randy Winn, who'd been the Devil Rays' lone All-Star in 2002, batting .298 with 14 homers and 75 RBI. After the deal was announced, Lincoln bragged, "Wilpon shot himself in the foot. He thought he was the only bidder," and added, "Piniella got what he wanted—to manage close to home."

"Fred did everything humanly possible to get Lou," said Nero. "It just wasn't meant to be. The timing just wasn't right. Once it became evident Seattle wasn't going to let Lou go to New York, Fred had to get a manager. I was also representing Art Howe and that's how that happened."

I have to admit, I was astonished Naimoli agreed to give up a player of Winn's caliber for me. I also had to laugh. All those years in Seattle, the front office could never get a left fielder for me. Now they had.

I am immensely proud of my ten years in Seattle. I'd like to feel I made a difference there. The only thing I would add is that Howard Lincoln remained CEO of the Mariners for fourteen years after I left, during which time they went through nine different managers and never once made the postseason, much less the World Series.

CHAPTER 13

Out at Home

In the summer of 1998, I was drowning. On the field, I was enduring my first out-of-contention season in Seattle, exacerbated by Randy Johnson's contract issue. This, however, was nothing compared with the financial crisis wreaking extreme duress in my personal life.

The weight of all the debt and liens from my failed investments in the condominium project in Connecticut, the car dealership in Ossining, and my restaurants was crashing down on me. I was constantly answering depositions through my attorney, and 25 percent of my take-home pay from the Mariners was being garnished by the State of Washington. It was at this absolute worst time in my life when I turned to God.

For years, Anita had always been urging me to try and get closer to God. She prayed for me to be reborn again. I had never sought to have a more personal relationship with God, but it appeared He was using my finances to get me to pay more attention to Him. God uses our worst of times to summon us to Him. During that time, I started doing a lot of praying. My close friend Mondy Flores got me to start attending Bible-study classes, and I began reading different verses on a daily basis. What a calming experience. Little by little, I was starting to handle things so much better. Although I'd grown up in the Catholic religion from the first through the twelfth grade, Mondy encouraged me to join another church, a half mile from my home in North Tampa, where the senior pastor, Ken Whitten, became a profound influence on my life, strengthening my Christian beliefs. There's a saying in the Bible that when you're at your weakest, you're at your strongest. In 1998, I was at my most vulnerable, but I learned to get my strength through God. It set me free and allowed me to dwell on the things that were important and eternal. It's been a tremendous transformation for me, making me a better person and a better manager.

I bring this all up now because my faith in God, and the network of friends and spiritual advisers surrounding me in my hometown, helped me enormously as I coped with all the losing in the three trying years I spent as the manager of the Devil Rays.

In the negotiations leading to my exit from Seattle and my return home to Tampa, Alan Nero and I had a series of meetings with Vince Naimoli designed to firmly gauge both his commitment to winning and to me. The answer to the latter was quickly established when we agreed on my four-year, $14 million contract. In addition, Vince gave me a free hand with my coaching staff. I hired my old Mariner warhorse Chris Bosio as my pitching coach and brought Uncle Lee Elia, John McLaren, and Matty Sinatro over from Seattle, joining the holdovers Tom Foley, a great third base coach who in my opinion could have been an excellent manager in the big leagues if only given the chance, and Billy Hatcher, the first base/outfield coach who's one of the best people I've ever been around in baseball.

But my last hire turned out to be one of the most important hires in the history of the Tampa Bay franchise: Don Zimmer. Zim was a longtime Saint Pete resident whom I'd known and respected from when he was briefly a coach with the Yankees under Billy Martin in

1983, and whom I'd periodically run into at the dog track or Tampa Bay Downs when I was home. Like me, he'd left the Yankees after a falling-out with Mr. Steinbrenner, after eight years and four rings as Joe Torre's right-hand man, and I just felt he was a great person and a great baseball mind to have around. I said to Vince, "This is a guy who's immensely popular here, who's got an encyclopedic baseball mind. The players all love him and the coaches can all learn from him. He'll be a great goodwill ambassador for the team, as well as a tremendous help to me. We need to hire him." Vince didn't hesitate. He gave Zim a contract for $100,000 along with the title "special adviser," and I had myself an extra coach and a valuable asset. Like the man who came to dinner, Zim never left, working in the same all-purpose capacity as one of the faces of the Rays' franchise until the day he died in 2014.

As to Vince's commitment to winning, he explained that the team's payroll my first year would be in the low $20 million range, including some deferred money, but he promised to increase it in $10 million increments until it reached $50 million in the last year of my contract. Even though the Yankees and the Red Sox in the AL East had respective payrolls of $132 million and $70 million in 2003 (and my "second son" Alex over there in Texas was making more than my entire team), I believed that with the gradual $10 million yearly increases, I could still compete with them. That first year I even deferred $1.1 million of my salary to help out on the payroll, which was still only $19.6 million. Still, being home and taking care of my family was a good situation for me, and I truly thought I could do the same thing in Tampa Bay that I did in Seattle. Before a game against the Yankees, at Yankee Stadium in April, after we'd made 16 errors in our first 11 games, I told my players, "It's easy to say, 'We're a team with a $15 million payroll playing a team with a $180 million payroll, so how are we gonna beat them?' If that's how you feel, or what you believe, then don't play. If you help them beat you, you get what you deserve. You have to *make* them beat you!"

That was before I knew the payroll disparity in the American League East would never get better for us. For unbeknownst to me, there were problems within the Devil Rays' ownership. Though Naimoli was the majority owner and managing general partner, the five other primary partners, and specifically the Outback Steakhouse partners, Bob Basham and Chris Sullivan, had grown disenchanted with the way Vince was running the team. Of particular dismay to them were the onerous long-term contracts given out to the veteran sluggers Greg Vaughn, Vinny Castilla, and Jose Canseco, who all turned out to be busts. An in-house insurrection resulted in the Outback partners telling Vince they were withdrawing their financial support to increase payroll. I remember early on, Chris Sullivan telling me flatly, "You never should have come here."

So I had sufficient warning, but it was too late. The more I realized what a mistake I had made, at least I was home when my dad, Lou Sr., passed away on February 27, in Saint Joseph's Hospital in Tampa. He was eighty-six and his heart just gave out.

In the weeks leading up to my first spring training at home, I had made a study of the Devil Rays' roster and had seen a lot of promise. By virtue of finishing last in their first five years of existence, the Devil Rays, under the guidance of GM Chuck LaMar, had done well with their high draft picks. Their entire prospective outfield for 2003, two first-round picks, Josh Hamilton and Rocco Baldelli, and a second-round pick, Carl Crawford, were all ready to blossom, while Aubrey Huff, a fifth-round pick in '98, had a breakthrough 23-homer season in 2002. Equally promising was the catcher Toby Hall, a ninth-round pick in 1997 who had an excellent throwing arm and hit .258 with 42 RBI in just 85 games in '02. In addition, LaMar had signed as free agents Travis Lee, a proven Gold Glove first baseman, and Marlon Anderson, an excellent second baseman who'd hit .293 with 11 homers for the Phillies two years earlier. So starting out, my everyday lineup looked more than decent, and in mid-May it became even better when LaMar signed Julio Lugo, a plus defensive shortstop who hit 15 home runs that first season for me.

What we didn't have was pitching—and that became a nagging, futile situation my entire three years there.

That first spring we had a record seventy-two players in camp, half of them pitchers. It was a nightmare, way too many to fully evaluate everybody, but I think Chuck wanted me to get a look at as many players in the organization as possible. In all my spring trainings, I always made an effort to give everyone an opportunity to make the team, which is why I scheduled a lot of B games. But this really pushed the envelope. Not included in that original seventy-two was Wayne Gomes, a thirty-year-old right-handed pitcher who'd been released by three different clubs in the previous two years. Every day I came to the complex, Gomes approached me in the parking lot, asking for a tryout. I'm not sure if he was sleeping in his car or what, but every morning, there he was. Finally, I got tired of this guy bothering me and started feeling sorry for him, so I told Chuck to just give him a damn tryout. It was Chuck's feeling that, in our situation, anyone who'd had any success in the majors was worth giving a look. By this time, Gomes had become a bit of a human-interest curiosity story for the writers and I told them, "I just hope this doesn't turn into Campground for America." Fortunately, we didn't have any more vagabond walk-ons descend on us, and Gomes actually pitched pretty well at first, but then hurt his arm so we had to let him go.

The one player I was most eager to see that spring was Hamilton, the 6' 4", 240-pound left-handed slugger whom the Rays had made the first overall pick in the 1999 draft. Even though he had played only in A ball in 2002 and had been plagued by injuries throughout his four years in the minors, everyone told me he had supreme talent and could definitely be my right fielder in 2003. For the first couple of weeks of camp, I could see what they meant. He was playing well, working hard, and everything was very good—a five-tool talent. At one point I told Hamilton, Crawford, and Baldelli, "I don't want you to worry about trying to impress. I recognize your talent. You're all on my team."

Toward the middle of spring, however, Hamilton started coming in late to camp, which led me to have a couple of talks with him. One day, he didn't show up at all. Then, he was missing for three or four days, and we finally found him in a Bradenton crack house. We had no choice but to suspend him for the year. He never played a game for the Devil Rays.

In the years I played, drugs were really not that prevalent—or at least around my teams. Hamilton was a guy who would stand out on a field with a hundred other players on it. It never dawned on me that he could have a problem. This really caught me by surprise, and I had no idea how to deal with it. It was a failure on my part not to learn more about addiction. My attitude was, let the people who know about this stuff handle it. All I knew was that it really put a dent in our plans. Those three kids were the lure for me taking the Tampa Bay job. I envisioned building a competitive team around them. It wasn't until 2008 with the Texas Rangers, after numerous drug-related setbacks and suspensions, that Hamilton finally began to fulfill his vast potential, leading the American League with 130 RBI. Two years later he was the American League MVP.

With Hamilton gone, I had to revamp my projected lineup, moving Ben Grieve to right field and replacing him as my designated hitter with Al Martin, whom we'd signed after he'd been twice previously released that spring. At $5.5 million, Grieve was our highest-paid player—seventeen players on my opening-day roster were making the major-league minimum $300,000—and with five fairly productive seasons in the big leagues, I looked to him as one of the team's leaders. That's probably why I got so upset with him on June 26 when he took a very questionable called third strike on a pitch from the Yankees' Mariano Rivera for the final out in a 4–3 loss, and chose to walk away without saying anything to the home plate umpire. From my vantage point in the dugout, the pitch was clearly high, and the replay confirmed as much. When Grieve got back to the dugout, I asked him, "Was that ball high?" and he said he thought so.

"So why didn't you say something?" I demanded, to which he replied, "It didn't matter."

That was when I really lost it in front of the whole team.

I said, "Doesn't matter? What the hell do you mean it doesn't matter? It matters to *me*! And it matters to everybody else! You're the highest-paid player on this team. These kids take their lead from you!"

Afterward, I told the writers, "Rivera's a tough pitcher. I understand that, and I'm not expecting anything. But I *am* expecting if you think the ball is high to tell the umpire it's high instead of walking off to the damn dugout. Getting a response like that after we busted our damn asses out there for nine innings trying to win a baseball game, it damn well *does* matter. It matters to me and matters to a lot of damn people in that clubhouse."

I then added, "And when it matters to everybody, we'll start winning more damn baseball games here."

A big part of my being upset was that we'd lost 18 of our last 20 games to fall to 25–52—already 22 games behind in late June. Grieve was so shaken by my outburst he called the *St. Petersburg Times'* baseball beat writer, Marc Topkin, later that night, insisting he never said "it didn't matter." His dad, Tom, who was an outfielder with the

Rangers in the '70s and was now one of their broadcasters, called me to express his anger for embarrassing his son. He really got on me, but he was merely defending his son. I later explained to him the circumstances and my reasoning, and I think he understood.

Barely three months into the 2003 season, the reality hit home that this was a far more impossible situation in Tampa Bay than it had been in Seattle ten years earlier. Our pitching simply couldn't compete. Because we'd started executing in the field, we were in a lot of games, but we had no real stoppers in our rotation. At the end of June we had not been able to win more than two games in a row, which prompted me to issue a challenge to my players: "The first time we put together a three-game winning streak, I'll dye my hair." Not long after, we won three in a row, July 3–5, and I fulfilled my promise. The players brought in a hairstylist and they picked the color—a kind of ash blond. The stylist arrived at the clubhouse at nine o'clock Sunday morning, whereupon he spent about forty-five minutes dyeing streaks into my hair. Anita had begged me not to make it too drastic, but it really was quite dramatic, and when I looked in the mirror afterward, I thought, *What the hell did I do here?* The point was, I wanted to do something to loosen things up, to give the players a fun thing to shoot for.

The three-game winning streak was short lived. Beginning that Sunday, we lost six of our next eight games. From August 20 to the end of the season we went 12–26, finishing with 99 losses. The pitching staff led the majors with 639 walks and 95 hit batters, and had a collective ERA of 4.93.

I understood this was a young team that had never experienced anything remotely close to winning, and, to that end, I admit I drove them hard. I was especially hard on Toby Hall, my catcher, but for a reason: The catcher is the most important player on the field. Nothing happens in a baseball game until the catcher puts down his fingers. I had a lot of respect for Bill Parcells and how he went about things, and he was just as hard on his quarterbacks as I was on my catchers. They're the guys who run the game. Toby had a very young staff to work with, and as the year went on, he got better and better. But in the end, our pitching betrayed the effort to change the losing culture in Tampa Bay.

"We had a bunch of young guys, many of whom were complacent about just being in the big leagues," said Hall. "It just seemed like every other day, compared to ours, the opposing pitcher was a future Hall of Famer. It was very frustrating, and Lou was constantly on me to work to make our pitchers better. It finally all came to a head in a game in August against the Indians in Cleveland. We had just gone ahead, four to three, in the top of the eleventh inning, and now the Indians had a runner on third with one out and Casey Blake batting in the bottom of the inning. Our closer, Lance Carter, was pitching, and I called for a fastball low and away to guard against the sac fly. But Lance's fastball came in high and Blake drove it into right field for a sac fly that tied the game. After the game—which we wound up winning—Lou called me into his office and aired me out. 'How the hell could you call a damn high fastball in that situation?' he screamed. I looked at him, feeling my blood boiling, and hollered back at him, 'Do you think I have a damn PlayStation joystick back there to control the pitches to go anywhere I want? Look at the damn video and see where I set up!'

"I stormed out of his office. Lou never yelled at the pitchers, and I was tired of taking the bullet for them. The next day, John McLaren came up to my locker and told me Lou wanted to see me in his office. 'Uh-oh,' I said to myself. 'I'm traded.' But when I walked in, Lou was sitting there behind his desk with a smile on his face. 'Son,' he said, 'close the door. I just wanted you to know I looked at the video and you were set up right.' Then he got up from his chair, walked around the desk, and gave me a big hug. 'I love you, Toby,' he said. 'I just want to make you a better player.' From that day on, we never had another problem. And he absolutely did make me a better player."

I told Toby many times that if the pitcher was not locating, it wasn't his fault. His other job was to control the running game, and he did that extremely well. Toby had a cannon for a throwing arm. I really didn't call many pitches as a manager, only doing so if my catcher looked over to me. That was another thing I learned from Billy Martin. Billy didn't like opposing hitters teeing off on his pitchers' fastballs. Whenever that did happen he'd yell over to our pitching coach, Art Fowler, "What was that?" and Fowler would holler back, "A slider!"

Year two in Tampa was only slightly better than year one. Over the winter we acquired Tino Martinez in a trade with the Cardinals to replace Lee (who'd left as a free agent) at first base. We also signed John Halama, my former number four starter with the Mariners, to give us some veteran pitching depth. But while the payroll did increase $10 million, to $29.5 million, I had expected the first-year payroll to be in the midtwenties, as Naimoli had indicated. Our fate was pretty much decided when we lost 19 out of 22 games from April 25 to May 19. We were on pace for a 117-loss season, and after a Tuesday-night game in Texas in early May, Bill Parcells, who was then coaching the Cowboys, visited me in the clubhouse.

"This is really different for me," I told him. "Everywhere I've ever been, I've won."

"If you can't win here, you've got to get out of this thing, you know?" Bill said.

I knew. A week later, it was announced that Stuart Sternberg, a Wall Street investor and partner in Goldman Sachs, had purchased 48 percent of the Devil Rays from the Outback boys and the rest of the limited partners. The announcement further said that Naimoli would remain in charge of the team until sometime in 2005. I asked Vince what this was going to mean in terms of the payroll and he couldn't give me an answer, other than for 2005, his hands were tied.

It wasn't what I wanted to hear. But then at least things began to turn around on the field. We started June 18–32, and finished it 38–37, thanks in no small part to a franchise-best 12-game winning streak. In the middle of that streak, on June 16, I won my 1,410th game to tie the Tampa native and Hall of Fame manager Al Lopez. Even though I was never one to pay much attention to milestones or records, tying and passing Al on the all-time wins list was something that meant a lot to me. So, too, had breaking Al's American League record of 111 wins with the 1954 Indians, when we won 116 in Seattle in 2001. Al was a true gentleman and an inspiration to all the kids like myself growing up in Tampa in the '50s and '60s. It was because of him I rooted for the Indians when I was a kid. Many years later, I'd play golf with him—"El Senor"—at the Tampa Terrace Country Club, and we were both proud of our Tampa heritage.

As encouraging as our play in June was, I knew we didn't have the kind of pitching to sustain it. At the trading deadline, we sent our number one starter, Victor Zambrano, to the Mets for their top pitching prospect, the Long Island–bred lefty Scott Kazmir. It turned out to be one of Chuck LaMar's best deals, although I wasn't fully the beneficiary of it. In his first full season for me in 2005, Kazmir was 10–9 with a 3.77 ERA, but he was still learning and led the league in walks. Two years later, he led the AL in strikeouts and seemed on his way to stardom until he hurt his arm. The reason we traded Zambrano was because we'd gone 8–15 from July 4 to July 30 and we knew we weren't going to be contending. It was an opportunity to get a prize pitching prospect for the future.

Although a 12-game losing streak from August 27 to September 10 sealed a seventh-straight losing season for the Devil Rays, there was a silver lining. The team was able to finish out of the AL East cellar for the first time, and it also won 70 games for the first time in franchise history. When we beat the Tigers, 7–4, on the last day of the season for our 70th win, I decided to throw a little impromptu party and ordered a few bottles of champagne for the players. It was a fun finale for everyone—with the notable exception of my old-school senior adviser. When Zimmer came out of the coaches' room and saw all the champagne bottles, he was aghast.

"What the hell is all this?" he demanded.

"Oh, I just thought it would be nice to have a little celebration for winning seventy games for the first time," I said.

"My god," Zim said disgustedly. "What the hell are you gonna do when they get over five hundred? Buy 'em all Mercedes?"

I couldn't help laughing. Those 70 wins were the hardest I ever got. After just two years in Tampa Bay I was already burned out. I knew there was no way I would ever have to worry about reaching .500, especially when Vince's warning words about his hands being tied were confirmed that winter. Our major-league-low $29.5 million payroll in 2004 was going to remain essentially the same for 2005.

An eight-game losing streak from April 24 to May 2 put us in last place and we stayed there the rest of the '05 season. Our pitchers led the league in runs allowed per game (5.78) and walks (615) and were next-to-last in ERA (5.39). In particular, our pitching had their problems with the Red Sox who, besides beating up on them pretty good, complained about the way they were being pitched to. Tensions boiled over during an 11–3 beating the Red Sox put on us on April 24, when six players were ejected in two bench-clearing scuffles. A couple of days later, Curt Schilling ripped me on a Boston radio station, essentially accusing me of ordering my pitchers to throw at the Red Sox's hitters. "The problem is when you're playing a team with a manager who's somehow forgot how the game is played, there's problems," Schilling said. "Lou's trying to make his team into a bunch of tough guys, and the telling sign is when their players say, 'This is why we lose 100 games a year because this idiot makes us do stuff like this.'"

I was astounded. Curt Schilling calling *me* an idiot. After hearing those remarks, I called a team meeting in Toronto and issued a statement in which I said, "Forget how the game is played? I've forgotten more baseball than this guy knows. On the idiot subject, I'm appalled he would actually say something like that. I had a meeting with my team and to a man they denied saying it. He's questioning my character and integrity and that's wrong. He's never played for me, never really talked to me, so he doesn't know what I stand for."

Schilling was still under my craw when, on July 18 in Boston, I engaged in a very heated argument with the umpires over a reversed call at first base and got myself another ejection. Julio Lugo had been called safe at first base on an infield hit when Dana DeMuth, who was an excellent umpire, ruled that Schilling, covering first on the relay, missed the base. Schilling immediately raised a beef and even appeared to have bumped DeMuth who, after also hearing it from the Red Sox's manager, Terry Francona, agreed to consult with home plate umpire Laz Diaz to see if he had a better angle. When Diaz subsequently reversed the call, I charged out onto the field, screaming in protest and later had to be restrained by my first base coach, Billy Hatcher. I had never seen a home plate umpire overrule a first base umpire, not when the first base umpire was right there on top of the play. As I said at the time, "You've got one base to call; make the call, and stand by it!"

A week later in Saint Pete, David Wells, another Red Sox pitcher with a big mouth, popped off to the writers, saying my players were "petrified" of me—which prompted a quick rebuke from Francona, who said, "I do wish we would stay away from doing stuff like this.

I definitely do not agree with our players. I'm sure I'll make a pass by Lou today to apologize."

He did, and let me say right here, I have a tremendous amount of respect for Terry, who is one of the class acts in baseball. He's also one heckuva manager, who did a tremendous job in 2016 getting the Indians all the way to the seventh game of the World Series without the services of one of his best players, Michael Brantley, all year long, and two of his top starting pitchers, Carlos Carrasco and Danny Salazar, down the stretch.

At the same time, the entire imbroglio with the Red Sox underscored the problem I had with our pitchers. I assured Terry I did not instruct my pitchers to throw at anyone. The problem was, they were young kids who didn't have command and, as a result, issued a lot of walks and hit a lot of batters trying to pitch inside. And unfortunately, as Toby Hall explained, he didn't have a joystick to control the direction of their pitches. A few years ago, at a dinner in Boston, I made my peace with Schilling, who I know regrets the things he said. I wish him luck now in his political career.

Going into the All-Star Break, we lost 14 of 16 to fall to 28–61. I was beaten up physically and mentally. Right before that losing streak began, I let my feelings be known, while laying down the gauntlet to Sternberg after Marc Topkin asked me when we were going to start to win. "I'm not going to take responsibility for this," I said evenly. "If I had been given a forty- to fifty-million-dollar payroll as I was promised, I'd stand up like a man and say it's my fault. Well, I'm not going to do it. So if you want answers about what's going on here, you call the new ownership group and let them give them to you."

Well, that created quite a firestorm. Immediately, the media interpreted that as my farewell address, especially when, the next day, I stood by my words, adding only that "the new people who bought this baseball club, they're nice people. I have absolutely nothing against anybody. It's a tough business and what I said, I said." I wasn't offending anybody. I was just telling the truth.

It was when we were in New York in mid-August, playing the Yankees, that I asked Sternberg himself. He was sitting in the third base box seats, next to the visiting team's dugout, and I wanted to know exactly what his vision was. He told me success was going to take a while, that he couldn't do it right away, and that his priorities were to build up the ballpark in Saint Petersburg and build up the minor-league system. The payroll was not going to rise much, to which I told him, "I can't compete like this." He said he understood, but that he still had to do things in the order of preference. "It's just not going to happen for a while," he said.

That was it for me. I knew I had to get out of there. I had come home to Tampa in hopes of turning the franchise around like we'd done in Seattle, and I was even willing to give it a couple of years. But I never had a chance—and now Sternberg was confirming I wasn't going to have a chance any time soon either. It had gotten to the point where I didn't even like going out to restaurants and having friends, associates, and just plain people asking me when the team was going to start winning. (I was almost relieved when Malio closed down his landmark restaurant on Dale Mabry Boulevard in September 2004, so I wouldn't be constantly running into Mr. Steinbrenner.) Joe Torre, Tony La Russa, and Bobby Cox, who all went into the Hall of Fame in 2014, are three of the greatest—and winningest—managers of all time. But I guarantee you if they'd managed in Tampa Bay, with the payrolls I had, they'd have lost just as many games as I did.

Years later, after Sternberg changed the name of the team to the Rays and the farm system started to deliver another core of young players in Evan Longoria, David Price, James Shields, and Ben Zobrist, who got them to the World Series, a lot of the people in Tampa and around baseball asked me if I had any regrets leaving when I did. My response was to look at the record of my successor, Joe Maddon, his first two years in Tampa Bay: 61–101 in 2006 and 66–96 in 2007. There wasn't enough money in all of Tampa for me to endure two more years of that kind of losing.

After that conversation with Sternberg, I called Alan Nero and told him to see what he could do to get me out of the last year of my contract. I told him, "The new owners probably deserve to hire their own manager and not pay him what they're paying me." Alan worked out an agreement in which I would forfeit one-half of my salary and sit out the 2006 season, at least in terms of a uniformed or baseball management position. That was fine with me because I needed the year to "detox." In the meantime, the Fox network hired me to do color commentary on the 2005 World Series games, and they liked my work enough to give me a full-time job for 2006 on the backup Saturday *Game of the Week*.

I really enjoyed my year in the booth, especially working with Thom Brennaman, whose father, Marty, is the longtime Hall of Fame radio announcer for the Reds. Marty and his broadcast partner, Joe Nuxhall, were two of my dearest friends my three years in Cincinnati. Some of my most favorite times in baseball were my dinners with Marty and Joe. It was not surprising that Thom and I hit it off right away. He's a top-notch broadcaster who helped me a lot. We had a lot of fun together—just as I did with his dad—and we played off each other really well.

In June 2006, my life in my first season out of uniform unexpectedly intersected with one of my favorite prodigies. I was at Yankee Stadium the night of June 27, doing a charity event in one of the suites, when who should walk in but Cynthia Rodriguez, Alex's wife. She was quite eager to talk to me. I guess I should let Alex tell the rest of this story.

"I was really struggling at that time, in a 4-for-31 slump that had dropped my average nearly 10 points to .276," he said, "and I'd gone like nine games without a homer. We were playing the Braves, and during the game I got a text message that Lou was in the ballpark, up in one of the hospitality suites. It was comforting just knowing he was in the ballpark. It had been so long since I'd seen him. So I called Cynthia, who was sitting in the stands, and told her I needed her to go up to the suites, find Lou, and tell him it was very important I see him after the game. Cynthia said, 'How am I gonna get up there with all the security? They're liable to arrest me!' I said, 'The way I'm hitting, they're gonna throw me out of the stadium! Just tell any guy with a badge up there who you are, show 'em your ID, and get to Lou.' Somehow she worked her magic, talked to Lou, and told him that I'm massively struggling with the bat and desperately needed his help. Could he meet us for dinner or a drink after the game? Lou had Anita with him and said he'd love to get together but that he had dinner plans in the city. Cynthia called me back and explained the situation and I said, 'Tell him I don't care what time of night it is. I need to see him.'

"Cynthia brokered the meeting and Lou showed up at my apartment in Manhattan at twelve thirty—we had a day game the next day but it didn't matter. As soon as he got there, he launched into a hitting lesson. He's going, 'Here's how you have to do it, you gotta have f-ing weight shift,' . . . getting into all that stuff . . . and Cynthia's sitting there with Anita and can't believe what she's seeing: Lou Piniella giving me a batting lesson in my apartment at twelve thirty in the morning! After a while, Lou asks me, 'Do you have a bat?' I didn't, but I found a broomstick. 'What about a ball?' he asked. I said, 'Wait a minute,' and went into my bedroom and came out with a rolled-up sock. Now Lou starts throwing the sock to me and I'm hitting it all over the apartment with the broomstick with shit flying everywhere. Finally, Lou left around 2:00 a.m. I got to the stadium the next morning with only a few hours' sleep."

I was obviously really happy to see Alex, as was Anita, who was very close to both him and Cynthia. The next day, Anita and I rented a car to drive over to New Jersey to visit some of our old friends from Allendale. We had the Yankees game on the radio, which was now in the twelfth inning, and here comes Alex, with one out and one on, and he hits a game-winning walk-off two-run homer! I pulled the car over, and we just listened to the crowd cheering and John Sterling going wild. We both had tears in our eyes.

"After the game," said Alex, "Cynthia met me outside the Yankee clubhouse and she's screaming, 'Oh my god! Lou Piniella is Jesus!'"

CHAPTER 14

Billy Goats to Bartman to Chance

Toward the end of the 2006 baseball season, as the bad taste of three losing seasons in Tampa Bay slowly began to dissipate, I started getting the feeling back. There was no way I wanted my managing career to end on such a downer. I had prided myself on winning for most of my entire life, going all the way back to my high school Pony League days with Tony La Russa in Tampa, and I needed to start doing just that once more before I reached retirement age. At the same time, I wondered: Do I still have appeal to any teams?

That question was answered when I started getting feelers from four or five teams, in particular the Giants, the Yankees, and the Cubs. Long after we'd gone our separate ways from the Yankees, the Giants' general manager, Brian Sabean, remained a close personal friend. Whenever I would be in San Francisco for a game, I would make a point to stop up to Brian's office and we would spend the time in nonstop laughter, retelling our war stories about Mr. Steinbrenner, whom we both referred to as "the commander." After two straight losing seasons, Felipe Alou, at seventy-one, was planning to retire as the Giants' manager at the end of 2006, and Brian was looking for a replacement. He asked me if I would be interested. My initial reaction was "hell yes!" The Giants, under Brian's leadership, were one of the best organizations in baseball; he and I had a wonderful relationship; and San Francisco was one of my favorite cities. It was also, like Seattle, on the other side of the continent, some three thousand miles away from Tampa, and therein lay my dilemma. I told Brian I'd have to think about it and discuss it with Anita. A day or so later, he had Peter Magowan, the Giants' managing general partner, call me in Tampa to make his pitch to me. Anita and I talked about it. She was pretty firm about my not taking another West Coast managing job. She just didn't want to go across the country again, and there were more and more family considerations that would require being a shorter distance from home. I told Brian all this, and he understood. Instead, he hired Bruce Bochy, who after losing seasons his first two years with the Giants, went on to win three world championships from 2010 to 2014, and is still there looking for more. Great move on my part.

"That will always be one of my biggest regrets," said Anita, "talking Lou out of going to San Francisco."

I had just finished broadcasting the first round of the American League playoffs between the A's and Tigers when Alan called and told me the Cubs' general manager, Jim Hendry, was flying down to Tampa to meet with me. I picked Hendry up at the Tampa Airport Marriott and we went over to the nearby Ruth's Chris Steak House, where, over a few martinis and steaks, we really hit it off. Jim was easy to talk to. He said he needed to turn the Cubs' situation around real quick—they were coming off a 96-loss, last-place season under Dusty Baker—but that the parent Tribune Company was prepared to put a lot of money into it to make it easier for him. The reason for that, which neither of us knew at the time, was because they were getting ready to sell the Cubs along with all their newspapers, and a winning team would enable them to command a much higher price.

In the meantime, I had heard that after two straight eliminations of the Yankees in the division series, there was some friction between Joe Torre and Mr. Steinbrenner. I could relate to that, except with me it had taken only one year; Joe had been there ten and won four world championships. No matter. With Mr. Steinbrenner, it was always a "what have you done for me lately" proposition. Alan Nero had heard that Mr. Steinbrenner wanted to talk to me, but since we were already in talks with the Cubs, I wanted to see where that was going.

In the year I'd been out of baseball, I'd run into Mr. Steinbrenner a couple of times in Tampa, and one day when I had lunch with Malio and him, I could see he was slipping somewhat. His memory seemed to be failing and he wasn't nearly as sharp as he'd always been. I also heard he was scaling way back with the Yankees, turning most of the decision making over to his sons, Hal and Hank, and his son-in-law. So when Nero said the Yankees might be interested in talking to me, I was skeptical. Even though the hard feelings I'd felt toward Mr. Steinbrenner were gone, I didn't want any part of revisiting them. I told Nero not to pursue anything with them.

It was the right decision, because let me say something right here: managing the Cubs is something everyone should do—at least once.

During our conversation, Jim did mention the superstitions surrounding the Cubs but said that if I ever went to a Cubs convention I'd see how rabid and loyal their fan base was. We talked about the makeup of the team, a coaching staff, free agents, and the fact that the Cubs had not been in a World Series since 1945 and had not won one since 1908, and by the end of the night I was pretty much committed to taking on another great challenge. Chicago was only a two-and-a-half-hour plane flight from Tampa and a great city to live in during the summertime. All that was left was for Alan to work out the contract details with Hendry's boss, John McDonough. Before we called it an evening, Hendry and I went over to SideBerns, another Tampa eatery, for a nightcap. While we were at the bar, a couple of friends of mine came over and, out of the blue, said to me, "You know, Lou, you should manage the Cubs!" They had no idea who Hendry was, and I said to myself, *If these guys only knew.*

Once the news started leaking out of my possibly going to the Cubs, I got a call from Bob Castellini, the new owner of the Reds, whom I'd gotten to know during the 2006 season through my Cincinnati ties. He's a terrific guy—whom I now work for as a special assistant—but on this particular phone call he was not too happy with me. "C'mon Lou," he pleaded, "you can't take a managing job in our own division! Come back to Cincinnati!" It was tempting. I'd have loved to try and win another championship in Cincinnati—especially for Bob Castellini—but it was too late.

A few days later, Alan worked out a contract that was three years and an option for $14 million. A press conference was called for October 17 at Wrigley Field. After being introduced by McDonough and Hendry, I made the statement, "Long-suffering Cub fans, we're going to win here, and that's really the end of the story." If only it was.

Instead, it opened up a whole line of questioning to me about the Cubs' tragic history: The supposed billy goat curse, in which a local tavern owner was said to have put a curse on the Cubs after he and his pet goat were ejected from game 4 of the 1945 World Series because the goat's smell was bothering the fans. What did I know of billy goats—or for that matter Steve Bartman, the Cubs fan who interfered with a foul pop Moises Alou was about to catch with the Cubs just four outs from clinching the pennant in game 6 of the 2003 National League Championship Series? It was pointed out to me that the Bartman interference, which led to Miami erasing a 3–0 Cubs lead and scoring eight runs in the inning, was merely another extension of the billy goat curse.

This was nuts! In all my years in baseball, I'd never seen such media negativity. At first I laughed at the silly questions, but then I realized they were serious. Hendry had casually warned me to expect periodic talk among the media and fans about curses surrounding the Cubs, but I had no idea how pervasive all this stuff was through the organization. I quickly came to realize this was going to be a challenge in itself, keeping the players insulated from the curse talk.

In welcoming me to the Cubs, John McDonough made a point of saying, "We brought you here to win and we're going to make sure to give you everything you need starting out. We're not into rebuilding. We're into winning now." That was what McDonough was all about. I told him, "This is the third straight time I've taken over a team with the most losses in the league the year before, and I have the same urgency you do. I don't see myself managing in my seventies."

After the press conference, Anita and I took a stroll around Wrigley Field. It was a cold, gray, dreary day and the ivy on the outfield wall, which is a beautiful lush green in the summertime, was all brown. We took some pictures and then walked around outside the stadium, where I couldn't help noticing all the bars in the area. "From the way it's being portrayed to me by the media," I said to Anita, "these fans seem to do a lot of drinking here."

Once again, I was able to put together a really nice coaching staff. Larry Rothschild, whom I'd had in Cincinnati and felt was second to none as a pitching coach, had already been in place with the Cubs since 2002, and I brought in Matty Sinatro, who'd been with me in Tampa and Seattle, as my first base coach, and Gerald Perry, whom I'd had in Seattle, as my hitting coach. Hendry asked that we promote from the organization Mike Quade to coach third base, and Lester Strode as my bullpen coach. We also had Ivan DeJesus, one of the best infield coaches I've ever been around. Now it came down to a bench coach. Jim and I discussed a bunch of names but the one that kept coming up was Alan Trammell, who'd managed the Tigers from 2003 to 2005 but had sat out the 2006 season. I didn't know Trammell all that well other than as a respected opponent and a Hall of Fame–worthy shortstop when he played for the Tigers in the '80s. I called him to ask if he would be interested in the job, and he said yes.

"Great," I said. "I'll have Jim Hendry call you about a contract."

"Don't I need to interview?" Trammell asked.

"Heck, no," I said. "I know you'll do a good job here."

That was the truth. He did a great job for me. Though he was passed up for the Cubs manager job after I left, he deserves another chance and I hope he gets it.

Hendry was right about essentially having an open checkbook from the Tribune Co. to buy players. Right after the general managers' meeting in late November, he signed outfielder Alfonso Soriano, one of the preeminent free agents that winter, to an eight-year, $136 million contract, and utility man Mark DeRosa for three years, $13 million. In December he added to his booty lefty Ted Lilly for four years, $40 million, and right-hander Jason Marquis for three years, $20 million to bolster our rotation behind the staff's ace, Carlos Zambrano. In addition, Hendry signed our third baseman, Aramis Ramirez, to a five-year, $73 million extension. That was a total haul of $282 million in new contracts. The Lilly contract in particular showed Hendry's doggedness. We were at the winter meetings in Orlando when, in the middle of his negotiations with Lilly's agent, he suddenly started feeling dizzy and having chest pains. He kept putting it off, maintaining he was all right, just a little fatigued, until finally I insisted on taking him the hospital to have him checked out. I drove him right to the emergency room at the hospital in Orlando, whereupon they determined he was having a heart attack. I'm sure a lot of that had to do with the pressure Jim was under from the Tribune Co. While he was in the hospital, he was still trying to sign players, and on the day before he was discharged, I walked into his room and he was sitting up, completing the Lilly deal over the phone. I looked at him and said to myself, *These guys really are committed!*

We went to spring training in Mesa, Arizona, with the idea of playing Soriano in center field, DeRosa at second, and Cesar Izturis, who'd been a backup for the Dodgers and Cubs the year before, as our everyday shortstop. Our catcher, Michael Barrett, was a good hitter but subpar defensively. It didn't take long, however, for us to realize that it might be asking too much of Soriano—who had just been converted from a second baseman to a left fielder by Washington the year before—to now move to center. I had always operated on the premise that to win, you need to be strong defensively up the middle, and even though we started out with that alignment—Barrett behind the plate, DeRosa at second, Izturis at short, and Soriano in center—I had reservations about all of it. I loved DeRosa a lot. He was a smart, versatile, hard-ass player who knew how to play the game, but he wasn't a natural second baseman and I didn't like the way he turned the double play. Where we were really strong was the infield corners, with Derrek Lee, a Gold Glove, 30-homer man at first base, and Ramirez, a .300, 100 RBI hitter at third.

At the end of the spring I told Hendry, "You did your job, Jim. Now I'll do mine. Go out and relax and play some golf!"

By the quirk of the schedule we opened the 2007 season on April 2 in Cincinnati, and I'm sure Bob Castellini got a lot of enjoyment watching the Reds beat us on Opening Day and taking two of three in the opening series. On April 3, an off-day, it was announced that Sam Zell, a Chicago-based equity investor, had completed an $8.2 billion deal to purchase the Tribune Co., and all its newspapers and properties, including the Cubs and Wrigley Field. I had suspected the Tribune Co. was getting ready to sell the team, but happening this soon caught us all by surprise. What this meant for us going forward was uncertain. I only knew that Zell's prime interest was in real estate and therefore it probably didn't bode well for the Cubs. In any case, I couldn't worry about it. I had enough problems with my team's play on the field.

When we lost a fourth straight game on April 13 to start out 0–3 at Wrigley and 3–6 overall—a game in which Zambrano blew a 5–0 lead in the fifth inning, and the reliever I replaced him with, Will Ohman, threw only nine pitches, eight of them balls—I had my first temper flare-up as Cubs manager. What set me off was one of the writers asking me after the game what wasn't working. "What the hell do you think isn't working?" I said, adding, "I can start to see some of the ways this team has lost ball games."

We continued to flounder most of April, and when we were 10–14 at the end of the month, Hendry came to me and said, "I thought you said I could play golf!"

"I always thought Lou was the most interesting manager I ever had," said DeRosa. "Bobby Cox was like a father figure, same as Bruce Bochy. Buck Showalter was more like a military guy where everything had to be in place. But Lou was pure theater. He was the biggest star on the team, even though we had guys like Derrek Lee, Ramirez, and Soriano. I actually enjoyed the way he'd kick you in the rear. Lou figured out by May 1 what was wrong and what his players were made of. He'd manipulate you if he thought you were soft, and if you were, you wouldn't be around long.

"He had me in the lineup on Opening Day against the Reds, versus Aaron Harang, and then the next day, with Bronson Arroyo pitching for them, he had me benched. I was really pissed. I was a guy who always wanted to play all 162. I went out to the dugout and called my father in New Jersey and told him I wasn't in the lineup. I told him that I'd heard Lou was a guy who, if he got on you, he respected you if you pushed back. I asked my father if he thought this was too early in the season to test that. He said, 'If you want to play, go get it!' So I marched back into Lou's office and said, 'I want to play!' He walked outside to the bulletin board, tore the lineup down and announced to the whole clubhouse, 'I have to put a new lineup up because De-Rosa here wants to play.'

"Another time, I was at the plate with a 3-1 count and a runner on first base. Lou sent the runner, who was thrown out when I swung through the ball. After the inning I came into the dugout and Lou jumped me. 'What the hell were you doing, not taking there?' he screamed. I fired back at him, 'Damn, Lou, it's a 3-1 count, I got leverage there! I'm trying to go deep!' He scowled at me and said, 'Deep? You haven't gone deep in two years!' With Lou, you just had to laugh it off."

When things only got worse in May, I knew I had to start making changes. We were in the throes of a five-game losing streak and 22–30 on June 1 when Zambrano had another fifth-inning meltdown. After allowing five runs on five hits, he engaged in fisticuffs with his batterymate, Barrett, in the dugout. Zambrano went to the locker room and Barrett followed him up there, which was a big mistake. Zambrano was a big dude with big fists who reminded me of Rob Dibble, and Barrett took the worst of the fight. Zambrano was irked with Barrett for committing a passed ball and a throwing error on the same play in that fifth inning. It may also have been a culmination of Zambrano's frustrations the first two months. He was in the last year of his contract and upset that the Cubs' front office was seemingly dragging its feet on an extension. His fastball had lost a few miles per hour, and he wasn't pitching well. That June 1 loss, in which he gave up 13 hits and 7 runs in five innings, left him at 5–5 with a 5.62 ERA for his first 12 starts. He was pressing and made it clear he just didn't want to pitch to Barrett.

From that point on, I matched up Zambrano with our backup

catchers until June 20, when we traded Barrett to San Diego. Four days earlier we'd acquired Jason Kendall, a proven, veteran catcher who'd been a three-time All-Star with the Pirates. The fact was, the Zambrano-Barrett fight was embarrassing and left the impression with some of the media that things were spinning out of control. In my office afterward, one of the writers noted that I hadn't been kicked out of a game yet, to which I replied, "It'll happen. I just haven't seen anything on the field that I thought was flagrant enough to go out there and really argue about."

The next day it did happen. Before the game, John McDonough came into my office to talk about the team. He was an involved boss, and I liked that. He said to me, "You came here with a reputation as a firebrand, but you've been pretty calm and don't argue. If there's a close play, maybe you should go out there and light a fire under these guys!" Then, like Mr. Steinbrenner, he said, "Don't worry, we'll pay your fine."

So, in the eighth inning of a 5–3 loss to the Braves that day, Angel Pagan, one of my reserve outfielders, was thrown out trying to steal third base on a ball that had bounced away from the catcher. I thought he'd beaten the throw, and stormed out to confront the third base umpire, Mark Wegner. In the aftermath of my dirt-kicking, cap-tossing tirade, it was reported I made contact with Wegner. I didn't think so—even in my wildest rages I was always aware of getting physical in any way with umpires. Nevertheless, the imbroglio with Wegner earned me a four-game suspension and a $4,000 fine. Wegner is a really good ump—he lives near me in Brandon, Florida, a suburb of Tampa—and he got the call right. He just happened to be my foil that day. I later sent him a note of apology.

But as McDonough had reminded me, sometimes you have to get yourself ejected for the good of the team. I knew I had to change my thinking. The year away from managing had caused me to reflect on my wild ways while also devoting more time to my spirituality. When the 2007 season began I made a conscious effort to maintain a calmer disposition. But we were playing badly—too many errors and bonehead plays, which I just couldn't tolerate. There was also an ESPN report—which Derrek Lee termed "completely false"—that my players were griping about my criticisms of their poor play. I knew if we were going to get untracked and start playing up to our ability, I had to shore up our up-the-middle defense (while also hoping Zambrano would get his head together).

I had started that process on May 1 when I moved Soriano to his more comfortable position in left field and replaced him in center with Jacque Jones, a fine defensive outfielder who'd hit 27 homers for the Cubs in '06. Then, on June 1, I installed Ryan Theriot, who'd been playing all over the infield, as my everyday shortstop, and on June 9 turned second base over to our other utility infielder, the 5' 9", 165-pound "flyweight" Mike Fontenot. Theriot gave me some much-needed speed, and Ivan DeJesus did a great job getting him ready to play shortstop. Theriot and Fontenot had played together at LSU, so teaming them up was kind of a natural and they really stabilized the middle of the infield. Earlier, I'd moved DeRosa from second to third when Ramirez was on the disabled list for two weeks. After that I moved him all around while keeping him in the lineup for the most games he'd ever played—149. DeRosa had a terrific first season with the Cubs as my all-purpose man (.293, 10 HR, 72 RBI) and proved to be worth every penny of the contract we gave him.

By late June we had started playing much better, inching closer and closer to .500. We reached it on June 29 with a dramatic 6–5 win against the Brewers that was decided on Ramirez's two-out, two-run homer in the ninth inning.

"That game was when we all came together," said DeRosa. "Lou had made all his moves and it was like we all said, 'Okay, let's win the division now!'"

Once we got the defense and catching straightened out, everything began to turn around. We were 17–9 in July and 62–59 overall when we climbed into first place to stay when we beat the Cardinals, 2–1, on August 17. In addition, Zambrano, who finally got a five-year, $91.5 million extension on August 16, provided a huge boost to the pitching, going from 5–5 with a 5.62 ERA on June 1 to 18–13, 3.95, at season's end.

Admittedly, the NL Central was the weakest division in baseball in 2007, which is why it took only 85 wins to finish first. While I was gratified to have been able to make a 96-loss, last-to-first turnaround, it was a long first season in Chicago. On the other hand, the postseason was all too short. We were swept by the Diamondbacks in the division series, managing a total of only six runs in the three games. I was criticized by the media for removing Zambrano in game 1 after six innings, with the score tied 1–1. But I had what I thought were good reasons. For one thing, the reliever I replaced him with, Carlos Marmol, had been unhittable all season (5–1, 1.43 ERA, 96 strikeouts in 69⅓ innings). My other reason was I wanted to preserve Zambrano as much as I could since he would be coming back on short rest for a game 4. Before I made my move on Zambrano I talked it over with Larry Rothschild and he agreed. But Marmol gave up a home run to Mark Reynolds, the first batter he faced in the seventh, and the Diamondbacks added another run off him in the inning to seal the deal on a 3–1 win.

In the second game, Arizona roughed up Ted Lilly for six runs in 3⅓ innings, which we were unable to overcome. Game 3 at Wrigley Field—in which we managed just one extra-base hit in a 5–1 loss—was a field day for all the billy-goat-curse theorists. For one thing, sometime overnight before the game, someone had actually hung the skinned carcass of a goat over the statue of the Cubs' beloved, iconic broadcaster Harry Caray outside the ballpark.

When it was over, the media was still talking about my game 1 decision on Zambrano. The media are like the fans. They want results. But I would do the same thing today. No regrets. What I do regret is not having a meeting with my team before the series, to try to take the pressure off them by telling them we were the underdogs. That's what Joe Torre always did with his Yankees teams. We had scored runs most of the season, and I should have taken it on my shoulders to tell them not to pay attention to all this billy goat superstition stuff and just have fun.

Years later, I told Alan Nero, who was also the agent for the future Cubs' manager Joe Maddon, the same thing. When Maddon was the manager who finally broke through all the curses and jinx talk to get the Cubs to their first World Series since 1945 in 2016, I knew from past experience the billy goat stuff would still be hovering over the Wrigley fans and media with every Cubs misplay. I'm not sure if Alan ever transmitted that to Maddon, but I couldn't help noticing after the Cubs fell behind 3–1 to the Indians in the World Series, he told his players not to show up to the ballpark until 5:30 p.m., skipping batting practice, and to "just go play." They didn't lose another game.

A month after the 2007 season, a shock wave went through Wrigley Field when John McDonough announced his resignation as the Cubs' president to take a similar position with the National Hockey League's Chicago Blackhawks. Though it was spun by McDonough as an opportunity he just couldn't pass up, Hendry and I both knew it was more a result of the uncertainty of what Sam Zell was going to do with the Cubs. In any case, this was troubling news because McDonough had been so supportive of Jim and me, giving us all the resources we'd asked for, and we didn't figure to have the same rela-tionship with his successor, Crane Kenney, a high-level Tribune Co. exec whose main concentration had been on the business side of the operation.

When Hendry and I regrouped after the '07 NLCS to map out plans for the next year, we both agreed a major deficiency had been the predominance of right-handed hitters in our lineup. Our only two lefties, Cliff Floyd and Jacque Jones, were both free agents whom Hendry didn't want to re-sign. Instead, like Gillick in Seattle, he looked to the Far East, and, for four years and $48 million, he signed Kosuke Fukodome, a Japanese left-handed-hitting outfielder who'd batted over .300 in four of his last six seasons with the Chunichi Dragons and never had fewer than 13 homers in a season. I obviously knew nothing about Fukodome, but Bobby Valentine and Trey Hill-man, who had seen a lot of him when they managed in Japan, both said he could handle major-league pitching and would potentially be a big asset for us.

The Fukodome signing was our only major outside off-season ad-dition. Internally, however, we made a decision that proved to be far more meaningful in 2008, and that was to move Ryan Dempster, who'd done a nice job as my closer in 2007, into the starting rotation. Dempster was the ultimate team player. He'd been a starter his whole career until 2004, when the Cubs moved him into the bullpen and then asked him to be their closer because they essentially had no-body else with his experience and know-how.

To replace Dempster as closer we embarked on a bold but calcu-lated experiment with Kerry Wood. Signed by the Cubs out of Grand Prairie High School in Texas as the fourth overall selection in the 1995 draft, Kerry burst into the majors in spectacular fashion, tying the major-league record of his fellow Texan Roger Clemens with 20 strikeouts in his fifth career start, in May of '98. He went on to win

National League Rookie of the Year honors, but soon afterward he blew out his elbow and missed the whole '99 season with Tommy John surgery. He was able to come back from the elbow surgery with three stellar seasons from 2001 to 2003, including leading the league in strikeouts in '03, and was on his way to establishing himself as one of the all-time great Cubs pitchers when he started experiencing shoulder issues.

When I got there in 2007, Kerry was recovering from a torn rotator cuff. Hendry and I agreed that, with his durability a question, Kerry might be better suited for the bullpen. But then he encountered more elbow pain in spring training and we had to put him on the 60-day disabled list. When he finally did come back, in August, he pitched exceedingly well as Dempster's setup man—enough so that Hendry and I felt, with his velocity and plus breaking ball, he could possibly be a dominant closer for us. Kerry was such a popular player in Chicago—just a super guy—that I took some heat from the media and the fans when we activated him from the DL on August 3, and I brought Bob Howry, our other setup reliever, into the game that day instead of him. Howry actually got a standing ovation from the Wrigley fans, who just assumed it was Kerry coming in from the bullpen. I later explained I wanted Kerry to "have a softer landing" from his long stint on the DL, delaying his return until two days later when we were down by four runs against the Mets.

Our other significant internal move for 2008 was to turn the catching over to the rookie Geovany Soto. Soto was an excellent "catch and throw" guy who knew how to call a game and had hit .380 down the stretch in '07 as a September call-up.

Looking over the team in 2008 spring training, I felt we had a good nucleus of professionals, none more so than Derrek Lee, my first baseman, who finished his career with a lifetime .281 average and 331 homers. What a wonderful young man. Came to the park prepared to play every day and cared only about winning. I just had a good feeling about 2008. Managing at Wrigley Field is special—it's like playing in the British Open. You never know what the weather is going to bring, with the wind blowing off nearby Lake Michigan. When the wind is blowing out, you can play long ball and at 1:00 p.m. have a nice, sunny, warm day, only to end up cool and rainy with the wind blowing in at the end of the day, forcing you to do more hit-and-running and stealing. You always had to be prepared to play two different games in one day. It's such a wonderful carnival-like environment, with the fans right on top of you. I used to get tears in my eyes when they'd play the Cubs' fight song, "Go, Cubs, Go." I'm sure the whole environment is very similar to Ebbets Field in Brooklyn.

My message to the team in spring training was, "We have unfinished business. Let's get after it."

Initially, we were hoping Fukodome could take over in center field for the departed Jacque Jones, but after a couple of weeks of watching him out there in spring training, I could see he clearly wasn't comfortable. With all the other adjustments he was trying to make, I moved him to his more natural position in right field and turned center over to Felix Pie, who'd shown defensive skill there in his rookie '07 season, but who really struggled with the bat.

After losing three of our first four games, we started to take off, finishing April 17–10 and tied for first place with the Cardinals. We jockeyed back and forth with the Cardinals for a week and then on May 9 began a stretch of 9 wins in 11 games to go into first place for good. About the only concern I had was Pie's inability to get on base often enough. So on May 14 Hendry resolved the problem by signing Jim Edmonds, who had been released by the Padres five days earlier. I had never really liked Edmonds. I thought he made a lot of catches in center field look more difficult than they were—which earned him a lot of play on the ESPN highlight tapes. Little did I know that, in my team's uniform, I would have a whole different opinion of him. Edmonds, like Derrek Lee, was a consummate professional. At thirty-eight, he had his best days behind him, but he could still play the heck out of center field. He also provided us another left-handed bat, which we needed. Edmonds came over to us with a bit of a chip on his shoulder after being released by the last-place Padres, and finished the season with 19 homers and 49 RBI in 85 games.

Hendry made one other meaningful midseason acquisition, trading for right-hander Rich Harden from the A's for a reserve outfielder, Matt Murton, and three prospects. Harden had once been a young phenom for the A's but missed significant time from 2005 to 2007 with arm issues. He was enjoying an excellent comeback season with the A's when we made the deal for him, and down the stretch for us he was about my most effective starter (5–1, 1.77 ERA, 89 strikeouts in 71 innings). I suppose I should mention here that one of the prospects we gave up in the Harden deal was a third baseman named Josh Donaldson who, at the time, was hitting .217 for our Class A Peoria team. There was no way to foresee that, seven years later, after the A's also traded him, Donaldson would become the American League Most Valuable Player for the Blue Jays.

On Saturday July 12, two days before '08 All-Star Break, I was feeling really good about the way the season was going—we'd been in first place since April 20 and had stretched our lead to 5½ games over the Cardinals—when Peter Chase, the Cubs' media relations director, informed me that my closest buddy in baseball, Bobby Murcer, had passed away from a brain tumor he'd been battling for nineteen months. He was only sixty-two. Poor Bobby had put up a tremendous fight and had even made what we thought was a miraculous recovery when, after extensive treatment at the M. D. Anderson Center in Houston, he'd returned to the Yankees' YES Network broadcast booth in May. A month later, however, the cancer had come back and we talked on the phone about life, fate, and God. Bobby said he'd made his peace with the Lord and was prepared for whatever He intended for him. He said that if the Lord kept him around, great; otherwise, he'd be going up to see Him. It was sad, but it was also comforting for me, knowing Bobby was at peace. Still, even though I knew the gravity of Bobby's situation, I wasn't prepared for it to happen so fast.

So many thoughts and memories began rushing through my head: That last night Bobby and I had shared with Thurman in Chicago; the home run Bobby hit at Yankee Stadium the night after we got back from Thurman's funeral; our running "where's my bunter?" joke; the image of him sitting in his rocking chair in front of his locker—the one Sparky Lyle cut the legs off—just gazing around the clubhouse with that impish smile on his face. I thought back nine years earlier, to that September morning in 1999 when we all had gathered in Hertford, North Carolina, to bury Catfish, who'd fought a similar courageous battle with an equally dreaded affliction—ALS. Little did we know that two years later Anita's dad would die of the same devastating disease. My three best friends with the Yankees, Thurman, Catfish, and now Bobby, all gone, way before their time. I knew I would no longer have that feeling of being forever young.

We finished the 2008 season 97–64, the most wins in the National League, 7½ games in front of the Brewers. We led the league in runs, OPS, and walks, while Rothschild's pitchers were third in ERA and WHIP and led the league in strikeouts. Soto hit .285 with 23 homers and 86 RBI and was named NL Rookie of the Year. Five of my regulars—Lee, Ramirez, DeRosa, Soriano, and Sosa—hit 20 or more homers. Dempster, in his return to the rotation, emerged as the ace of the staff (17–6, 2.96 ERA). Ted Lilly was 17–9, Zambrano, 14–6, and Wood saved 34 games with 84 strikeouts in 66⅓ innings in his first season as a closer. About the only disappointment was Fukodome, who was hitting .280 going into the All-Star Break and went into a major fade the second half, ending up at .257 with 10 homers, with only three after July 13. Overall, however, it was one of the best teams I ever managed, which is why a second straight losing sweep in the NL Division Series—this one to Joe Torre's Dodgers—remains one of the biggest disappointments of my entire career.

Before the series, I told my team, "Just play like we did all season and good things will happen," and I fully expected they would. But in the first game, Dempster uncharacteristically struggled with his command and I had to get him out of there in the fifth inning after he'd walked seven. By that time, we were down 4–2 and were never able to overcome that. Game 2 was just a blowout, 10–3, starting with the Dodgers scoring five runs in the second on Zambrano. Because he had pitched so well for us the last three months, I gave Harden the game 3 start, passing up Lilly, and while this one went much better, the two-run double by James Loney off Harden in the first inning proved to be all the runs the Dodgers needed to complete the sweep. Just like the year before against Arizona, our hitters almost completely shut down, scoring only six runs in the three games. I don't have an explanation for it except maybe we played tight, but I didn't sense that. It was truly baffling to me. We didn't see a single left-handed pitcher in the entire series. I was experienced in the postseason, used to competing and winning, and that damn Torre beat me again. He probably sold that same "underdogs" theme to the Dodgers before the series.

There's not a whole lot you can do when your best pitchers have back-to-back bad days and your hitters don't hit. My one other big disappointment is that I didn't get Lilly a start. Lilly was such a competitor—remember, we'd paid $40 million to sign him in 2007—and when Soriano struck out for the final out of the game, Lilly let his anger and frustration be known, taking a bat to the plumbing on the runway up to the clubhouse. After a few swings, he broke one of the pipes and water came cascading down the runway as we were trying to make our way back to the clubhouse. Far be it for me to say anything to him!

"Lilly was one of our favorite guys on the team," said DeRosa. "Everybody loved him for his competitiveness and his dry humor. One of the funniest incidents in my two years with the Cubs was early in the '08 season. We were playing the Pirates in Pittsburgh, leading seven to nothing in the fourth inning, when Lilly suddenly started losing it. He was really getting knocked around, so much so that Lou finally had to come get him. But as Lou walked to the mound, he didn't realize his fly was open. I'm watching from second base and I'm cracking up. When he got to the mound, Lilly pointed to Lou's fly and said, 'What are you doing out here? Selling hot dogs?' Lou looked down and tried to stop from smiling. 'No,' he said, 'I'm here to take you out because you're getting your ass kicked!'"

After the season, it was pointed out to me I was only the second manager in history, along with the Hall of Famer Dick Williams, to win 90 or more games with four different teams, and I'd also been the first Cubs manager to have back-to-back first-place finishes since Frank Chance (of "Tinker-to-Evers-to-Chance" Cubs lore) way back in 1907–08. It gave me some measure of satisfaction having achieved something that hadn't happened in one hundred years—as did the Baseball Writers Association voting me my third Manager of the Year award. But I never went into professional baseball for awards or records. All that ever mattered to me was winning. As I took my seat on the plane next to Hendry for the long flight back to Chicago, I could hear Mr. Steinbrenner's admonishment ringing in my ears: "Ninety-seven wins. Not good enough."

CHAPTER 15

Alex Heartbreak, Bradley Madness, and a Windy City Farewell

I was still feeling the sting over the rude and abrupt ending of the 97-win 2008 season when Jim Hendry called me in early December with more bad news: the Tribune Co. under Sam Zell was filing for Chapter 11 bankruptcy protection, which meant we were probably going to have to start trimming payroll.

I turned sixty-five in August 2008 and I was thinking how, when Sam Zell sold the Cubs, I would be working for the fifth different owner in seven years. The lure of the Cubs job had been to do what no manager had done in one hundred years—win a World Series—and the Cubs' ownership at the time, the Tribune Co., had made a commitment to spend whatever it took to try and accomplish that. I could see now we were already starting to take a step backward in that direction. When I took the Cubs job, I made it clear I wasn't going to be a "lifer," that there was just as much urgency on my part. I always felt—foolishly, I guess—that I could win under any circumstances. But given all this new uncertainty, I began to seriously wonder if that was going to be possible, and I could see my career soon coming to a close.

We had already decided we were not going to be able to afford the two years and $20 million our closer, Kerry Wood, would likely get in the free-agent market. Instead, Jim had traded a prospect to the Marlins for their closer, Kevin Gregg, who was not nearly as dominant as Kerry but who would be making only $4.2 million in 2009. In addition, Hendry told me, he was going to have to unload at least one other contract if he were to have any financial flexibility to get us a much-needed left-handed-hitting outfielder. I was skiing in Colorado Springs on New Year's Eve when Jim called to tell me he had traded Mark DeRosa to the Indians for three low-level prospects who would not see the lights of the major leagues for at least three years. (As it turned out, seven years later, one of those prospects, the right-hander Chris Archer, became an All-Star starting pitcher, though not with the Cubs but Tampa Bay.) A week later, in another money dump, Jim traded Jason Marquis—who'd won 23 games for me as my number four starter over the previous two seasons—to Colorado. Marquis was owed $9.8 million in the final year of his contract.

Needless to say, I especially hated to see DeRosa go, but it would not be for another eight months that his essential replacement would prove to us what an absolute catastrophe the exchange had been in terms of clubhouse chemistry.

At the 2008 winter meetings in Las Vegas, Jim had talks with numerous clubs and even more player agents in an effort to find us a left-handed-hitting outfielder. In addition, he was working on a big deal with the Padres to get us Jake Peavy, the 2007 National League Cy Young winner, when Zell called and told him no more payroll. So we crapped out in Vegas. After the New Year, we had narrowed down our outfielder search to Adam Dunn, who was much better suited for first base or designated hitter, and Milton Bradley, the thirty-one-year-old switch-hitting right fielder who'd already been with six different organizations and had left most of them under less-than-amicable circumstances. We both agreed signing Dunn would create a very untenable defensive situation in our outfield, which was already reshuffled with the retirement of Jim Edmonds, and the necessity of moving Fukodome from right to center. So with the money saved from the DeRosa and Marquis trades, Hendry signed Bradley for three years and $30 million. Before he came to Texas in 2008, Bradley had developed a reputation for being a problem in the clubhouse after numerous verbal clashes with the media, fans, and teammates on his five previous teams. There was also a stamina issue, in that his 126 games with Texas in '08 were the most he'd played in four years. At the same time, if he stayed healthy, Bradley was a talented guy who got on base a lot, and who I could hit almost anywhere in the lineup.

"I knew it was a gamble," Hendry said. "Half of our scouts were against it. Bradley had had all sorts of problems in the past with his temper, but with Texas in 2008, he'd had his best season (.321, 22 HR, 77 RBI, a league-leading .436 OBP, and .999 OPS), and made the All-Star team. Putting his other problems aside—which hadn't appeared to manifest themselves in his one year in Texas—he was the perfect fit for us."

After meeting Bradley for the first time at the Cubs Convention shortly after we signed him, I was inclined to agree. He was very friendly and seemed genuinely excited to be a Cub. I was especially impressed with his knowledge of Cubs history.

Despite the newly imposed payroll constraints that prevented us from making the Peavy deal, I felt that the team we gathered in Mesa in the spring of '09 was, on paper, potentially as good or better than the '08 team. The lineup, with the exception of Bradley, was the same, with everyone still in their prime. In Gregg and Carlos

Marmol, the back end of the bullpen was covered with two guys who could each close, and I looked forward to having a full season of Rich Harden in the starting rotation.

The day before camp was to open, I was in my hotel room in Scottsdale watching an ESPN *SportsCenter* broadcast of a press conference Alex Rodriguez was holding at the Yankees' spring training camp in Tampa. There had been reports about a book that was coming out about Alex and his alleged involvement with steroids, but I hadn't paid much attention to it. Now, however, here he was in an interview with ESPN's Peter Gammons, admitting that in his three years in Texas, 2001–2003, he had in fact been using performance-enhancing drugs. I sat there, watching at first in disbelief, then in utter consternation, and finally in anger, listening to Alex:

> When I arrived in Texas in 2001, I felt an enormous amount of pressure. I felt I had the weight of all the world and I needed to perform and perform at a high level every day. Back then it was a different culture. It was very loose. I was young. I was stupid. I was naive. And I wanted to prove to everyone that I was one of the greatest players of all time. I did take a banned substance, and for that I am very sorry and deeply regretful. . . . I couldn't feel more sorry, because I have so much respect for this game and the people who follow us. And I have millions of fans out there who won't ever look at me the same.

When it was over, all I could feel was a tremendous sense of disappointment. My thought was, *Why? The pressure of the contract?* Watching Alex's admission, I was brought back to that phone call I got from Mr. Steinbrenner in August of '79 informing me that Thurman was dead. Why did Alex have to do this? To prove to everyone he was one of the greatest players of all time? He was already well on his way to proving that in Seattle! The more I thought about it, the more I was mad at Alex for getting involved with that damn stuff, just like I was mad at Thurman for not getting rid of that damn plane.

Alex was in the glory years of his career, both physically and mentally, and all he had to be was himself. There was no reason whatsoever to partake in this foolishness, especially in a smaller hitter's ballpark like Texas'. I thought we'd taught him better in Seattle. People make mistakes. The huge contract I suppose made him feel like he had to be superhuman when, in fact, you're always being paid for what you did in the past. At the same time, the steroids culture was more and more prevalent, and neither the commissioner's office nor the players association had been inclined to do much about it. You had to really stay grounded and disciplined while at the same time being around the right people. We had that for Alex in Seattle, with mentors and role models like Edgar Martinez and Jay Buhner, but when he left us he apparently went astray. He got bad advice.

But as upset as I was at Alex, I also had empathy for him because I knew this stigma was not going to go away. It would haunt and dog him the rest of his career and after it. He was insecure in Seattle and I was aware of that fact. That's why I would tell him almost every day, in Spanish, "You're the best player in baseball. I'm so proud of you," just to buck him up. He needed that encouragement. I wasn't blowing smoke at him. I meant it. He was raised by his mom, and she did a super job, shielding him from the dangers of everyday life. Alex was such a talented kid, but he was also very naive. I think without a father around it led to a lot of his insecurities, and I guess that's why he looked to me as a father figure. I can only guess, with the huge contract, he didn't get that kind of bucking up and reassurance in Texas. He was a super talent who wanted to be recognized that way.

I probably should have picked up the phone, but I've never been the best phone person in the world. I really didn't have a good grasp on the situation, nor did I know exactly the right thing to say to him. I was just deeply saddened.

"We never had any specific conversations about it," Alex said for this book. "But I knew that Lou would never condone that type of behavior by me and I knew that he would be disappointed in me. I knew I'd let him down. In many ways, I revered Lou, much like a dad. It broke my heart to disappoint him.

"If I had talked to Lou more, I know I probably wouldn't have made a lot of the mistakes I made. I always knew Lou's position—to be honest, to be transparent, and to do the right thing. Our conversations since have been a lot more progressive. I have so much love for Lou. I always look at him as a consigliere—if there's any major decision to make, Lou will be my first phone call. In my tough moments, I always hear Lou's voice. He was my professor, my teacher, from my formative years. To this day, when I'm on the field I still hear his voice on how to handle a tough day, how you think about the game, how you put things together. All those things I learned from him. I remember early on, he would be on me, making the double plays the proper way, being in the right place, hit-and-runs. If you missed any of those things it would drive him nuts. But for me, the one thing he especially taught me was accountability. Looking back, I wish maybe I could have had a few more years with him. Some things might have turned out differently."

I didn't talk to Alex for a long time afterward. Just like with Josh Hamilton and the drugs in Tampa, I really didn't know what to say to him. Much as the news about Alex upset me, I still had to focus on my own team.

It did not take long into the 2009 season for Jim's and my concerns about Bradley to be realized. Against the Brewers, on April 12, he came up with a sore groin and I had to limit him to pinch-hitting duties. On April 16, he was called out on strikes in a pinch-hitting appearance and was then ejected—and subsequently suspended for two games—after bumping the home plate umpire, Larry Vanover, in a vociferous argument. At that point, he announced he would not be talking to the media. When I returned him to right field against the Reds, April 22, he went 0-for-4 with three strikeouts, and on his one groundout, he didn't run to first base, even though the throw was bobbled by the first baseman. For that, he was booed repeatedly throughout the game, which we lost, 3–0. At that juncture, he was 1-for-23 with seven strikeouts. When the writers asked me after the game about Bradley not running out the ground ball, I gave him the benefit of the doubt, saying I would not be starting him again until he was healthy.

The next day he ended his boycott of the media, insisting he was "a positive person, an upbeat person," but from then on it seemed that whenever he had any extended sessions with the writers, it was always to complain about the way he was being treated. On May 25, in particular, he made the grievous mistake of suggesting the umpires were out to get him after the Vanover incident: "We're going to get him any time we can. As soon as he gets two strikes, we're going to call whatever and see what he does. Let's try to ruin Milton Bradley."

He ended April hitting .118 and did not get over .200 until May 27. Just prior to that, an eight-game losing streak had put us one game under .500, in fourth place, and I was becoming more concerned with our overall play than I was with Bradley. On May 8 in Milwaukee, we suffered a devastating loss when Aramis Ramirez tore a muscle in his throwing shoulder and was sidelined until July 6. During his absence, we were 24–26 and were saved from falling out of the race before the All-Star Break only by the subpar play of the Brewers, Cardinals, and Reds ahead of us. Besides Ramirez,

Geovany Soto was out for a month in midseason with a shoulder injury, Soriano missed most of September with knee and hamstring issues, Derrek Lee missed 20 games with a back problem, and Bradley missed nearly 40 games. As a result, I was able to use my Opening Day lineup only three times.

My tensions with Bradley boiled over during the Cubs–White Sox interleague game at US Cellular Field on June 26, after he threw a fit in the dugout, throwing his helmet and smashing a Gatorade cooler, causing an eruption of water all over. Not that I hadn't thrown similar tantrums in my day, but I was just tired of Bradley's seemingly constant rage and told him to take off his uniform and go home. I should have let him sit there and stew. Instead, I followed him up the runway to the clubhouse and after he gave me some lip, I yelled at him, "You're the biggest piece of shit I ever managed!" Justifiably mad as I was, that was over the line, especially since it was in earshot of the other players and later leaked out to the press. That night I got a call at home from Peter Chase, the Cubs' media relations director. "We have a problem," he said. "The media all know what you said to Bradley and it's all over the place."

I told Peter I'd address it in the morning. When I got to the White Sox's park the next day, I called Bradley into my office, apologized to him, gave him a hug, and said, "I hope you accept this. I said what I said out of anger and frustration."

It had been building. On June 12, in a game against the Twins, after hitting a two-run double in the sixth, Bradley made a baserunning mistake in the same inning, lost a ball in the sun, and was charged with an error when he caught a ball for the second out in the eighth and threw it to a fan in the bleachers. As I told the writers, "I've looked the other way a lot. I'm done with it."

In addition to my issues with Bradley's temperament, I was just as disturbed with his performance on the field. By June 25, he'd gotten his batting average up to .237 and finished the season at .257, but he wound up hitting far better from the right side (.373/.830 OPS) than he did from the left (.231/.757 OPS)—which is what we got him for. Offensively he didn't do the things we were expecting him to do, and defensively he made a lot of bonehead plays. He had this chip on his shoulder and seldom smiled. He seemed happiest when he didn't play.

My first two seasons in Chicago, we had great clubhouse chemistry. Mark DeRosa and Kerry Wood were a big part of that. That all changed in 2009. I hate to put it all on one player—the clubhouse is my responsibility—but, boy, it was tough. Carlos Zambrano (who was once again suspended six games without pay and fined $3,000, after bumping a home plate umpire, Mark Carlson, on May 27) was temperamental, too, but he was always fighting himself and didn't create problems. Bradley's antics affected the whole team. After a game against the Nationals at Wrigley in August he accused the Cubs fans of being racist, claiming he'd been constantly subjected to racial slurs from the fans in the right field seats, even though our other players maintained they'd seen no evidence of that. "All I'm saying," he told the writers, "is that I just pray the game is nine innings so I can be out there in the least amount of time." Yet another firestorm.

The final straw for us was when Bradley pulled himself out of the starting lineup on September 19 against the Cardinals, then refused to pinch-hit later in the game. That prompted my hitting coach, Von Joshua, to get in his face, and they nearly came to blows. After the game, he launched into another angry diatribe about the media, the fans, and the organization: "You understand why they haven't won in one hundred years here. I need a stable, healthy, enjoyable environment. There's too many people everywhere in your face with a microphone, asking the same question repeatedly. Everything is just bashing you. It's just negativity."

To that, Ryan Dempster responded, "I've been here six years and never had a problem with anyone. The city's great. The fans are great. Sometimes you have to realize the consequences of your actions."

Those consequences were Hendry suspending Bradley for the rest of the season while stating, "It's become intolerable to hear Milton talk about our great fans the way he has."

I fully supported Jim. Bradley wore me out. It was a long damn summer dealing with this every day, and on top of all that, he just didn't perform. He was an angry, troubled young man. In 2013, he was convicted on a domestic violence charge and sentenced to thirty-three months in jail.

Right before the '09 All-Star Break, Zell made it official: he'd agreed to sell the Cubs to the Thomas Ricketts family of Chicago investment bankers, for $845 million. For me, that was another unwanted record: three owners in three years. For Hendry, it likely meant a further hold on payroll and an eventual dismantling of what we'd built there.

We were at .500, 43–43, at the All-Star Break but still only 3½ games out of first place. From July 11 to July 30, we won 13 of 17 and even climbed into first place for six days, from July 26 to August 4. August had often been the cruelest month for me, and this one was no different. After we beat the Rockies, 6–5, in Colorado on August 8, to remain just one game back, I was reminded of the remarkable run the Rockies had made in 2007 when they won 14 of their last 15 regular-season games and then won all seven of their playoff games to get to the World Series. Up to now it had been an up-and-down season in which we never could get a good streak going to take charge of what was a mediocre division. I was feeling somewhat buoyant when I said to the writers, "In 2007, did anyone think the Rockies could get to the playoffs? We're a lot better off than they were that year at this time. It's amazing what a nice winning streak will do for you to make up ground in a hurry." The next two days the Rockies beat us by identical 11–5 scores, and we wound up going 11–17 in August.

There were many reasons for our eventual 83–78 second-place finish in 2009: the fact that we scored 148 fewer runs than in 2008; the loss of Ramirez for two months; Soto (.218) falling victim to the sophomore jinx; Carlos Marmol (65 walks in 74 innings) incurring an alarming lapse of command that gave me pause to use him in the closer's role; Zambrano's being disabled twice with back issues; Soriano battling leg problems all year and driving in only 55 runs; our inability to acquire any substantial help at the trading deadline because of financial constraints; and the absence of any substantial major-league-ready prospects in the farm system. All of those were contributing factors, but none was more so, in my opinion, than the constant clubhouse upheaval caused by Milton Bradley. Good-chemistry teams have a way of playing through injuries and adversity. We just didn't have that in 2009.

Shortly after the 2009 World Series, the Cubs had their organization meetings in Mesa. Ordinarily, we used these meetings to plot our course over the winter—trade possibilities, free agents we planned to target—but as Hendry noted, we were pretty much locked in with the roster we had, the one major objective being to trade Bradley. Rather, the highlight of the meetings was the appearance of Tom Ricketts and his family. On the first day, Ricketts addressed us and outlined his objectives. He talked about how, as a Cubs fan who grew up in the left field bleachers at Wrigley Field, he was so proud to be the team's owner now. He was very passionate about doing what was necessary to finally get the Cubs to the World Series. At the same time, however, he said he was going to do it the right way, which meant building from the ground up. He talked about necessary major renovations to Wrigley Field and our outmoded spring training facility in Mesa, and he talked about restocking the farm system. I was very impressed with everything he said, and I knew in time the Ricketts ownership was going to be successful.

The only major acquisition Jim made that winter was the signing of the free agent center fielder Marlon Byrd, who'd hit 20 homers with 89 RBI for Texas in 2009. Then, on December 18, Hendry made everyone's day by trading Bradley to Seattle for the right-handed starter Carlos Silva in a straight salary-dump exchange.

I wish I could say the jettisoning of Bradley made everything well again. There was no question the clubhouse chemistry was greatly improved, but we just didn't play very well. After flirting around .500 for most of April, we fell under it May 4 and never got back. After a string of 9 losses in 11 games in May, Hendry came down to the clubhouse for a talk with me and our hitting coach, Rudy Jaramillo, whom he'd hired away from Texas over the winter. At the time, we were at the bottom half of the league in runs and Hendry wanted to know what was wrong and what could be done about it.

"This is a three-year program," Jaramillo answered.

"Three years?" exclaimed Hendry. "I'm on a three-*month* program!"

I guess Rudy thought he had more time.

As it turned out, I, too, was on a three-month program. As the losing continued—by June 12, we were 27–35—I was growing more and more frustrated. The team was trying, giving me effort, but it was clear that my veteran core—Lee, Ramirez, and Soriano—were all beginning to slow down. At the same time, there was almost constant media speculation about my future, with my contract expiring at the end of the season. It seemed like there was always some sort of blowup when we played the White Sox in the intracity interleague series. Before the first game against the White Sox, on June 11, I was asked a question about my two rookies, the shortstop Starlin Castro and the center fielder Tyler Colvin, who were gradually working their way into the lineup. This reminded me of some critical remarks made about me by a White Sox TV broadcaster, Steve Stone, a former Cy Young Award winner. Three days earlier, Stone had suggested I was retarding the progress of Colvin, who he maintained should be playing every day.

I explained to the writers I had four other proven, veteran outfielders—Soriano, Fukodome, Byrd, and Xavier Nady—who also deserved to play, and that it was just not fair to abandon one or two of them. Then I laid into Stone by saying, "What job has he had in baseball besides talking on television or radio? What has he ever done? Why isn't he farm director and bringing some kids around? Why isn't he the general manager? Why hasn't he ever put the uniform on and been the pitching coach? Why hasn't he been a field manager? There are thirty teams out there who could use a guy's expertise like that. I'm tired of some of these guys."

Stone maybe had a point that Colvin was providing some young energy for us. But he was also striking out a lot and I was trying to bring him along slowly. Stone was very opinionated and I was never one to take criticism well. In this case I just felt he should stick to commenting on his own team, the White Sox. I actually like Stone. I'd admired his competitiveness as a pitcher, and he does know his baseball. With my pal Hawk Harrelson, the Sox's lead broadcaster, serving as mediator, we were able to patch things up.

Two weeks after my flap with Stone, in the first game of the second Cubs–White Sox series, my ever-volatile number one starter, Carlos Zambrano, had another temper tantrum, this one with my team leader, Derrek Lee. Zambrano had apparently gotten upset when Lee, who was playing in for a possible bunt, was unable to make a play on Juan Pierre's hard-hit leadoff double down the right field line in the first inning. After the inning, in which the White Sox went on to score four runs, Zambrano went after Lee in the dugout and we had to separate the two. For me, this was just another thing I'd had enough of, having to explain to the media why these periodic meltdowns by one of my players weren't symptomatic of discord on the entire team. In announcing he was suspending Zambrano indefinitely and sending him to anger-management classes, Hendry said it all: "His conduct is unacceptable. We'll play with twenty-four before we tolerate that kind of behavior. His actions toward his teammates and staff were unacceptable. This has become a bit of a tired act."

It was around that same time Hendry approached me about my contract situation and asked me if I would be interested in signing an extension. I told him I didn't think so, that after the season I was probably going to pack it in. He wasn't happy. From that point on our relationship began to deteriorate. But I had my reasons. I was sixty-six and wasn't sure what direction the team was going in, although I suspected from Ricketts's comments that the Cubs would probably want to start tearing it down and building it back up from within. In addition, my mom's health was failing and I was anticipating needing to spend more time closer to home.

As the season approached the All-Star Break with no substantial improvement in our play, my blood sugar was going through the roof. In 2004, I had been diagnosed with type 2 diabetes, which was a bit of a wake-up call for me and, among other things, caused me to give up smoking cold turkey. During the course of my time with the Cubs I had many discussions about diabetes with Ron Santo, the Cubs' iconic third baseman and broadcaster who had suffered from the disease since he was a teenager. Ronnie was my favorite dinner companion on the road, just a super guy, who fought diabetes gallantly and without complaint after it had necessitated the amputation of the lower half of both his legs in 2001 and 2002. After the first amputation, of his right leg, he joked, "It was just a flesh wound!" Poor

Ronnie. He bled Cubbie blue, and I think he suffered more than I did after losses. We'd go out to dinner after a bad loss and I'd wind up having to console *him*! We'd talk about the Hall of Fame and how it kept eluding him, and of the 1969 season when the Cubs were overtaken by the Mets and how that fed even more into the superstitions surrounding the Cubs. In 2010, I could see that he was really starting to struggle. The bladder cancer he'd been diagnosed with in 2003 had come back and the diabetes was continuing to wreak havoc on his system. But he soldiered on, until finally surrendering to it all on December 3. The real tragedy of Ronnie's life was that he didn't live to see the day, December 5, 2011, when he was finally given his due with his election to the Hall of Fame by the Golden Era Veterans Committee.

I was in my apartment in Chicago the morning of the 2010 All-Star Game, July 13, watching ESPN's *SportsCenter* when the news came across that George Steinbrenner had died of a heart attack in a Tampa hospital, a little more than a week after his eightieth birthday. I knew Mr. Steinbrenner's situation had been deteriorating, but not to that extent. The previous winter Malio and I had gone over to his house with some stone crabs from Malio's restaurant, and he seemed genuinely happy to see us and didn't appear frail or ill. As I watched the coverage of Mr. Steinbrenner's death, with all the highlights of his career, I felt a tremendous sense of sadness. In one way I thought of him as my dad. Other times, I hated him. He was very tough on me. He could be one of the most entertaining and fun people to be around, but also a royal pain in the ass. He knew how to get under your skin when he wanted something. We got along much better after I left the Yankees. Whenever I brought my teams to Yankee Stadium, if he was in town, I'd try to stop up to his office, just to say hello.

I thought about all the good times I'd spent with him in New York and Tampa—the three-year contract he gave me when I was almost done . . . and the World Series we won together. I tried not to think about the bad things. He always hated the All-Star Game. Never wanted us to participate in it for fear of injuries. Rather, he wanted us to take those three days to rest. Remembering that brought a smile to my face. *Leave it to Mr. Steinbrenner to upstage the All-Star Game*, I thought. Later that day, I called the Yankees to find out about the services. I was informed there would be none and that the funeral was going to be private. Suddenly, I felt very empty. I had never gotten the chance to tell him how I felt about him, never really gotten proper closure. So this one really hit me hard. It hurts to this day, every time I think of him.

The death of Mr. Steinbrenner only further fortified my decision to retire after the 2010 season. After talking it over with Hendry, we decided it might be best to announce it right away, so my contract situation wouldn't become a lingering distraction the rest of the season. Before our game with the Astros at Wrigley, July 20, I shared with the media that I would be hanging it up at the end of the season. I told them managing the Cubs had been a wonderful experience—which it was—and that there was no way I wouldn't cherish my memories in Chicago. "But I've been away from home since 1962," I added. "That's about fifty years."

When I was asked why I didn't just step down immediately, I replied, "I signed here for four years. I'm going to honor my contract."

Hendry was happy I'd made my decision public because it gave him more time to evaluate his options for a successor. In retrospect, it was one of the worst things I could've ever done. Once the players know the manager isn't coming back, there's a different attitude knowing they're playing for a lame duck. I could feel it. Then, on July 29, I got a call from my aunt in Tampa informing me that my uncle Joe Magadan had died of an aneurism burst. Even though he was ninety-two, his death was almost as big a shock to me as Mr. Steinbrenner's. Uncle Joe had been one of my earliest baseball coaches on the Tampa sandlots and had taught me the rudiments of the game—as he'd done with his son, Dave, who'd gone on to a very successful sixteen-year career in the big leagues, later becoming a batting coach for a number of teams. Now, within the course of just a couple of weeks, two of the men who'd been closest to me, Mr. Steinbrenner and Uncle Joe, were gone.

As soon as I got word about Uncle Joe, I packed a bag and headed right to the airport without going to the ballpark. I put Alan Trammell in charge of the team and asked him to give my apologies for leaving so abruptly. I knew the players weren't happy I hadn't informed them personally. When I got home to Tampa I saw firsthand how much my mom's heart was failing. She would have these periodic spells where she couldn't breathe, and for the next few weeks I'd get regular calls from my aunt, who'd become her caretaker, warning me about how grave her condition was becoming.

Two days after my uncle's death, Hendry traded Ted Lilly to the Dodgers for three prospects—a signal to everyone he'd given up on the season. From July 27 to August 22, we were 5–20 and fell into fifth place, 21½ games behind. The final death knell to the season was Hendry's trade of Lee to the Braves for three more prospects on August 18.

Between my concern for my mom and my own state of mind, I felt I needed to go home immediately, rather than waiting until the end of the season. I expressed my feelings to Jim, and he couldn't have been better about it. On August 22, the Cubs had a nice retirement tribute for me at Wrigley Field after our game against the Braves. In addition, they told me they were going to pay my salary for the season, something they certainly didn't have to do. It was one of the most emotional days of my life, not the least because of the presence of Bobby Cox in the other dugout, who was also retiring as a manager after the season. Coxie had been there at the beginning of my journey, as a Triple-A manager and spring training instructor with the Yankees when I joined them in 1974. He also coached first base for Billy Martin in 1977, and it was very apparent the high esteem with which he was held in the organization. Even then, there had been talk of Bobby being an heir apparent for the Yankees' managing job, but nobody was surprised that he went off and became one of the greatest managers in baseball history with first the Blue Jays and then the Braves. There's a certain bond among guys who worked for the Yankees and Mr. Steinbrenner, and that's why having Bobby there that day seemed all the more appropriate for me. I cry easily anyway and I was barely able to get through my postgame press conference. "I get emotional," I said, through my tears. "I'm sorry. This is the last time I'm gonna put a uniform on." Earlier, I had told the media, "My mom needs me home and that's where I'm going."

It turned out my mom was a tough old lady and lived another year and a half, but she really struggled. Periodically her lungs would fill up with water and she couldn't breathe, and we'd have to rush her to the hospital, where she'd spend a couple of days. Those incidents really frightened her. It was in mid-January 2012 when her heart really began to give out and she was admitted again to Saint Joseph's Hospital. Shortly thereafter, she lapsed into a coma and was put on a respirator. After it became clear she wasn't going to recover, we made the decision to remove her from the respirator. She kept fighting right to the end of her ninety-two years. I was right there with her when she breathed her last breath. Her suffering was over. I'm forever grateful I was able to be with her. She had always been my rock.

At the same time, I've come to really regret not finishing out that last season with the Cubs. I think about it a lot. I've never been one to walk away from the battle. I just got caught up in the moment. My mom was happy I came back home, but she even said I should've stayed and finished out the season.

I was sincere when I told the media at that last press conference how much I truly appreciated managing the Cubs. I enjoyed my time with Hendry. He was an excellent boss to work for and kept all his promises to me. The Cubs are a landmark organization, with intensely loyal fans and a long tradition of special players. One of the great pleasures of my time there was having iconic Cubs like Ernie Banks, Billy Williams, Fergie Jenkins, Andre Dawson, and Rick Sutcliffe come around in spring training. And those Cub Conventions in January! I never experienced anything in baseball of that magnitude, where the fans would come from all over, and the old Cubs would speak to them, hold seminars with them, and sign autographs for hours. Three or four days of absolute craziness—and that was when they were still working on that century-long drought without a World Series championship that finally ended in 2016. I only wish I could've been the one to end it for them.

It would have been nice to end on a winning season, to have won one more championship, but I am immensely proud of my 1,835 victories, which are the 14th most of all the managers in baseball history—and 355 more than my old nemesis, Weaver. (Sorry, I just had to point that out!) I was also flattered when three or four teams called over the next couple of years to inquire if I'd be interested in managing them. It would have been great to get 2,000 wins—and I would've, had I not gone home to Tampa for those three years with the Devil Rays. But I can't have any regrets over putting family first. I just didn't think I had the stamina to put up with the grueling eight-month baseball schedule anymore. That's why I was thankful to my old friend Brian Sabean for offering me a "soft landing" in 2011. I'd blown my chance to manage the Giants for Brian, but here he was again, wanting to hire me as a special assistant to scout for him out of Tampa, which I jumped at. The Giants, under Sabean, were like a Yankees' "old home society," with so many of my former Yankees teammates and Yankees I managed—Dick Tidrow, Chicken Stanley, Dave Righetti, Steve Balboni, Joe Lefebvre, Roberto Kelly, Hensley Meulens—all working for them in various capacities.

The 2011 season was one of the most enjoyable of my life. I was able to watch baseball games without the stress while still feeling I had something to offer. The only reason I gave it up after one year was because Brian wanted me to expand my role into a more full-time job. That would have required much more travel, frequent trips to San Francisco, and likely an extended period of time in Arizona for spring training. After a half century on the road, I spent 2012 getting used to honing my golf game, fishing with my sons, Derek and Lou Jr., and spending time with my daughter, Kristi, and my five granddaughters.

Home in Tampa, enjoying this life of leisure in the early months of 2013, I was reading the almost daily accounts in the local newspapers about another budding steroids scandal for baseball involving a Biogenesis clinic in south Florida. Until this time, I didn't even know what Biogenesis meant or was, but the more I read about this clinic and its activities, the more I came to realize it had everything to do with the distribution of performance-enhancing drugs, in particular human growth hormone. According to the newspaper accounts, a number of prominent major leaguers were linked to this clinic and its founder, Anthony Bosch—most notably, Alex. Had he once again become a prodigal son? Apparently so.

As the investigation by Major League Baseball dragged on through the spring and summer, more and more revelations came out about Alex's relationship with this fellow Bosch until, on August 5, it was announced that he and twelve other players, including Bartolo Colon and Nelson Cruz, had been suspended. The twelve other players received 50-game suspensions, but in Alex's case it was 211 games, which meant Commissioner Selig had determined he was the ringleader of sorts in this whole Bosch-Biogenesis mess. My reaction was surprise. All summer I'd been hoping it wasn't true. It was hard for me to believe that Alex would once again be involved with performance-enhancing drugs. The only explanation was that he was thirty-eight, had undergone two hip operations, and was starting to feel a natural erosion of his skills. Why else?

I was deeply saddened, but I was also very concerned about what this had done to his career and his reputation in baseball. In the weeks after, as Alex appealed his suspension and hired some high-powered lawyers to fight the case for him, I could see this thing was starting to get out of control. Then when I read the reports of him storming out of his hearing with the arbitrator, and his supporters demonstrating outside the commissioner's office, calling the Yankees' president, Randy Levine, "the devil," I winced. Levine and Alex had been going back and forth over Alex's physical situation all summer and how this latest suspension would affect the home run–milestone performance clauses in his contract. That was apparently a war within the war. I personally liked Levine, who I know was very close to Mr. Steinbrenner. He was instrumental in bringing me back into the Yankees' fold, as a part-time broadcaster for the YES network in 2012. He essentially told me I could do anything I wanted—scouting, advising, tutoring the minor-league hitters—in the organization. I told him how much I appreciated his offer but that I didn't feel comfortable working as an "outsider" in Yankee GM Brian Cashman's operation.

At the same time, Alex's lawyers were suing Major League Baseball, the Yankees' team doctor, and even the players association for supposedly not protecting his rights. I hated reading about this circus up there in New York. Alex was conducting a scorched-earth defense in which he was seemingly now at war with everyone. He was getting terrible advice. Alex was smart enough to make his own decisions, and for whatever reason, he wasn't.

It got to the point where I felt I needed to talk to him. It was sometime in early January 2014 when we finally spoke, and I told him, "You've got to face the music here. You have to come clean. And above all you've got to drop this suit against the union. The union is there to protect the players and you're part of it. If you don't drop this suit, you're going to lose the support of your best allies."

Of all the players I worked with, Alex was one of the most talented. Our friendship, which had begun as that of simply a manager and a player, had evolved into something far more meaningful for both of us. Over the years I'd been blunt with him when I had to. I'd been tough, I'd been funny, but I never told him something just because I knew it was what he wanted to hear. In baseball, there's an unwritten rule when you get into management—"Don't get too close to your players"—and I guess with Alex I violated that quite a few times, more with him than any other player. But remember, I had him as a pup and saw him grow into a man. In a way I felt responsible for his well-being, and seeing him now suing the union, well, I knew that wasn't going to benefit him, and I felt compelled to call and tell him.

I'm glad he listened. In February 2014, Alex did all those things. He dropped all the lawsuits, made peace, and came clean with Selig's deputy of discipline, Rob Manfred. He also wrote a letter of apology to the Yankees' fans and then, right before the start of spring training, held a press conference at Yankee Stadium in which he apologized *again* to the Yankees and the media. From that point on, as his career inexorably came to a close, I was glad to see he was nothing less than a great teammate and willing mentor to the younger Yankees players. It was truly a remarkable "rehabilitation" effort on his part, and I think he succeeded in winning the fans—and even most of the media—back. It did not surprise me at all either that he got rave reviews for his work in the Fox broadcast booth in the 2016 postseason. Alex could do anything he wanted in baseball.

When I saw him at a card convention in Chicago a couple of weeks after the Cubs won the 2016 World Series, he told me he was in the best place he's ever been in. He was free and it felt great. I couldn't have been happier for him. To me, he'll always be an "adopted son"—a good person who made mistakes and worked hard to earn our forgiveness.

CHAPTER 16

Lou-Pinions

At the same time that the scourge of steroids has resulted in inalterably changing the baseball record books, the game itself has undergone significant changes—to the point where it's almost an entirely different game today from when I first broke into the majors for good in 1969.

Free agency, salary arbitration, licensing money for the players, interleague play, wild cards in the postseason, even the designated hitter, those were *negotiated* changes that were all a necessary part of the evolution of the sport. And while there is still lingering debate over the latter, I think most everyone would agree that the other changes were all for the betterment of the game, enabling it to grow into the billion-dollar industry it has become. On the other hand, the newest changes (or rather innovations) have mostly kind of evolved. They, too, are also having a significant impact on the game, although I'm not sure it's been for the better. As with free agency and everything else, it's going to take time to fully assess the growing emphasis on sabermetrics, instant replay, pitch counts, innings limits for pitchers, and shifts. The same, I guess you could say, would apply to the steroids issue.

I have my opinions about all of them, and since I have the floor here, I'd like to take this opportunity to share them.

STEROIDS

I admit that because of my relationship with Alex, I am conflicted with this issue. I have been asked many times whether I would have done steroids as a player had they been so readily available as they were a decade later. I have also been asked whether I would vote for players who did steroids for the Hall of Fame. Here is my response to those questions: When I was a player, I was never in to bodybuilding and weight training. As such, I never equated adding muscle mass to increased success in hitting a baseball. (One winter, back in the '80s when I was playing for the Yankees, Mr. Steinbrenner sent a Nautilus machine to my house. I remember opening up the box and it looked like a torture machine. So I wrapped it back up and put it in my basement. Every day, I'd walk past it from the garage and tell Anita, "Remind me to call Goodwill about that.")

At the same time, I can understand those players, beginning in the mid '90s, looking around the clubhouse seeing their teammates bulking up and suddenly putting up big power numbers—which then translated into equally inflated contracts—and feeling compelled to do steroids themselves, just to be on an even playing field. I'm just glad I was never put in that situation. As I said, I was never into weight training, which is all part of the steroids regimen, so I probably wouldn't have tried them. But I also wouldn't have liked losing my job to someone who suddenly went from a 15-homer guy to a 40-homer guy. I always felt I was underpaid as a player.

Would I vote for players for the Hall of Fame who used performance-enhancing drugs? The answer to that is a qualified yes for those players who had unquestionably great careers, and here's why: For one thing, baseball had no rules in the book prohibiting the use of PEDs when the whole steroids era began, and the sport was in fact celebrating the home run race between Mark McGwire and Sammy Sosa. And even after such rules were in place, it took another few years before Major League Baseball could get the players' union in agreement on a truly comprehensive testing program. So I blame the entire steroids issue on the era and the fact that nobody—not the commissioner, the players union, the owners, or even the US government—was able to get a handle on it before it got out of control.

I know in Alex's case, he was a great player before he got involved with steroids and, by his natural ability alone, was a great player his whole career. He didn't need PEDs. I realize maybe I'm the one who's sounding naive here, but I truly believe he'd have hit as many homers as he did without PEDs. He was that great. On the other hand, Barry Bonds, who never tested positive, hitting 73 home runs at age 37? Therein lies the problem—especially when you stop to realize that there were a lot of very good, Hall of Fame–worthy players—Fred McGriff comes to mind—who didn't use PEDs and were hurt by the steroids era when their previously Hall of Fame career numbers were dwarfed by players who used PEDs but were not nearly as good. So it's really difficult. That's why, for me, I would just have to vote on what I saw. I think when it comes to steroids, we have to chalk up this regrettable era for what it was, baseball's version of the untamed wild, wild west, and be thankful that the powers that be were finally able to get a grip on it, and move on without looking back.

SABERMETRICS

Call it the invasion of the Ivy League mathematicians. Every team in baseball now has a small army of math wizards working in the front office, breaking down every aspect of the players to determine their value. When people say a pitcher's wins or a hitter's RBI are two of the most meaningless statistics in baseball because they are both dependent on the performance of other players, I get it. I understand in this new age baseball there are many far more comprehensive formulas to evaluate players, but in my opinion it's becoming way too complicated. The favorite stat among the sabermetric crowd is WAR, or wins above replacement, whatever that means. It's a stat so vague and complicated, even the creators of it can't seem to agree on what it should be made of. Yet most of the baseball executives and baseball writers today use it as gospel. What it is, essentially, is an approximation formula designed to lump everything about a player (minus makeup, instincts, and intellect, of course) into one number—which the sabermetrics folks have deemed an exact measurement. What they're doing is turning human beings into a statistic. Scary, if you ask me.

Meanwhile, do I really need to know how fast a struck baseball gets out of the ballpark? How does that help a manager win a ball game? It's interesting that we are now able to calculate such things as bat speed in baseball, but I could always tell which batters hit the ball the hardest just by the sound of the bat. You should be able to see bat speed with your own eyes.

Everyone is interested in winning baseball games, and data and stats are a big part of that. Every team has essentially the same data, but while technology is useful, you still have to rely on your basic instincts. When a critical decision comes up on the field, you're not going to be able to call Siri or Alexa to tell you what the best way to go is. Imagine Billy Martin sitting in the dugout with an iPad! You have to know what's in the player's head, and all the data in the world can't tell you that. I'm not dismissing data—I like percentages and used them frequently. The more you keep the percentages on your side, the more games you're going to win. What bothers me is that all this advanced technology baseball is using today doesn't account for the human element, and that's where scouting comes in. The most important criteria in evaluating a player is makeup, and you can find that only by watching players every day, learning their tendencies, and getting to know what's in their hearts and their heads. Whom do you value and rely on more—the guy with a PhD from Harvard who crunches numbers in his computer, or the scout who actually sees the player and gets to know him? I understand there's a value in both, but there seems to be more and more emphasis in baseball being put on the former, and I think that's a mistake. Example: During a game, managers will be sent defensive alignments from above which have been calculated by the sabermetrics staff. But these alignments don't take into account whether the pitcher is tired or what pitches are working best for him at that stage of the game. That's why I always gave my pitchers the final say on defensive alignments.

The sabermetrics folks are also at war with the bunt—which I always felt was one of the most important strategic weapons in my manager's toolbox. If it were up them, the bunt would become extinct—their argument being that sacrifice bunts result in outs about 96 percent of the time, along with the lead runner being thrown out 17 percent of the time, and a double play being turned about 8 percent of the time. At the same time, they point out that base stealers are successful around 72 percent of the time, so wouldn't you rather have that, with no outs, than an 83 percent chance of having a runner at second with one out? I'm not arguing with those stats. What I am saying here is that when it comes to using the bunt, it's not all just statistics. It depends on the circumstances and—again—the human element.

Let's be clear about this: I would never ask my 3-4-5 hitters to bunt. Nor would I try to sacrifice with a decent runner on first and a pitcher who's slow to the plate with his pitches and a catcher with a below-average throwing arm. But with no outs, runners at first and second, and a slow-footed double play guy at the plate, your options are either to hit-and-run or bunt the runners over. The idea is to advance the runners whichever way you can and put the pressure on the other team. Here's where you have to know your players' abilities. Does my batter have the ability to execute a bunt in this situation? That's why when I was managing, we spent a lot of time in spring training working on bunting. Ask Carlos Guillen if that didn't pay off for him in the third game of the 2000 American League Division Series when I asked him to drop a bunt down between the pitcher and White Sox first baseman Frank Thomas with Rickey Henderson at third base.

I probably hit-and-ran as much as any manager in baseball. Conversely, using the bunt in the right way, advancing runners to second or third, especially with no outs, is an important strategy. I don't need statistics to tell me scoring from second base is a lot easier than scoring from first, and when you put a runner on third, it changes a lot of the strategy. Now all of a sudden you have to guard against your pitcher bouncing a curveball. As I said, I like putting pressure on the other team to execute, and the bunt can help you do that. But I fear because of sabermetrics it's becoming a lost art.

INSTANT REPLAY

I understand the argument for getting the calls right, but baseball is a game, not a science. I don't think it was made to be perfect. Yeah, it's nice to get the calls right. I just don't like the idea of waiting for someone in the clubhouse to look at the tape and call the dugout to decide whether to challenge or not. There's a close play at second and the manager puts up his hand and shouts, "Stay right there until we review it!" It slows the game down and, in my opinion, demeans the umpires. It at least has to be more instantaneous, and I'm not sure how you can do that. At the same time, the game had been played for over one hundred years without replay booths.

One of the problems with instant replay is that managers began relying on the technology from the clubhouse video room during games to argue about balls and strikes, prompting an increase in ejections. I got a chuckle when, in 2016, Joe Torre, MLB's head of on-field operations, sent out a memo scolding the managers for using the replay video to bolster their arguments with the home plate umpire's pitch-calling. Calling this conduct "highly inappropriate," Torre maintained it undermined the integrity of the umpires on the field and delayed the games. Huh? Doesn't the very nature of instant replay undermine the umpires? The 2016 season was the first time more than 50 percent of the umpires' challenged calls were overturned, and it's continued to go upward. (When I saw that, I thought, *I should be getting 50 percent of my fine money back!*) As for this extra beefing by the managers over ball and strike calls delaying games, say it ain't so, Joe! Your 66 ejections are ninth on the all-time list, three more than mine!

That's what I really don't like about instant replay. It has eliminated managers coming onto the field to argue calls. Say what you will about this also slowing the game down, there was entertainment value in manager-umpire confrontations. Pretty soon we'll have four robots umpiring the games along with someone in New York looking at replays. Like sabermetrics, this is another example of the human element being slowly eroded from the game. It's never going to be a perfect game and all umpires are different, especially when it comes to calling balls and strikes—which are not replay challengeable. It's up to managers—and then by extension the players—to get a feel for the umps and then make adjustments.

I realize instant replay would have saved me tens of thousands of dollars in fine money, but it would have been at the expense of my passion. A lot of times I was more than willing to take the fine in an effort to demonstrate to my players that I was fighting for them. Can't do that anymore.

PITCH COUNTS

To me, putting an arbitrary limit of 100 pitches on starting pitchers and holding firm to it is downright foolhardy—especially when you're talking about your top-of-the-rotation starters. I was talking to Tom Seaver a few years ago about pitch counts. He knew in his head what his pitch count max was—about 150—and he was a power pitcher. Nolan Ryan's was about 160, he said. The point is, nobody knows better how many pitches a pitcher has left than the pitcher himself. The batters will tell you when a pitcher is losing his stuff by how they're fouling pitches off. The problem is, starting pitchers today are put on a pitch count limit the minute they sign their first professional contracts and in many cases were on pitch count limits going all the way back to Little League and Pony League.

A vast majority of games are won or lost in the eighth and ninth innings, when the starters today are no longer around, because it's been ingrained in everyone's minds that when they hit the 100-pitch mark, they're starting to lose it and you've got to get them out of there. If you've got a solid number one starter, wouldn't you want him in there in the eighth and ninth innings if he's showing no signs of losing it? I remember with the Yankees, Billy Martin would ask his pitching coach Art Fowler how many pitches Ron Guidry or Ed Figueroa had in the eighth inning and then say, "Good, take twenty off!"

I came up in the era of the four-man rotation and ten-man staffs, and I'd face a starter four or five times during the course of the season. Today, with the five-man rotation, starters get an extra day of rest but, for the most part, throw a lot fewer pitches in a game. Guys like Seaver, Catfish, Jim Palmer, Bob Gibson, Mickey Lolich, Steve Carlton, Jack Morris, and Bert Blyleven would be in open rebellion if they pitched today. The fact is, pitching has become way too specialized, with thirteen-man staffs to accommodate all the late-inning pitching changes that are the result of starters getting pulled after 80 or 90 pitches. That slows the game down more than anything.

I'm not advocating pushing starting pitchers to the limit. I'm just saying use common sense when it comes to trying to win a ball game. I had to do this all the time with Randy Johnson, whose pitch max was around 135 or 140. A few times Randy might have had over 120 or 125 pitches in the sixth inning, and if I had to push him over 140 to get him to the eighth inning, the next time out I'd shorten him up, or give him an extra day's rest. Bottom line: I think we've taken a big step backward in letting pitch counts dictate how a game is managed. How many games have been lost because the manager lifted a still-strong starter after 90 or 100 pitches and turned it over to an inferior reliever?

INNINGS LIMITS

By now you probably get the idea I'm somewhat baffled by the way pitchers are being babied in baseball today. Not only are starting pitchers being limited to 90 to 100 pitches a game, their innings are being even more drastically curtailed. In the '70s heyday of my playing career, it was not unusual for starting pitchers to log 300 or more innings. Rest assured it will never happen again. Even though this was before expansion (and therefore fewer pitchers in the majors), there were 62 pitchers with at least 200 innings in 1976. By contrast, in 2016, only 15 pitchers had 200 innings or more, which, according to the Elias Sports Bureau, was the lowest total in the modern era of baseball. Moreover, the 2016 Cubs-Indians World Series was the first time ever not a single starting pitcher pitched beyond the sixth inning. We've come a long way from Jack Morris–John Smoltz. In case you haven't noticed, six-inning starts have become the norm.

A few years ago, when Bert Blyleven was coming up to his last year of eligibility on the Baseball Writers Hall of Fame ballot, a writer, who had not voted for him up to then, explained to me why he had changed his mind. "It's a different game now," he said, "and pitchers aren't allowed to be what they used to be." He then noted how Blyleven had thrown 60 shutouts in his career, ninth on the all-time list. "How are we going to explain [that] to Bert Blyleven ten years from now when we start electing guys to the Hall of Fame with zero career shutouts?"

There's a reason this is happening, and it isn't just because teams are looking to prevent arm injuries. It's called survival of the fittest, and if baseball was really interested in preserving pitchers' arms, it would cut the season back to 154 games, or even less. With the introduction of wild cards and the expansion of the postseason to three tiers, starting pitchers can wind up getting as many as seven or eight additional starts and 40 to 50 more innings, depending on how far their teams advance in the postseason. That's why from day one of the modern baseball season, managers today are managing with an eye on the postseason and conserving their starting pitchers, especially the young ones, so they'll still have enough left in the tank come October. However, I don't buy the prevailing theory that once a pitcher goes over the 175-inning mark he runs the risk of getting hurt. If you've got good mechanics and you're in good shape, the chances of that are minuscule.

Even though I've always been an offense guy, I enjoyed seeing great pitching duels like Koufax-Marichal, Seaver-Carlton, Hunter-Palmer, or Randy Johnson–Greg Maddux. Sadly, those, too, are gone forever. When two great pitchers match up today, it's a reasonable assumption that neither of them will still be in the game in the eighth inning (and consequently a good chance of not getting a decision), and instead fans will be treated to an endless parade of specialized relief pitchers. Cat-and-mouse percentage strategy aside, is this really good for baseball? Be assured, we will never again see a 300-game winner and, with this trend, 200 wins will soon even be hard to attain. It was interesting to me to hear Baseball Commissioner Rob Manfred suggest in 2016 that maybe, as a way of speeding up games, baseball needs to look into a rule limiting the number of relief pitchers a manager can use in an inning. It would be a drastic measure—which is why I'm sure baseball will never do it—but I'd love to see that implemented. Not only would it serve to speed up games, it might force managers to once in a while ignore that arbitrary 100-pitch limit and let their starters get those critical outs in the eighth and ninth innings.

SHIFTS

What's most concerning to me about all these new innovations and sabermetrics is that so many of them are geared toward preventing runs. There is no better example of this than the preponderance of shifts, which are designed to take away base hits and runs. I don't think the fans want to see offense curtailed. When great hitters like Big Papi, Anthony Rizzo, or Robinson Cano come up, people don't go to the hot dog stands. Why take that away? The left-handed hitters are especially being penalized. With a runner on first, the first baseman has to stay on the bag, opening up a hole on the right side.

Except now, with the shift, the shortstop is playing on the second base side of the bag, the third baseman is at short, and the second baseman is in short right field, all but eliminating that hole.

If I were managing today, in close games I would order my left-handed hitters to bunt or slap the ball to third base, against the shift. I would demand that we work on this in spring training as part of our hitting drills, to use it to our advantage and force the other team to reconsider. No more a respected baseball person than Dodgers' two-time Cy Young pitcher Clayton Kershaw affirmed that when he said, "Mentally for me, I can live with a hard-hit ball getting through the hole as opposed to a soft, cheap ground ball that goes through a place where no one is playing because of the shift." I'm frankly surprised more teams aren't doing this, but as long as they're not, I think there needs to be a limitation on shifting. For one hundred years, teams have positioned players for a hitter pulling the ball, but I don't think playing them *out* of position is right. I think there should be a rule at least preventing the shortstop from playing on the second base side of the bag and vice versa for the second baseman.

In an April 2016 game, Yankees pitcher Nathan Eovaldi lost a no-hitter against Texas on a ground ball that went through the area where the shortstop normally plays because Yankees' manager, Joe Girardi, had the shift on. After the game, Girardi said what I maintain: "It's an illegal defense, like basketball. Guard your man, guard your spot. I just think the field was built this way for a reason—with two men on one side and two on the other." He went on to say if he were commissioner, he would ban the shift. I fully concur. In my twenty-three years of managing, I never once used a shift and somehow still managed to win 1,835 games.

EPILOGUE

As I reflect on my career and life, I recognize that God has blessed me, and I am extremely thankful. In April 2017, I celebrated fifty years of marriage, and I am the proud father of three children, Lou Jr., Kristi, and Derek, along with five beautiful granddaughters: Kassidy, Sophia, Anica, Mia, and Ava.

My whole adult life has been in baseball, as a player, coach, and manager, and I enjoyed every minute of it and learned a lot from my experiences. Losing my best friends, Thurman Munson, Catfish Hunter, and Bobby Murcer, taught me how fickle life can be and that nothing is guaranteed. You slowly realize there are things more important in life other than trophies, rings, and, yes, even the Hall of Fame.

I'd be lying if said I hadn't thought about the Hall of Fame, especially after I passed 1,800 victories and people began telling me that, in the history of baseball, only Joe Torre, Dusty Baker, and I had over 1,500 hits as players and 1,500 wins as managers. I also couldn't help noticing that, of the thirteen managers in history with more wins than I have, only one, Gene Mauch—who had a losing record and never made it to a World Series—was not in the Hall of Fame. (My friend Joe Torre, who's fifth on the all-time wins list with 2,326, played eighteen years in the big leagues and then managed fifteen more years with three different teams without ever getting to a World Series. It wasn't until he went to work for Mr. Steinbrenner that he started winning championships. I could have told him that and saved him a lot of time and anguish!) I am likewise proud of having over 200 more wins than my contemporaries Tommy Lasorda,

Dick Williams, Earl Weaver, and Whitey Herzog, who have all been elected to the Hall of Fame in recent years.

So I felt I had some worthy credentials, but I also knew it was very difficult to get the necessary twelve votes (or 75 percent) from the sixteen-member Veterans Committee. On December 4, I learned just how difficult when the Hall of Fame's president, Jeff Idelson, announced that Bud Selig, the longtime commissioner, and John Schuerholz, the highly accomplished former general manager of the Kansas City Royals and Atlanta Braves, had been elected. Schuerholz was unanimous with sixteen votes and Selig got fifteen. "The only other person on the ballot with more than five votes," Idelson said, "was Lou Piniella with seven."

In the hours waiting at home for the election results, I thought about how strange it was being on the same ballot with Mr. Steinbrenner, who was my boss. I felt sure he'd be elected after all he'd accomplished in baseball—restoring the Yankees dynasty with six world championships, founding of the YES network that sent the value of franchises skyrocketing, and being an early visionary on free agency—and I even wondered if he fell short by one vote if there was a way I could give him one of mine. But he didn't even come close, and I find that really puzzling. Nevertheless, I was particularly happy for Schuerholz, who was the assistant farm director under the highly astute baseball man Lou Gorman with the Royals my first few seasons with them in the early '70s. John and I were both young pups back then and were in the same National Guard reserves unit in Olathe, Kansas, a suburb of Kansas City. One summer, we shared a tent together at Fort Leonard Wood for our two-week active training. The memory of that got me to reflecting on all the great people who came through my life in baseball, many of whom touched me deeply and helped shape me into the player, manager, and person I became.

My passion in baseball was hitting, and I was fortunate enough to have had an excellent batting instructor in the minor leagues in Johnny Lipon (who taught me how to hit the breaking ball), and, on the major-league level, the greatest batting instructor of them all in Charlie Lau. I played for about twenty different managers from 1963 to 1984, but the two who stand out are Bob Lemon and Billy Martin. I played for Lem both in Kansas City and in his two terms with the Yankees. He was a man's man who didn't tolerate fools and he was just a great guy to play for. Billy was my mentor, a brilliant in-game strategist. Because of all the continual off-field drama with him, he wasn't always the most fun guy to play for, but I loved sitting next to him in the dugout watching how he ran a ball game. I will forever cherish the memory of those 1977–78 Yankees world championship teams, which Billy and Lem both managed.

The games I'll never forget: Opening Day, April 8, 1969, with the expansion Kansas City Royals. There I was, leading off, that noted agent of speed, going 4-for-5 and finally launching my career . . . My first and only All-Star Game, July 25, 1972, Atlanta. All three Royals' outfielders, Amos Otis, Richie Scheinblum, and myself, made it, only Earl Weaver, our manager, told me to leave my glove at home . . . I didn't play October 14, 1976, but what a beautiful sight from the bench it was, Chris Chambliss's home run disappearing over Yankee Stadium's right-center-field fence, carrying me to my first World Series . . . The playoff game with the Red Sox, October 2, 1978—this one they were glad I had my glove . . . The night Reggie Jackson became Mr. October, October 18, 1977, hitting three home runs and leading the Yankees to the world championship, which, for most of us, was our first . . . The game for Thurman, August 6, 1979, Bobby Murcer, 2-for-5, singlehandedly winning it with a three-run homer in the seventh and two-run single in the ninth.

When I think about the important dates in my professional life, however, one stands out above all the others: December 7, 1973. That was the day I was traded by the Royals to the Yankees. The best thing that ever happened to me. Were it not for George Steinbrenner, the managing part of my baseball career might never have happened. When it comes to people who had the most impact on my life and career, he was unquestionably number one.

A manager is only as good as the players he has and the people who got him those players. I am privileged to have managed *six* Hall of Famers—Dave Winfield, Rickey Henderson, Barry Larkin, Junior Griffey, Randy Johnson, Goose Gossage—and two more, Edgar Martinez and Alex Rodriguez, who should and hopefully will be in the Hall of Fame. And I was fortunate to have worked for many talented general managers, especially Woody Woodward and Pat Gillick, who made me look good with their knowledge and acumen in putting together a ball club.

I want to thank all those people, my teammates, my players, my coaches, my trainers, my general managers, the owners who hired me, the fans, and all my friends in the media, for being part of this wonderful journey. And while I would be honored to someday join so many of my contemporaries in Cooperstown, I am comforted by the fact that in my family's eyes, I am already in the Hall of Fame as a husband, father, and grandfather. I also realize that, approaching my midseventies, I am in the ninth inning of life, winning the game because of my faith—and that is the greatest comfort of all to me.

ACKNOWLEDGMENTS

The authors would like to thank the following people whose help was significant in the creating, writing, researching, and editing of this book:

Moss Klein, who lived a lot of this Lou history himself and was our dogged and scrupulous proofreader.

Sean Forman's Baseball-Reference.com, the new bible of baseball insofar as the history of the game goes. This book and just about any other future book on baseball could not be written without Sean's "bible."

Steve Hirdt, Tom Hirdt, John Labombarda, and Bob Waterman of the Elias Sports Bureau, who swiftly and diligently provided answers to all the statistical questions that came up along the way in the writing of this book.

Mondy Flores, who provided background history on the city of Tampa and the neighborhood and playing fields where Mr. Piniella grew up.

The Major League Baseball Media Relations Departments—Rob Butcher and Brendan Hader of the Cincinnati Reds; Mike Swanson and Curt Nelson of the Kansas City Royals; Randy Adamack, Tim Hevly, and Ben Van Houton of the Seattle Mariners; Rick Vaughn and Dave Haller of the Tampa Bay Rays; Peter Chase and Steve Green of the Chicago Cubs—which assisted in the procuring of pictures for the book.

Andrew Levy and Tim O'Neill of Wish You Were Here Productions who provided contact information for people interviewed for this book.

Steve Alexander of Octagon Sports and Entertainment Agency for his tireless work editing copy, procuring pictures, and coordinating this entire project.

Jeff Idelson, Jim Gates, and Bill Francis of the National Baseball Hall of Fame, who made available their files and photo resources.

And lastly:

David Hirshey, who had the vision at HarperCollins that *Lou* was a story well worth publishing . . . and Matt Harper, a "baseball guy" who did a superb job of editing the book.

APPENDIX

The Lou Lists

Managers All-Time Wins List

Connie Mack	3,731*	Casey Stengel	1,905*
John McGraw	2,763*	Gene Mauch	1,902
Tony La Russa	2,728*	Bill McKechnie	1,896*
Bobby Cox	2,504*	Lou Piniella	1,835
Joe Torre	2,326*	Bruce Bochy	1,789
Sparky Anderson	2,194*	Jim Leyland	1,769
Bucky Harris	2,158*	Dusty Baker	1,766
Joe McCarthy	2,125*	Ralph Houk	1,619
Walter Alston	2,040*	Fred Clarke	1,602*
Leo Durocher	2,008*	Tommy Lasorda	1,599*

* Hall of Fame

Managers All-Time Ejections List

Bobby Cox	161	Frankie Frisch	80
John McGraw	132	Jim Leyland	68
Earl Weaver	94	Joe Torre	66
Leo Durocher	94	Ron Gardenhire	65
Tony La Russa	87	Lou Piniella	63
Paul Richards	80	Bruce Bochy	61

LOU'S ALL-TIME TEAMMATES TEAM

CATCHER: THURMAN MUNSON—Gritty leader by example. Master handler of pitchers. Great clutch hitter. In many ways our idol on those '70s Yankees championship teams.

FIRST BASE: CHRIS CHAMBLISS—We called him "the snatcher" because of his ability to cover first base and all the incoming throws like a blanket. Quiet, steady, productive hitter, who hit perhaps the biggest home run in Yankees history.

SECOND BASE: WILLIE RANDOLPH—Made every play look smooth and easy around second base, and was no easy out at the plate either.

SHORTSTOP: FREDDIE PATEK—His size (5' 5", 148 pounds) belied his big-time ability. Superior range with great throwing arm afield. Pesky hitter with superior speed who was a three-time All-Star.

THIRD BASE: GRAIG NETTLES—Maybe the smartest player I ever knew and definitely the wittiest. Along with Alex, the greatest third basemen in Yankees history. Six-time All-Star, 390 career HR.

RIGHT FIELD: REGGIE JACKSON—Thought about making him my DH but knew he'd get the ass about that, so I'm starting him in right field. "Mr. October," one of the great postseason players of all-time—and also one of the greatest showmen the game has ever known.

CENTER FIELD: AMOS OTIS—In my opinion, one of the most underrated players of his time. He could do it all. Three Gold Gloves, five-time All-Star. Had power (193 HR) and speed (340 SB). Ten straight seasons of 20 or more doubles.

LEFT FIELD: DAVE WINFIELD—Classy, smart, complete player who hit for average and power. Six 100-RBI seasons for the Yankees. I agree with those who said the most exciting thing in baseball in the '80s was watching him go from first to third with those long, powerful strides.

DESIGNATED HITTER: JOHN MAYBERRY—Big John was one of my favorite guys. Dangerous hitter who was a big ol' teddy bear off the field. My last year in KC ('73), he led the AL in on-base percentage (.417), with 26 HR and 100 RBI. Runner-up AL MVP in '75.

RIGHT-HANDED STARTER: CATFISH HUNTER—Hall of Fame pitcher and person. Money pitcher who won countless big games for the Yankees and, before us, the A's. His first year with us, 1975, led the league in wins (23), innings (328) and complete games (30). You read those last two stats right.

LEFT-HANDED STARTER: RON GUIDRY—His '78 season, in which he led the AL in wins (25–3) and ERA (1.74) and struck out 248, remains one of the greatest single pitching seasons in history. Loved his competitiveness. I always marveled at how all that power pitching could come out of that thin, small (5' 11", 160) frame.

CLOSER: GOOSE GOSSAGE and SPARKY LYLE—Sorry. It was impossible to choose just one here. They were both superior closers—one (Goose) who's in the Hall of Fame and the other (Sparky) who probably should be. Goose was the fiercest competitor I ever knew and Sparky was the coolest.

Lou's All-Time Opponents Team

CATCHER: CARLTON FISK and JOHNNY BENCH—Had to split this one too. Only played against Bench in the 1976 World Series, but it was more than enough to warrant being an all-time opponent: .533, 2 HR, 6 RBI, 4 runs in 4 games. From 1971 to 1979, when they both played against each other, Fisk and Munson were each named to seven All-Star teams, and you have no idea how much that pissed Thurman off.

FIRST BASE: EDDIE MURRAY—One of the most lethal switch-hitters in baseball history. Says it all that he was a first-ballot Hall of Famer despite spending nearly his whole career at war with the Baseball Writers Association.

SECOND BASE: ROD CAREW—Along with Tony Gwynn (whom I never played against), Carew was one of the best contact hitters not only in my time but also in baseball history.

SHORTSTOP: CAL RIPKEN—2,632 consecutive games played, 3,184 hits, 431 HR, 1,695 RBI, and two MVP awards says it all. With Murray and Ripken, it was no wonder Weaver won all those games.

THIRD BASE: GEORGE BRETT—I had the privilege of playing with and against him. We all know how he absolutely killed the Yankees (.358, 6 HR, 14 RBI in 17 postseason games against us, 9 career HR alone versus Guidry and Catfish).

RIGHT FIELD: AL KALINE—Made it all look easy. Complete player. Hit for average (.313 lifetime against the Yankees) and power, and had a rifle for a throwing arm in right field. Would be the captain of my all-class team.

CENTER FIELD: ROBIN YOUNT—Made the seamless transition from shortstop to center field, while collecting 3,142 hits and winning two MVP awards in the process.

LEFT FIELD: JIM RICE—With his short, compact, powerful swing, he hit .330 with 36 HR in 170 career games versus the Yankees. I'll never forget the colossal home run he hit off Matt Keough in July 1983. It was his second HR of the game and traveled nearly 500 feet, off the facade of the third deck in left field at Yankee Stadium.

DESIGNATED HITTER: PAUL MOLITOR—Best right-handed hitter I ever saw. His 3,319 hits are ninth all time.

RIGHT-HANDED STARTER: JIM PALMER—Smooth, fluid delivery with late pop. Won two Cy Young Awards and was 30–16 with a 2.84 ERA against the Yankees. Plus, he was at constant war with Earl Weaver, which made us kindred spirits.

LEFT-HANDED STARTER: MICKEY LOLICH—Don't be fooled by his dough-boy physique. He was a truly nasty curveball specialist, and one of the most durable pitchers of the modern era (four straight seasons of 300-plus innings, 1971–74).

CLOSER: DAN QUISENBERRY—Never gets his due as one of the great closers of all time, because he didn't throw hard. Led the league in saves four times when saves were really (often multiple-inning) saves. Only thing keeping him out of the Hall of Fame was that his career was short.

Lou's All-Time Managed Team

CATCHER: DAN WILSON—This was a real tough call over JOE OLIVER, with whom I won a world championship, but I had Danny longer. He epitomized all the ingredients needed for a field-leader catcher—he handled the pitching staff exceedingly well, had a strong throwing arm, worked hard to make himself into a decent hitter, and was tough as nails, like Thurman.

FIRST BASE: Have to split this one, a righty-lefty platoon, if you will, between DERREK LEE and DON MATTINGLY—They were both great hitters, for power and average, superb defensive first basemen, and team leaders. A privilege to have managed both.

SECOND BASE: BRET BOONE—Confident, cocky, highly productive hitter from a position not often associated with offense. Turned the double play as well as any second baseman I ever saw.

SHORTSTOP: Another position I have to split, this time between ALEX RODRIGUEZ and BARRY LARKIN—I raised Alex in baseball and he will go down as one of the greatest players of all time. Barry had a Hall of Fame career, was a twelve-time All-Star, and was the leader of my 1990 Reds world championship team.

THIRD BASE: ARAMIS RAMIREZ—Very professional hitter for average and power. Had two 100-RBI seasons for me in Chicago, was excellent defensively, and was another quiet leader in the clubhouse.

RIGHT FIELD: ICHIRO SUZUKI—One of the greatest all-around players in baseball history. Led the league in hits seven times, had a lethal throwing arm in right field, and stole 30 or more bases ten times. I was proud to be his manager in his first two years in the big leagues.

CENTER FIELDER: KEN GRIFFEY JR.—Best player I ever managed, who, in his prime, was the best all-around player in baseball. Had six 40-plus homer seasons for me and, with the possible exception of Paul Blair, was the best defensive center fielder I ever saw.

LEFT FIELDER: RICKEY HENDERSON—The greatest leadoff hitter of all time, he had some injury issues when he played for me with the Yankees, 1986–88, but still led the league in stolen bases two out of those three years, en route to being the all-time leader with 1,406.

DESIGNATED HITTER: EDGAR MARTINEZ—One of my last missions in baseball is to get him in the Hall of Fame. From 1990 to 2001 there wasn't a more lethal right-handed hitter in baseball. Had 8 homers and 24 RBI in 34 postseason games for me.

RIGHT-HANDED STARTER: JOSE RIJO—Despite some injuries, he won 44 games for me as the right-handed ace of my 1990–92 Reds teams and was 3–0 with a 2.28 ERA in the '90 postseason.

LEFT-HANDED STARTER: RANDY JOHNSON—When it's all said and done, the Unit will go down as the greatest, most unhittable left-handed pitcher of all time, with four ERA titles and leading the league in strikeouts nine times.

CLOSER: DAVE RIGHETTI—One of the most unselfish players I've ever known. Made the conversion from often-dominant starter to closer at the Yankees' behest in 1984 and led the AL in saves (46) for me in '86.

Lou's All-Red-Ass Team

CATCHER: RICK DEMPSEY—Got his red-ass start with the Yankees with the Pfister Hotel fight with Bill Sudakis in Milwaukee in 1974, then was greatly influenced by Earl Weaver in Baltimore in the art of ballbreaking.

FIRST BASE: DAVID SEGUI—He got the red-ass from both sides of the plate. Set records for throwing helmets when I had him in Seattle from '98 to '99.

SECOND BASE: BRET BOONE—Booney makes two of my all-time teams. Not only was he a productive hitter and elite second baseman, but when he didn't come through at times, the whole dugout heard about it.

SHORTSTOP: RICK BURLESON—There was a reason they called him the Rooster. Prided himself on his fiery intensity.

THIRD BASE: CHRIS SABO—He made me laugh with his tirades. Very unpredictable. You never knew when he was going to go off at something.

RIGHT FIELD: PAUL O'NEILL—He reminded me a lot of myself, but he was more talented. When it came to being a red-ass, he could do it all.

CENTER FIELD: MILTON BRADLEY—This was one red-ass I didn't find funny. Had a perpetual chip on his shoulder. Thought everyone was out to get him and set records everywhere he went for ill-conceived clubhouse tirades.

LEFT FIELD: LOU PINIELLA—Can't leave myself off *this* team. I'm quite proud of it.

DESIGNATED HITTER: ALEX JOHNSON—Boy, could he hit, but had major temper issues—fights with managers, coaches, teammates, sportswriters—that got him traded five times and sold once.

RIGHT-HANDED PITCHER: CARLOS ZAMBRANO—He could be captain of this team. Seemed like he was good for at least two meltdowns a year with the Cubs. He could pitch, but he was really exasperating.

LEFT-HANDED PITCHER: TED LILLY—Don't be fooled by the choirboy face. He had quite a temper if things didn't go his way on the mound and wasn't averse to taking it out on a watercooler or two.

CLOSER: ROB DIBBLE—*See:* our clubhouse wrestling match in 1992.

Lou's Five Best Umpires

NESTOR CHYLAK: He's in the Hall of Fame for a reason. He was at the end of his career when I first came to the big leagues but was still by far the best ump in the American League, especially on balls and strikes. He also had a great wit about him, and you could talk to him.

BILL HALLER: Extremely consistent, especially in the strike zone. Even tempered. You could talk to him too.

JOHN HIRSCHBECK: You never wanted to disagree with him, because he had a brother and that could lead to double trouble down the road. But he was very sound in all aspects of umpiring and would allow you some leeway if you had a beef.

STEVE PALERMO: As technically sound, especially with the rule book, as any umpire I ever knew. Commanded respect and did have a bit of a short fuse. Would've gone down as one of the best umps of all time had he not been cut down and partially paralyzed by a mugger's bullet in Texas in July 1991.

DUTCH RENNERT: One of the marks of a good umpire is that he's seldom involved in any controversial decisions or confrontations. That was Dutch. Unassuming and solid in every way.

(**NOTE:** *I'm not including "God," Doug Harvey, on this list, because I was around him for only a few games during my three years in the National League in Cincinnati.*)

Lou's Top Five Red-Ass Umpires

JOE WEST: "Cowboy Joe" could break balls with the best of them. One particularly hot day in Cincinnati I came running out to argue a call with him when he put up his hands like a stop sign. "Don't come any further," he said. "It's one hundred degrees and if I have to be out here all day, so do you. I'm not throwing you out of this game just because you're having a lousy day of managing. You should've taken your starting pitcher out two innings ago!"

BRUCE FROEMMING: When he was behind the plate, he always had one eye on the dugout. That June day in 2007 when I earned a suspension after getting into it with Mark Wegner, Uncle Brucie was behind the plate and was even more pissed off with me than Wegner was—but for a different reason. They'd had to delay the game to clean all the trash off the field, and after intervening, Uncle Brucie scolded me, saying, "Why didn't you argue with me instead of the young guy? I'd have thrown you out immediately and we wouldn't have all this trash on the field. Now you've made me miss my dinner reservation and I'm not happy with that."

RICHIE GARCIA: As fellow Latins from Tampa, we had a lot in common, especially our quick tempers. He had the ability to throw you out of the game in two different languages.

KEN KAISER: Kenny could have a quick hook and definitely didn't like being questioned. But if you wanted to be assured of a little more leeway with him, you agreed to go to his charity banquet in Rochester.

FRANK PULLI: He liked playing the ponies and having a few cocktails at night, and I always worried about his mood if he'd had a bad day at the racetrack or a long night before. One time, he was umpiring behind home plate and told me when I came out to exchange the lineup cards, "Just so you know, I've got a splitting headache, so I don't want to hear a peep out of you today."

(**NOTE:** *I want to make a point here that by "red-ass" I'm only saying these guys had short fuses with me. They were all respected umpires. They just didn't put up with my bullshit.*

I would also like to add here that I wish I hadn't created as many headaches for the umpires as I did. They have a very tough job—a no-win job—and I really respected them. I wish I had managed when they had instant replay. It would have alleviated a lot of arguments I had with umpires and saved me a lot of money in fines. I know I've missed a lot more good umpires here, but that's because, as I said, the best ones are the ones that don't get a lot of attention.)

ABOUT THE AUTHOR

Lou Piniella (nicknamed "Sweet Lou" partly as a description of his swing but more popularly as a facetious reference to his fiery demeanor) has been in Major League Baseball for more than fifty years. He played sixteen seasons with the Orioles, the Indians, the Royals—where he was American League Rookie of the Year in 1969—and, most notably, with the Yankees, where he had key roles in two World Series Championships, of 1977 and 1978.

After Piniella retired from playing, he joined the Yankees as hitting coach, and eventually became manager of the team. He later went on to manage the Reds, the Mariners, the Rays, and the Cubs.

His 1990 Reds team won the World Series championship, and he led the Mariners to four postseason appearances in ten seasons, which included a record 116-win regular season in 2001. His Cubs teams captured back-to-back division titles (2007 and 2008). Piniella was named Manager of the Year three times during his career (1995, 2001, and 2008) and finished his twenty-three-year managerial career ranked fourteenth on the list of all-time managerial wins.

Piniella serves as a special adviser for the Cincinnati Reds and lives with his wife, Anita, in Tampa, Florida.

Bill Madden has covered the Yankees and Major League Baseball for the *New York Daily News* for more than forty years. In 2010, Madden was the recipient of the Baseball Hall of Fame's J. G. Taylor Spink Award. He has written several books about baseball, including the *New York Times* bestsellers *Steinbrenner: The Last Lion of Baseball* and *Zim: A Baseball Life*.